LORD ASHFIELD'S TRAMS

HOW LONDON LOST A WORLD CLASS TRAMWAY SYSTEM

ROBERT J. HARLEY

Capital Transport

I dedicate this book to the memory of Ken Glazier and John Gent. Both have assisted the present author on numerous occasions in the past. They were always willing to share the results of their meticulous research. The study of the history of London's transport is much the poorer for their passing.

ISBN 978-1-85414-384-6
Published by Capital Transport Publishing
Printed by Parksons Graphics
Designed by Tim Demuth
© Robert J. Harley 2014
www.capitaltransport.com

right Under new ownership, former West Ham Corporation Tramways car 68 has received the suffix letter H from the LPTB. Pictured on Greengate Street outside the depot, this vehicle will shortly be repainted in standard London Transport colours.

previous page A line of tramcars is illustrated during rush hour at the terminus in Grays Inn Road, Holborn. Two examples of the UCC/Feltham luxury type tram can be seen on route 21 to North Finchley. At this time of the day a quick reversal was imperative for vehicles connecting central London with the northern suburbs of the capital, including Hampstead, Wood Green, Stamford Hill and Edmonton. London Transport Museum

front cover illustration Trams were no strangers to the streets of London's East End. Here at Church Crescent in Hackney car 1205 traverses the one way system to emerge on to Lauriston Road. The passers-by, the corner shop, the colourful advertisements and the distinctive Penfold letter box evoke a bygone era. It is the summer of 1939 and work has already started on planting new traction standards in anticipation of the introduction of trolleybuses later in the year at this location. From a painting by Richard Berridge

CONTENTS

INTRODUCTION
AND ACKNOWLEDGEMENTS

M Y FATHER, John Harley, worked as a civil engineer from 1932 until the mid-1960s. His field of expertise lay in the construction of highways and houses. He prided himself that he had advanced further in society than his father, whose physical labour was once employed by the permanent way department of Wolverhampton Corporation Tramways. My father strongly believed that trams were a relic of the past, unsuited to the new, modern, post Second World War Britain. I begged to differ, but in an effort to open my eyes to the reality of the situation, extracts from two large tomes from the paternal bookcase were quoted at me.

The COUNTY OF LONDON PLAN by J. H. Forshaw and Patrick Abercrombie, published during the Second World War, gave the capital's railbound vehicles very short shrift:

Having in mind that trams were to have been removed from the roads by 1943, we have assumed, in preparing this report, that they will be replaced by other means of transportation at an early date after the war. Such a removal will contribute in no small way to the reduction in casualty figures.

By the time the official report of a Government steering group appeared in 1963, the work of the tram scrappers had been almost completed. The authors of TRAFFIC IN TOWNS express mild astonishment, when referring to the contemporary German view of public transport:

... Most cities have not merely retained their tramway systems, but propose to elaborate them. In some cases new tracks are being laid down in the central reservations of new roads; and in many towns there are plans for putting the tramways underground in central areas. This policy seems to have been most carefully thought out in the years after the war. It was adopted and pursued in the face of the knowledge that most other countries were planning to do away with trams.

We British, it appeared, had got it right. But I remained a sceptic. I wanted to know why a public transport policy, centred on the bus and aggressively pursued in London from the 1920s onwards, had so influenced town planners in the UK that, save for the honourable exception of Blackpool, the tramcar had been wiped out.

The original idea of writing a history of tramways in the London Transport era arose out of conversations between the author and Ken Glazier in the winter of 1995. Ken was a transport professional, who had held several official posts in the complex organisation based at 55 Broadway. He was renowned for his scholarship in the field of documenting the development of London's motor bus services. His meticulous research resulted in a series of books, which remain the standard reference works for the subject. Ken also had a soft spot for the trams he had known in the south London of his youth. Unfortunately, work commitments prevented his active assistance and it was agreed that I should go ahead on my own. The result was the publication in 2000 of LONDON TRAMWAY TWILIGHT, which detailed the last three years of the system to the final closure in July 1952. The plan that Ken should rejoin the project was ended by his untimely death in 2007. I lost a friend as well as a co-author. I dedicate this current volume to his memory.

It was always our intention to follow the story back to the inception of the London Passenger Transport Board in the late 1920s and early 1930s. Under the guidance of Lord Ashfield, ably assisted by Frank Pick, the new organisation became a bench mark for style, design and efficiency. Lauded at home and abroad, the buses, underground railways and trolleybuses attracted attention from town planners across the globe. Excluded

Lewisham Town Hall forms the background of this view of standard E/1 class car 1037 on route 54, as it pulls away from the tram stop with a full load on board. There was a triangular junction here at Rushey Green, Catford outside St Laurence's Church. Tracks lead off left towards Dulwich, Dog Kennel Hill and Camberwell. A. V. Mace

from this paean of praise was the extensive tramway network. It was the subject of an abandonment programme, calculated to rid the capital in less than 10 years of the 'encumbrance' of the railbound vehicles. The trams were also the target of what would now be termed 'a hostile press' and this negative impression influenced academics and writers. Professor C. D. Buchanan in MIXED BLESSING: THE MOTOR IN BRITAIN states bluntly:

It was about 1931 that policy finally crystallised against trams and tramlines as incompatible with the new motor traffic, and from this date there started a drive against trams which has now gone a long way to completion.

In his otherwise splendid book on postwar Britain, NEVER AGAIN, the author Peter Hennessy asserts:

crawling trams, running on rails down the middle of many a high street, were epic jam-makers.

Anti-tram propaganda of the period was often strident. In order to counteract some of these critical views, a fairer and more balanced picture is now needed.

In the 1930s London was blazing a trail; however, it was not alone. In New York and Paris rails were being ripped up from the streets in a vision of an all-bus future. In contrast to the Ashfield world view, wiser counsels prevailed in many other major European cities. They were less profligate with their transport infrastructure and sought to retain the services of their trams in the face of attacks from the motoring lobby, aided and abetted by vehicle manufacturers and powerful oil companies.

Planners for urban regeneration in the 21st century take a rather different approach from that adopted in the UK in the 1930s. Avoidance of congestion, allocation of road space, parking restrictions, traffic calming, environmental concerns and efficient public transport all come high on the agenda. Many contemporary experts now echo the views of those who, few in number, championed the cause of the tramcar in the decade before the Second World War. These maligned 1930s visionaries maintained that the hasty annihilation of trunk routes and the closure of the Kingsway Subway under central London constituted major errors of judgement. The campaign, such as it was, was ineffective and the opponents of Lord Ashfield and his Board failed. A mass transit system offering cheap fares and reliable operation in all weathers just faded away.

At the time of the great tramway extinction in London the reason for the abandonment was summed up in one word 'obsolescence'. It was stated that a more modern service could be offered by buses (originally of the petrol variety and later diesel powered) and trolleybuses. Although the red liveried bus has evolved into a universally recognised symbol for the capital city, its electrically powered fellow, the trolleybus, had a relatively short run for London's money from 1931 to 1962. It was later castigated as possessing the same faults of 'inflexibility' as the trams it replaced.

One of the purposes of this book is to analyse the thinking behind the decisions taken by Ashfield and the LPTB. In this task I have been greatly helped by Dr Gerald Druce, an engineer by profession, who has given eye witness accounts of the tramways in their last years. Gerald also studied developments in tramcar technology from North America to the continent of Europe, which led directly to the modern vehicles now in service in the Croydon area on London Tramlink.

The author also acknowledges Dr Druce's help in collating information for the appendices at the end of the main text. Two of Gerald's closest associates in the campaign to retain and modernise the London system were Julian Thompson and Alan Watkins. Both have contributed significantly to this book. In the case of the latter his spirit lives on courtesy of his widow, Ann E. Watkins, who has edited her late husband's letters and notes for publication as THE CAMPAIGN TO SAVE THE LONDON TRAMS 1946–1952.

I must also thank Russ Powers of Colorado for his meticulous uncovering of information relating to the history of the PCC tramcar on the North American continent. David Voice, archivist of the Tramway and Light Railway Society, deserves an honourable mention for his assistance in locating textual and photographic matter.

My first research on this project was assisted in the late 1960s by the staffs of local history libraries at Bexley, Greenwich and Lewisham. I am also very grateful for modern facilities for research such as Hansard online with its detailed coverage of Parliamentary speeches. The staff at the archives of London Transport have extended me every assistance. In particular I would like to thank Stephanie Rousseau.

I wish to record my indebtedness to all those members of the two tramway societies – the LRTL and the TLRS – whose reminiscences have contributed to this book. I am very grateful to all the folk who have gone before me in the field of tramway authorship. Writers who have been crucial in documenting the daily life of the tramways include Frank Merton Atkins, Michael Baker, Geoffrey Baddeley, Vernon Burrows, Stan Collins, Charles Dunbar, Ron Gee, John Gent, John Gillham, Sydney Harris, Doris Hazell, Charles Klapper, Ted Oakley, John Price, Cyril Smeeton, Ken Thorpe, Geoffrey Wilson, Richard Wiseman and Colin Withey.

Interviews with Richard Elliott, former employee at Charlton Repair Works, and with George Tapp, sometime Erith Council motorman and later trolleybus driver, gave me a better insight into the routines of London Transport. George Gundry had a fund of reminiscences of tram services in the south and west of the capital; he was also a regular visitor to Paris in the 1920s and 1930s and observed the decline of the tramways in that city. North of the River Thames, John Barrie and Don Thompson were on hand to record the passing of the Metropolitan Electric system; both were able to recall vividly the trolleybus conversion years. David Bayes and Herbert Lingwood have contributed eye witness accounts of trams in the East End. Our man south of the River Thames on observation duty was John Wills, to whom I owe many thanks.

I am aware that many of those mentioned are sadly no longer with us. Another great loss was Tony Banks, Baron Stratford, whose enthusiasm for Londoners, London and its trams and trolleybuses was infectious. In order to remedy the sins of the past, the House of Lords was owed one fighter for the cause of tramways, but his career was tragically cut short. In a hand written letter to the author Tony wrote: 'Who were those idiots who got rid of London's trams?' – Well, I hope the present volume goes some way to answering the question.

As a passenger in the late 1950s and an avid explorer of my home town, I used the London trolleybus system frequently. As regards the history of this form of transport in the capital, I wish to thank Ken Blacker for answering all my enquiries and pointing me in new directions. Another expert, Mick Webber has also assisted me in the preparation of this book. In the same way Mike Horne has patiently tried to expand my knowledge of the Underground and tube railways. Further information on the immediate postwar tram scene has been given by John Meredith and B. J. 'Curly' Cross.

As always, Jim Whiting, founder of Capital Transport Publishing, has offered valuable assistance in bringing the whole project to fruition. His support has been much appreciated. I would like also to record my appreciation to Tim Demuth for his invaluable contribution to the artwork and layout of this book. A special note of thanks goes to Dave Jones of the LCC Tramways Trust for his advice and expertise in locating rare photographic material.

Finally, I wish to thank my wife, Janet, my children and grandchildren for being very understanding while I was researching and writing this book.

A MATTER OF PREJUDICE

LONDON HAS been the inspiration for countless books, academic theses, official reports, newspaper articles, films and TV programmes. Documentary and factual works about the capital city, when referring to the daily journey to work of the inhabitants, often restrict their view to those two icons of London's transport – the red double decker bus and the Underground train. Of the large tramway system that survived for almost a hundred years until the middle of the 20th century there is scarcely a mention. Aside from a false start in the 1860s, the reign of the tramcar on London's streets began on 25th April 1870 and continued uninterrupted until 5th July 1952, with a resumption of operation on 11th May 2000, when Croydon Tramlink was opened. Unfortunately, in spite of this lengthy association with the capital city, for many authors and social commentators the role of the tram in metropolitan urban development has either been ignored completely or has been relegated to a mere footnote in history.

One the reasons for this oversight lies in the fact that boroughs such as Kensington, Chelsea, St Marylebone, Hampstead and the cities of London and Westminster never permitted any significant tramway encroachment on their territories. Oxford Street, Whitehall, Piccadilly, Trafalgar Square, The Strand and almost every thoroughfare serving the square mile at the commercial heart of the metropolis were quite firmly out of bounds. Thus the notion was perpetuated that those fortunate enough to reside in wealthy and fashionable areas had no use for tramways. Antipathy to this form of transport enlivened local politics and then coalesced into powerful lobby groups, which sought to influence legislators and town planners.

Fear of the 'lower orders' certainly lent credence to a world view that trams were vehicles for the working classes, and as such their spread should be resisted. However, on the other side of the coin their utility to London could not be disputed. The electrification of the major routes from 1901 onwards had given an impetus to expansion. Ten years after the inauguration of electric traction the constituent parts of the network numbered two company tramways – London United (LUT), South Metropolitan (SMET), one joint public/private enterprise – Metropolitan Electric (MET – lessees of Middlesex County Council), and no fewer than 11 municipal operators – London County Council (LCC), West Ham, East Ham, Barking, Ilford, Leyton, Walthamstow, Bexley, Erith, Dartford and Croydon. The London County Council Tramways formed the centre of the system and had concluded through running agreements with an increasing number of other operators. The passenger figures for 1911 showed a ridership of 822 million people, which equated to 43 per cent of all passenger journeys in Greater London (bus use was 21 per cent and the suburban and Underground railways registered 36 per cent). Cheap fares coupled with reliable services tell their own story. Looking at the figures it seems incredible that there were forces at work wanting to scrap the whole system, and that these forces would later dictate policy to the unified body, the London Passenger Transport Board (LPTB), which was formed in 1933.

In the years leading up to the establishment of the LPTB conspiracy theorists saw the issue quite clearly. To them the argument concerned the affluent, reactionary 'carriage folk' versus the urban proletariat and their favourite conveyance. In plain terms to many folk it was a straight fight between capitalism and municipal socialism. However this scenario does not tell the full story. There are common threads running through the whole debate. Decisions on investment, competition policy and revenue from fares are crucial to the understanding of what later transpired. It would be too simplistic to suggest that the decline and disappearance of the trams can be laid solely at the door of the rich and powerful. Personalities and policy decisions played an important role and into the arena step three rather larger than life characters. All had successful careers and all came from humble backgrounds.

It is 9:35am on a summer's morning in the early 1930s. An instantly recognisable scene depicts buses and trams crossing Westminster Bridge. The morning peak period is over as the two leading tramcars head for their suburban termini at Abbey Wood and Kew Bridge respectively.
London County Council

The queues at Blackfriars in 1914 give a good idea of the major role the tramways played in transporting Londoners. At this location the waiting throng consisted mainly of office workers, many of whom worked in the square mile of the City of London. Shortly this line of tramcars will proceed from the Victoria Embankment on to Blackfriars Bridge.

Albert Henry Knattriess was born on 8th August 1874 at Normanton, Derbyshire. His father, Henry, was a coachbuilder, who later emigrated with his family to Detroit. Having changed his surname to Stanley, the young Albert forged a career in the American street railway industry, first in Detroit and then as general manager of the Public Service Corporation of New Jersey. He returned to his native land in 1907 in order to become general manager of the Underground Electric Railways Company of London (UERL); he later achieved the position of chairman of the 'Combine', a group of private companies encompassing buses, trams, tube railways, electric power generation and commercial motor vehicle manufacture. On 29th July 1914 he was knighted for services to transport. Conservative by political persuasion, he was MP for Ashton-under-Lyne (1916–1920) and President of the Board of Trade (1916–1919). In 1920 Sir Albert Stanley was created Baron Ashfield of Southwell.

Lord Ashfield seems to have been an affable individual, who had learnt to practise the fine art of diplomacy. Of course, he had detractors, but there was very little talk of his having any enemies. He was widely considered as the only natural candidate for the new post of chairman of the London Passenger Transport Board. As the DAILY TELEGRAPH noted on 5th November 1948:

He was the undisputed choice. With its railways, tramways, omnibuses and coaches, carrying 4,000 million passengers a year, the vast organisation represented a capital of £120 million. To take charge of it Lord Ashfield gave up a salary of £30,000 a year for one of £12,500.

In his professional life Lord Ashfield often relied upon his deputy and trusted advisor, Frank Pick, who was born in Lincolnshire

on 23rd November 1878. The eldest son of a Stamford draper, Pick came to London in 1906 and became commercial manager of the UERL in 1912. His career then mirrored that of his boss, Lord Ashfield. Often acknowledged as the power behind the throne, Frank Pick was widely considered to be a 'bus man' through and through. His antipathy to trams probably began with his appointment in 1909 as claims officer for the London United Tramways. As Charles White, an official in the Combine, later wrote in article dated 25th April 1957:

Under Pick the LUT claims tended to increase financially, through Pick's tendency to fight claims to no purpose. Tramway claims were naturally more numerous relatively than those on the railways, owing to the tramway tracks being in public thoroughfares and thus susceptible to incidentals from which the railways were free.

On the credit side among town planners and connoisseurs of 1930s building styles Frank Pick is still highly regarded as the architect of London Transport and the instigator of a new school of urban design. However, in spite of his obvious talents, he retained an unfortunate habit of polarising opinion about him. It can fairly be stated that he managed to offend some very important people in his life time, including rather unwisely the Prime Minister, Winston Churchill. Frank Pick's wartime job as Director General of the Ministry of Information came to an abrupt end, as the EVENING NEWS of 14th December 1940 relates:

Mr Pick's four months at the Ministry have not been smooth. Mr Pick likes to play the part of a dictator and the many conflicting interests of the MOI have not taken kindly to his iron hand in an iron glove. Tact is not one of his strongest points.

The last member or our triumvirate also shared with Frank Pick the unhappy knack of apparently making friends and enemies in equal measure. Herbert Morrison was the son of a police constable and was born in Lambeth on 3rd January 1888. An astute observer and critic of contemporary social conditions, he set out to improve the lot of the working classes by joining the London Labour Party and then by making a career for himself in local authority politics. First elected to Parliament in 1923, he later became Minister of Transport in the minority Labour administration of 1929. He was widely regarded as a tireless worker and skilled administrator, qualities which he used to mastermind the Labour victory in the London County Council elections of 1934.

In the unfolding saga of the destruction of London's tramways Messrs Stanley, Pick and Morrison all play leading roles. Other cast members include peers of the realm, the Metropolitan Police, trade unionists, motoring organisations, highway engineers, town planners, oil and tyre companies, bus and commercial vehicle manufacturers. The outlook would eventually turn distinctly gloomy, but in the years preceding the First World War there had always been a balance between the anti-tram brigade and those with power and influence, who acknowledged the usefulness of the railbound vehicles to the economy of the capital city of the nation.

In the second decade of the twentieth century consolidation was the main theme. Improvements in rolling stock design had resulted in the widespread adoption of top deck covers (qv – Rolling Stock Appendix). In contrast to bus passengers, most tram users on the trunk routes into town could expect to be shielded from the elements on the 'outside' of the vehicle. On the debit side there were still several districts in the centre of the metropolis, where no trams dared to venture. At the edge of the urban area construction of new routes into the expanding suburbs had virtually ceased, with the LCC being the only operator interested in extending its tracks to new housing developments.

The balance between competing transport systems was always fragile. In his 1912 election address for a seat on Lambeth Borough Council Herbert Morrison summed up the problem:

We think there should be equal treatment as between trams and motor vehicles. The heavy motors tear up the roads, create a nuisance to the rate paying shop keepers, and generally destroy the safety and quietness of any neighbourhood wherein they travel, without contributing a single penny to the local rates for the upkeep of the roads they are continually destroying. On the other hand, the London County Council pay for the construction of the tram track, keep it in repair, and in addition, contribute to the rates of the Lambeth Borough Council.

At this early stage in his career there could be no doubt as to the transport preferences of the aspiring local councillor.

The whole network of metropolitan railways, tramways and buses was about to be tested in the time of national emergency. On the face of it London's tramways were in pole position, having assumed the mantle of the capital's major supplier of public transport. Large numbers of munitions workers, dockers and other personnel vital to the war effort filled the tramcars. The downside of all this increased traffic manifested itself in reduced maintenance to track and rolling stock, due to shortages of men and materials. Restricted coal deliveries to power stations also resulted in electrical supply problems, which interfered with the efficient running of services.

Streets devoid of the usual throng of motor buses were a strange sight for many Londoners. In theory vehicles were required for military duties on the Western Front.

Mobilisation of the armed forces in the first week of August 1914 was a prelude to the requisition by the War Office of 300 buses, together with 330 drivers from the metropolitan area. Petrol rationing from August 1916 further decimated the ranks of the London General Omnibus Company and its fellow operators. In practice, however, the situation was not nearly so dire for the bus company. A discreet arrangement between Frank Pick of the LGOC and the government was negotiated. Subsidies were granted to bus services for munitions workers attending Woolwich Arsenal, but the LCC Tramways received no such largesse from the public purse. The cloak and dagger veil of secrecy on these handouts, plus Pick's lobbying to curtail certain tram services in favour of the bus company soured the affair, when the facts became public.

Mutterings about the complicity of Sir Albert Stanley, a minister in the government, and Colonel Wedgwood of the Ministry of Munitions were deemed unhelpful to the war effort, although awkward questions were asked in Parliament and the whole affair then unravelled. The secretary of the Metropolitan Municipal Tramways Association, T. B. Goodyer, had no doubt about the legitimacy of the matter:

The principle of the whole thing is questioned. The tramways were, and are, capable of carrying much of what was creamed off by the LGOC. Some of the services which received subsidies never went anywhere near Woolwich.

The allegation that the LGOC had committed fraud found few supporters outside the tramway fraternity, but the suspicion lingered that the buses were getting preferential treatment. Albert Stanley appeared to confirm the rumours, when he lobbied the government in the hope that the London General, would be awarded a monopoly of operating rights in the capital. He suggested this perk should be granted in recognition of the 'patriotic' services rendered by his buses transporting troops on the Western Front. Even though nothing came of the suggestion, in a sense Stanley was only cashing in on widely felt sentiments. He foresaw correctly that in the five years after the end of the Great War the motor bus would come of age. Commercial advantage and profits were there for the taking. The guns may have fallen silent on the continent of Europe, but the starting pistol had been fired for a mass invasion of London's streets.

War surplus motor lorries were hastily converted into crude and uncomfortable public transport vehicles. They proved a stopgap until production of conventional buses, based on improved technology, fuelled a veritable stampede of new operators.

The Kingsway Tram Subway was the jewel in the crown of the London County Council Tramways. It was cited as an example of municipal enterprise at its finest, and, as such, featured on many contemporary postcard views. In the first decade of the twentieth century car 582 accelerates up the ramp on its way to the northern half of the LCC system. The crew have forgotten to change the indicator. Kennington Gate was one of the southern termini and lay in the opposite direction!

LONDON. - Kingsway, The Underground Tramway

Groups of ex-servicemen clubbed together to buy as many buses as they could afford. The competition for passengers threatened to get out of control, as rival drivers jockeyed for the best position on the crowded thoroughfares of central London. Accidents caused by speeding and plain bad driving were commonplace in this unregulated omnibus survival of the fittest. The Metropolitan Police, as guardians of law and order on the streets of the capital, were definitely not amused. Even the supporters of free enterprise began to take fright.

The trams were not immune to this competition. Although cheap fares ensured that those on the lowest incomes continued to use the service, valuable revenue was lost to the 'pirate buses' as they became known. Coupled with dissatisfaction over pay rates, the matter of the 'pirates' boiled up into a *cause célèbre* that resulted in Ernie Bevin, the General Secretary of the Transport and General Workers Union, advising his members to withdraw their labour. According to H. A. Clegg in his 1950 book LABOUR RELATIONS IN LONDON TRANSPORT:

16,000 tramwaymen and the LGOC's 23,000 busmen were on strike, transport in London was disorganised, and the tubes and the 300 'pirate' buses, whose staff enjoyed the benefits of non-unionism, were heavily overcrowded.

The B type motor bus, which first appeared in 1910, would emerge as a serious competitor to the tramways. Although a single tramcar could carry more passengers than its internal combustion engine rival. By 1913 around 2,500 mass produced buses of this type had entered service. As is apparent in this scene, the fight for road space was well under way, even before the outbreak of the First World War in 1914. The motorman of London United Tramways car 196 stands at his post, while the driver of the Crouch End bus has the benefit of a seat, although both men have precious little protection from the elements. Dave Jones Collection

Government legislation in the form of the London Traffic Act 1924 offered a way out of the impasse. Initially, there was general political consensus that order would be brought to chaos by some form of control of the anarchic melee of vehicles and services. The situation was made more urgent by the threat of supportive strikes on the railways and tubes. Industrial action began at midnight on 21st March 1924 and lasted 10 days. The strike had hastened the day when London would have coordination of passenger traffic in the metropolitan area. As a consequence of the legislation a consultative body, called the London and Home Counties Advisory Committee, was established to oversee the workings of the 1924 Act and the 'restricted streets' orders in particular. These related to the number of buses allowed to ply for trade at certain locations. In practice all roads equipped with tramways fell into this category.

What appeared outwardly to be a common sense measure, then provoked political divisions within the Labour movement. Obviously, independent bus operators, ostensibly non-political, but supported by free enterprise Tories, were deeply unhappy. They found unlikely allies in Herbert Morrison and his London Labour Party. Morrison, who was fiercely campaigning for the LCC and other municipal tramways, saw the 1924 Act as a way of consolidating the power of the LGOC and the Combine. He feared that cheap fares and workmen's concessionary fares would disappear if the trams were forced off the road. He made his feelings perfectly clear in a Parliamentary debate on 16th June 1924:

We shall have given a protected monopoly to Lord Ashfield for which he has been fighting and for which Hon Members opposite have been fighting . . . Hon Members opposite may trust the London Traffic combine, but I do not, and I think it is a thing London would do better without. I do not like its American methods and involved finance and secrecy. . . It would be very charming, it is true, to know all about the dark side of omnibuses and their finance, but there is not the least value in knowing about Lord Ashfield's omnibus finance unless we know the inside finance

A crowded traffic scene such as this could be interpreted in different ways. At Gardiners Corner, Aldgate those apostles of the 'coefficient of obstruction' would probably find enough evidence here to condemn the tramways. However, the question was: 'Who is obstructing whom?' It can be argued that the trams with their fixed track exerted a form of lane discipline on other road users.
London Transport Museum

11

of the Associated Equipment Company, of the Underground Railways, and of the Metropolitan Electric Tramways . . .

Herbert Morrison was alluding here to the common fund, whereby money was shifted around the constituent parts of the Combine. Predictably he directed his fire at the complicity, as he saw it, of the tube railways and the AEC bus manufacturers, but what did raise a few eyebrows was his inclusion of the Metropolitan Electric Tramways (MET) in the plot. He was well aware that the three Combine tramways had a separate legal status as members of the London and Suburban Traction Company, although of course the common fund pool of resources also existed for their benefit. Of these three it was the London United (LUT) that was most in need of investment. In modern parlance it was on the road to becoming a financial 'basket case'. Tellingly for the future of the trams, at the very time the London Traffic Act came into force, the LUT had abandoned route 69 from Twickenham to Richmond Bridge. General buses took over the service.

The South Metropolitan (SMET), lying tucked away in north Surrey, was less troubled by bus competition and, besides, it had a very profitable electrical supply business. Indeed, cynics suggested that the SMET was more interested in lighting homes and boiling kettles than running a tram system. The MET, on the other hand, was a large scale operator of trunk routes into central London. It had a close relationship with the county councils of Hertfordshire and Middlesex, and as such hardly fits into Morrison's target group of rapacious capitalists.

Morrison's fellow socialist, Ernie Bevin, took a different point of view. On many crucial issues the two men had never seen eye to eye and the enmity between them was to endure. Bevin had a decent working relationship with Ashfield. Conditions for his TGWU members were good and the London General busmen were paid higher than their tramway colleagues. The prospect of the Combine ruling the roost could bring the advantages of more favourable employment conditions to all transport workers in the capital. The demise of the 'pirates', staffed by non-union personnel, was also regarded with favour by the TGWU.

Local authorities within the metropolitan area may have had mixed views as to tramways, but they welcomed the income they received from them in the form of rates. Operators were also obliged by the provisions of the 1870 Tramways Act to maintain the roadway between the rails and for a distance of 18 inches outside them. Thus, in a very real sense, the trams paved the way for competing motor buses. The latter were subject to road fund tax, but there was an imbalance as pro-

tram MPs pointed out. In a speech by Sir Joseph Nall in the House of Commons on 5th July 1927 the argument was set out:

Some hon Members might say 'Scrap the Trams!' but what would be the result of that policy? An omnibus with a capacity comparable to that of a tramway car pays about £108 a year in licence duty. The contribution which a tramway makes to the maintenance of the roads varies from £200 per car per annum to as much as £400, and in some cases £500.

Although Sir Joseph was not the first individual to quote financial information, the next crucial years for the survival of the tramways were punctuated by frequent revelations of figures plucked from accounts, which were intended to influence the argument either way. Pro and anti-tram factions took solace from their own reading of balance sheets, where costs, revenues and debt charges varied according to the source of the information. In the mass of frequently conflicting information the task of establishing a definitive, realistic set of accounts became all the more difficult.

While the trams were contributing to municipal coffers all over London, the restricted streets orders certainly helped to relieve the adverse financial situation, but as Morrison suspected, the Combine consolidated its position. Frank Pick and his LGOC acquisitions team made offers that many independent operators could not refuse. Buses and operating staff disappeared into the ranks of the Combine, while erstwhile omnibus entrepreneurs turned their energies and their pay off moneys to other fields of commercial activity.

The London and Home Counties Advisory Committee, as established by the 1924 Act, was enjoined to publish annual summaries on the progress of solving congestion and traffic problems. The committee was subsequently asked to produce a series of reports on the public transport facilities in different parts of the metropolitan area. These contributed a body of knowledge crucial to the establishment of a unified transport authority. The merits of each mode of transport were considered impartially, but the impression is given that the trams were least capable of adapting to modern circumstances.

An example of this changed situation occurred in the 1926 public inquiry, conducted by the Advisory Committee into the travelling facilities to and from east London. Particular attention was paid to the new Becontree Estate, which was begun in 1921 on 300 acres of compulsorily purchased farm land. This LCC estate of 27,000 dwellings was the largest public housing project in the world. Although the 1926 report talks encouragingly about the

When the London United inaugurated electric traction in 1901, there appeared to be limitless possibilities for the expansion of tramways throughout the metropolitan area and beyond. Even narrow streets, more attuned to the horse and cart era, could accommodate tramways, as witnessed here in Brentford. LUT cars 249 and 92 represent the latest in Edwardian transport technology. However, there would be precious little further investment in track layout or rolling stock, thereby ensuring that the presence of trams at this location would later be condemned as anachronistic and obstructive to motor traffic. *Dave Jones Collection*

prospect of express tramways to serve the needs of residents, nothing concrete was achieved. Segregated rights of way were already common in several UK cities and the construction of reserved tracks for tramcars had considerably speeded up the service. Birmingham and Liverpool had led the way, but tramway operators in London were more cautious. In the end, much to the LCC's embarrassment, they were unable to supply public transport to their own housing development. London General omnibuses quickly filled the transport vacuum.

Becontree was an 'out county' estate and

as such could not be reached by a simple extension of one of the LCC's existing lines. The nearest trunk route terminus was at Barking, but that local authority was on the brink of ditching its tramway commitments. The northern approach to the new housing lay through Ilford territory. Their stubborn refusal to entertain new ideas is mirrored by the following extract from the 1926 report:

There was a considerable amount of cross-examination by Counsel for the London County Council on the subject of through running on the Ilford and LCC Tramways, but the Ilford witnesses held to their opinion that through running would be of no benefit to their system, on the grounds that the service and its punctuality would be prejudicially affected and that the Ilford track was not suitable for the heavy LCC cars.

Ilford's isolationism effectively killed any hope of trams serving Becontree. It also sent a strong signal to the watching politicians and town planners that buses would not be subject to the same sort of short sighted parochialism. Their routes could cross municipal boundaries to cater for the travelling public. They were flexible in adapting to changing needs.

The 1924 Act may have granted protection from excessive motor bus competition, but the increase in motor traffic still posed a constant threat to passengers. They needed protection in the form of bye laws, which obliged motorists to stop, when people were boarding or alighting from a tramcar. Loading islands and pedestrian refuges in the metropolitan area were few and far between. Consequently, the trams were unfairly blamed for the mounting accident rate. In a debate in the House of Commons on 28th March 1927, Thomas Naylor, the Labour member for Southwark South East, pressed the need for more street refuges for the main roads in south London. He asked the Minister of Transport:

if his attention has been drawn to the necessity of splaying tramlines in the main roads of south London at certain points to enable refuges to be erected between the two sets of rails; and whether he will make representations to the responsible authorities with a view to such alterations being made?

The Minister replied that he was awaiting the report of the London Traffic Advisory Committee. Members of Parliament were aware that several Scottish towns had enacted bye laws to ensure the safety of tram passengers and the practice of passing stationary trams on the nearside was already outlawed in many countries. However, the Advisory Committee firmly squashed the idea.

The official view, courtesy of the 1927–28 Annual Report, sums up the objections in the following statement:

[If we were to enact this bye law] . . . there might be temptations to drivers of vehicles to race a tramcar to a stopping place in order to avoid having to pull up while the tramcar sets down or picks up passengers. Further, drivers of following vehicles, even though aware that the tramcar is about to stop, cannot always know whether it is to pick up or set down passengers or for any one of a variety of reasons.

No wonder tram operators and road safety campaigners were dismayed at the flimsiness of the report's conclusions. They appeared to fly in the face of logic and they also suggested that the committee members had been 'got at' by the motoring lobby. There seemed to be no political will to change the highway code. In fact, in the columns of motoring journals and in interviews with prominent members of the AA and the RAC it was openly being stated that the tram's fatal flaw was that it could not get out of the way of the private motorist! Much use was made of a rather bogus 'scientific' analysis of traffic called the 'coefficient of obstruction'. Marks were awarded out of 10 and vehicles were assessed as follows:

Electric Tram	9
Motor Omnibus	4
Motor Cab	1
One Horse – fast	3
One Horse – slow	7
Two Horse – fast	4
Two Horse – slow	10

Strangely, there were no figures available for private cars, commercial vehicles or lorries, nor was there any attempt to assess correctly the passenger carrying potential of each mode of transport. Here the tram outperformed its rivals by some margin. Large crowds of spectators attending football matches at Tottenham, West Ham, Charlton and Wembley Stadium could attest to the shifting power of lines of tramcars. At Wimbledon Greyhound Stadium in Plough Lane trams ferrying punters were often packed with over 100 souls each. It was noted that two conductors were required to collect the fares and that passengers were obliged to stand on both decks and on the stairs. However, in spite of these positive advantages offered by railbound traction, the coefficient of obstruction mud stuck. Tramways in the capital were under attack throughout the 1920s.

The last words in this chapter were spoken in the House of Lords on 27th April 1926 by David Lindsay, 27th Earl of Crawford, former Tory Minister of Transport. The debate was on London Traffic Regulations. The

The LCC adopted an expansionist tramway policy, when it came to supplying quality public transport to its housing estates. Here at the end of the Downham line at Grove Park, car 1172 reverses at the start of its return journey to Southwark Bridge. An authorised extension would have linked Grove Park with Westhorne Avenue, Eltham, but the LPTB abandoned the scheme. Although the vehicle sports a traditional appearance, the pantograph on the car roof is anything but. It represents an attempt to modernise the overhead current collection system, then based exclusively on the trolley wheel and pole. Right up to the end of their stewardship in 1933 the LCC management were planning for the long term retention of the tramcar. London County Council

noble earl was vehemently anti-tram and he sought to support the argument of another likeminded individual, Lord Montagu of Beaulieu:

The tramcar is the only vehicle that has to stop in the middle of the road, it is the only vehicle that must block anything coming behind it, it is certainly the noisiest form of traffic and, in a hundred and one ways, experience drives one to the inevitable conclusion that the tramway has got to go.

HANDS OFF THE PEOPLE'S TRAMS!

IN THE THIRD decade of the twentieth century the future of the capital's tramways became a hot political issue. On the national scene the General Election of December 1923 had produced a minority Labour administration. This lasted until the Conservative victory in October 1924. The Tory hold on power ended in May 1929, when the Labour party secured the most seats, but lacked an overall majority over the other two major parties. Meanwhile, in the unelected House of Lords many of the noble members continued with their anti-tram hostility. In local authority politics the Progressives had lost control of the LCC in 1907 and power now resided with the Municipal Reform Party, which was closely allied to the Conservatives. Labour did not secure power at County Hall until 1934, by which time, as we shall see, the LCC had ceased running its tramways.

Credit does belong to the Municipal Reformers in pressing ahead with the LCC's route electrification and expansion scheme. Although elected on a platform of reining in public spending, they did not espouse the general ethos of the right of the Tory party, which condemned 'municipal trading', as it was called by those favouring private enterprise. It is a moot point whether the Progressives would have been more adventurous in constructing cross town routes, together with further tram subways on the Kingsway model.

On 27th July 1927 the BLUE REPORT was published under the auspices of the Advisory Committee. It was entitled A SCHEME FOR THE COORDINATION OF PASSENGER TRANSPORT FACILITIES IN THE LONDON TRAFFIC AREA. It envisaged a working arrangement lasting 42 years between the existing operators. However, for many observers the report represented an unsatisfactory halfway house with the threat that the municipal tramways would be absorbed into a private monopoly.

Although the battle lines in Parliament were not as fixed as some commentators have suggested, the main pro-tram lobby was supported by London Labour MPs, including Herbert Morrison. The nightmare scenario for them was that the municipal tramways would be handed over lock, stock and barrel to Lord Ashfield and his 'wicked' combine. Further fears centred on the cost of travel. It was known that there was no statutory obligation on bus companies to provide concessionary workmen's fares. Above all, it was a tenet of ideological faith that the trams were an instrument of socialism and therefore belonged to the people and definitely not to shareholders and private investors.

More and more the message comes across that the poor and financially disadvantaged would be hardest hit by the scrapping of the tramways. An impassioned speech was given in Parliament on 18th June 1928 by John Jones, MP for West Ham, Silvertown, a working class community in the East End. He was particularly incensed about a government plan to give rate relief to private industries:

I live in a district where we have run a tramway service for nearly 30 years. It only pays occasionally. It has not paid from a commercial point of view, as profits are reckoned by private companies, but it has paid as a public service in carrying people at cheap rates to their work in factories and industrial establishments in the neighbourhood. If we were a private company instead of a municipal undertaking, we should have to charge increased fares to cover our losses.

The government are simply saying to us that it is wrong for us to subsidise a public service, a utility service. It has been wrong for us in the past to pay a halfpenny rate in West Ham to subsidise our tramways and to support our industry by giving the people who have to work in the factories cheap facilities for getting to their employment, but it is right now to give 75 per cent in relief of rates to the productive manufacturers. In a few years from now all the debt that we have accumulated in

Advertising the benefits of municipally owned public transport, this tramcar is about to play its part in enticing the public on board. Who could resist the fare bargains on offer by the London County Council? The shilling all day, ride-at-will ticket is also being promoted. Although very much built to a traditional design, this particular vehicle – 'One of the 150 new and better trams for south London' – offered passengers upholstered seats, plus brighter interiors with improved lighting.
London County Council

In a scene to gladden the hearts of John Jones and the other pro-tram MPs, the full panoply of municipal pride is on display at the inauguration of West Ham Corporation Tramways. This local enterprise was to bring mobility to all classes of society. Various dignitaries await their tour of the borough in a tramcar suitably bedecked with bunting. Already the talk was of cheap fares and further extensions to developing areas. Municipal control of local tramways disappeared with the setting up of the LPTB.

West Ham as a consequence of improving a public service will be redeemed and the property will be ours. This has been done out of the sacrifices of the people of our own district. We never come to Parliament for assistance. If we did we know that we would not get it.

We want to know, however, why, when we have struggled against such fearful odds, we should be cut out of the advantage of the proposals now before Parliament. Why should we carry the men to the docks? As one of my hon Friends has said, you cannot produce goods without men, and you cannot get men to the place where goods are produced unless you have proper means of transport. The great railway companies are to be relieved of 75 per cent of their rates, but our tramways will not get any relief at all. Municipal tramways and municipal omnibus services are feeding industry.

Why are they not to come into this scheme? I cannot for the life of me understand why a set of private capitalists, who have their money invested in a particular form of transport, should have assistance to the extent of 75 per cent of their rates, whilst

another form of transport, organised under a public authority, is to receive no assistance at all. Take the docks in West Ham, the Albert, Victoria and King George Docks. The Port of London Authority is to be allowed 75 per cent of the rates and omnibuses owned by private companies will get similar relief, but, as I understand the Bill, our tramways will have to pay the full rates. Moreover, we have to maintain not merely the road that we use, but 18 inches on either side of the outer rail, which means practically 80 per cent of the total road surface. Yet there is no relief for us.

I want to know why you should discriminate against these transport services, whether

passenger carrying or goods carrying. They are rendering a great public service. Those who live in London know the tremendous service which our tramway system has rendered to the people of London and the great advantage it has been to the residents of the Metropolis. Yet we are being left out of the scheme. The poor can keep the poor as usual . . .

It is worth noting that the County Borough of West Ham, then situated in Essex, had a compact and efficient network of routes interconnected with the LCC and other east London operators and in the financial year 1928–29 the West Ham trams transported 61 million people. As with other municipal systems in the London area it had failed to secure Parliamentary powers to run motor buses. Lobbying from the LGOC and other companies had been most effective in preventing local authorities from owning this mode of transport. Had permission been forthcoming, then buses would have been used as feeder services to the main tram routes.

The inference in John Jones' speech is clear. He felt that a vital public service was the subject of discrimination. It certainly appears unfair that proposed measures to stimulate the nation's economy by granting rate relief to transport operators and other private companies should exclude the tramways. Mr Jones expressed sentiments felt by many in the poorer areas of London that the local trams provided a social service to the community, a function which many of his fellow Members in the House of Commons chose to ignore.

The Tory press was predictably on the

The public versus private contest was played out daily on the streets of the capital, as different modes of public transport competed for passengers. In Romford Road car 23 of West Ham Corporation Tramways is working the Ilford to Aldgate trunk service 63. Joining the fray are two buses. The leading vehicle is on route 25 to Victoria Station. When it rains, at least the tram passengers on the top deck will have the advantage over their fellows sitting 'outside' on the bus. There was definitely no love lost between tram and bus crews.

opposite side of the fence to Mr Jones. The leader writer of the EVENING STANDARD of 26th October 1928 stated:

Municipal control of the tramways has not so far been much of a success. We shall now be able to see whether Lord Ashfield can do any better. If he does, the tendency is not likely to stop at trams. There are other services at present controlled by municipalities or by the State which will at once come under review . . . Private enterprise and Socialism will be on their trial in the experiment, and the result may be of the highest importance for our future economic development.

The ideas expressed by the EVENING STANDARD provoked a swift response. They were quickly dubbed 'scaremongering', to be countered by the straightforward message of 'People before Profits', which became a rallying cry for the London Labour group. However, the 'scare' element soon became a very real threat to the trams. It did not take a genius to work out that the Municipal Reform leaders of the LCC had been consulting with Lord Ashfield *et al* to formulate a common policy for the future of London's public transport. A motion was tabled by Labour on 1st December 1928 expressing alarm at the proposal of the London County Council to transfer management of London's municipal tramways to a private trust.

The London Labour Group went into battle against two Bills promoted in the

Parliamentary session of 1929 – the London County Council and the Combine had both submitted Bills for the 'coordination of passenger traffic'. Herbert Morrison led the charge against them under the banner of 'Hands Off the People's Trams'. In January 1929 he published a 24-page pamphlet entitled THE LONDON TRAFFIC FRAUD. It had a foreword from J. Ramsay Macdonald, Leader of the Parliamentary Labour Party.

Morrison castigated the LCC Municipal Reformers:

They have little civic pride; they have no ambition to increase municipal influence and municipal property; they are always willing to kow-tow to the vested interests, which largely finance their Party organisation, and to eat out of the hands of any Tory Government. These London Traffic Bills involve wide public interests. For this is no mere tramway question. What is in the balance is the question of an almost complete monopoly of London passenger transport.

An objective observer to all this might have been left wondering which side was telling the truth on the economic argument. Were the tramways a drain on the public purse and could they be run more efficiently by private enterprise? Would a change of management require higher fares? What about the investment needed to upgrade track layouts and to modernise rolling stock in the light of substantial state subsidies for new highway schemes and road improvements? How much would it cost if the trams were scrapped and replaced by buses?

Several eminent Parliamentarians purported to have some of the answers. Sir Percy Harris, MP for Bethnal Green South West, weighed in with his own figures in the debate on 19th February 1929:

I have a document signed by the Clerk of the London County Council, and issued from County Hall, which shows that in the year ending March 1928 there was a surplus of £522,000 on working, after paying all expenses, the whole cost of running the

An ex-MET single deck tramcar is photographed on Station Road, Wood Green to mark the award of a charter to the Borough of Wood Green. The date is 20th September 1933 and this vehicle probably represents the last of a long line of decorated vehicles, which were so adorned to celebrate a civic event. Although on this occasion a former Combine tram was used, this tradition was widespread in the heyday of London's municipal tramways.
London Transport Museum

cars, providing power, paying wages, paying all the outgoings, maintaining the cars in proper condition and maintaining the rails.

Against that surplus had to be set charges for debt and charges for sinking fund to wipe out the whole of the capital cost of the tramways in 25 years, amounting in all to £745,000.

Opponents of the tramways were quick to underline the debt referred to in Sir Percy's last sentence. They were not prepared to wait another quarter of a century to see the matter resolved. They were of the opinion that, if buses took over, the whole operation would then be on a sound commercial footing. Unfortunately for the less well off in society this would probably mean unacceptable fare rises. Conveniently forgotten in the anti-tram argument was the fact that all of London's supposedly debt ridden municipal tramways had paid several decades' worth of surplus revenue into local authority coffers as a relief on the rates.

Parliamentary skirmishes over the two Bills were interrupted by the General Election on 30th May, when the Labour Party with 287 seats was asked to form a govern-ment. J. Ramsay Macdonald, the new Prime Minister, who had written the foreword to the 'Hands Off The People's Trams' tract, appointed Herbert Morrison as Minister of Transport. On 17 July both Bills were killed off in Parliament. In the winding up debate, John Scurr, MP for Stepney Mile End and a staunch supporter of the trams, uttered some very prescient words about the future:

The right hon Member for Woolwich West (Sir Kingsley Wood – Conservative) said that if anybody suggested that there was any desire to scrap the tramway system of London, he would be labouring under a delusion. No one here has ever suggested that they wanted to scrap the tramways of London. What the Combine wants is to get full control of the tramways of London so that in any possible further extension of London traffic facilities the tramways shall be left out and remain precisely as they are today. Traffic extensions will be tube, omnibuses, and things of that kind, and the tramway system will be relegated to the past. All we should get would be our present tramway system, which gradually would deteriorate and in the end be scrapped.

Herbert Morrison in his book Socialisation and Transport puts the outcome of the two Bills quite succinctly:

they were rejected by 295 to 172. With the authority of the Government, I agreed that a responsibility rested upon us to produce alternative proposals and undertook that this should be done. The Conservative Opposition regarded this as the traditional empty Ministerial promise – but they were wrong.

London's trams now appeared to be safe, but in reality they had only been granted a stay of execution. Outside the capital the tide had already turned against the railbound vehicles. Many medium sized towns, whose tramways had received little or no modernisation since the first decade of the twentieth century, now found it more convenient to switch to motor buses or trolleybuses. The latter had the advantage of running on home produced electricity. Questions were even being asked in large cities such as Manchester as to the viability of long term tramway operation. All in all it was a worrying time for the pro-tram lobby and the outlook was about to get a lot worse.

THREE AFTERNOONS AT THE MINISTRY

AFTER ALL the political wrangling, the question remains as to the real state of affairs regarding London's tramways at the end of 1929. Frank Pick and his associates at the LGOC might have given a clear answer. They sensed a lucrative future in relieving operators of their tramway burdens. As has been mentioned previously, on 1st October 1924, Mr Pick's buses ousted trams on one of the LUT's services.

A further conquest came in Croydon, where the Addiscombe line had closed on 28th March 1927, to be replaced by bus route 178. Barking Council got out of the tramway business on 16th February 1929. Red liveried London General buses on service 623 (later renumbered 100) took over from the green and cream painted trams on the line to Beckton. On the outskirts of the metropolitan area, 12 days after Barking's demise, the tramways at Gravesend and Northfleet breathed their last. Maidstone and District Motor Services supplied the requisite buses. In all these cases the costs of

fleet upgrades plus track renewals influenced the decision to abandon.

In order to counteract this gloom and doom, the LCC had put aside the Becontree debacle and had focused on expanding the network. On 15th November 1928 the final section of the Grove Park route through the Downham Estate was opened for traffic. Unfortunately, as the highway infrastructure was built new at the time, the opportunity was missed to place the tram tracks on a central reservation. On 14th January 1931, the rebuilt Kingsway Subway was opened for traffic, thus enabling new trunk services, worked by double deck cars, to link the northern suburbs with those south of the River Thames.

On the edge of the Epping Forest, well away from the urban grime of the central area, a new through running service was inaugurated on 5th March 1931, when LCC (ex Leyton) tracks were joined with those owned by Walthamstow. A connection was also projected via a new line linking the

Walthamstow, Ferry Lane terminus with MET rails in Tottenham. Meanwhile in south east London plans were in the pipeline to extend past Grove Park terminus towards the Eltham tramways at Eltham Green. Part of this new route was completed along Westhorne Avenue on 30th June 1932. This was the last major tramway construction in the capital until the inauguration of Croydon Tramlink in May 2000.

It might have been expected that new lines would require new vehicles to run on them, but improvements in rolling stock came at a price. The management of the LCC system was nothing if not conservative in its devotion to traditional looking vehicles. This anachronistic fixation with the tried and tested designs of the past – the eight wheel double decker was the norm – was becoming unattractive to many paying customers. Furthermore, hard wooden seats and open platforms were increasingly regarded as out of touch with passengers' demands. Part of the solution lay in more comfortable seating

London's most modern tramcars first appeared on the London United and Metropolitan Electric systems. The type UCC or Feltham tram offered a superior standard of comfort and they were immediately popular with passengers.
London Transport Museum

and a brighter interior décor, however, these innovations could not mask the fact that the Metropolitan Police, as licensing authority, had an aversion to the installation of driver's windscreens. Open fronted vehicles gave no protection against the elements for operating staff and they looked distinctly passé in the context of the late 1920s. The nett effect of all this was that tram design, in London at least, had not kept up with developments elsewhere.

The mould was eventually broken, not by the municipal tramways, but by the Combine. The General Manager of the Combine's three tramways, Christopher John Spencer, had been instrumental in inaugurating a research programme to produce a 'Super Pullman Car'. After the construction of several 'experimental' vehicles, the call went out for Lord Ashfield and his associates to inspect their latest assets. On 4th October 1929, they descended on Finchley Depot of the MET for a ride on two of the prototypes. The official party was not disappointed and an order was subsequently placed for a production batch of 100 vehicles. Built in house by Combine affiliate, the Union Construction Company of Feltham, Middlesex, the official designation for the trams was Type UCC, but they were known to the wider public as 'Felthams'.

It is worth quoting the words of W. H. Shaw, General Traffic Superintendent of the Combine tramways, in a 1932 scientific paper:

The UCC car designers and their advisers started out to design a car which, being of quite reasonable dimensions for a road vehicle, ignored the regulations. A bold policy and it succeeded in giving us a tramcar very much nearer the ideal and traffic requirements – a high degree of comfort for the slack hours with capacity in the rush. The principle must be the right one. So long, as in London, the omnibuses in their wisdom leave the workmen's traffic untouched, so long must there be a large capacity vehicle to carry those crowds.

Note that a deliberate attempt was made to challenge the antiquated Metropolitan Police regulations, which so hampered the LCC's design department. Lord Ashfield and his board obviously had influence in high places and their successful campaign later benefited other London operators. Public transport professionals from around the country were impressed with the modern features of the all enclosed Feltham tramcar, which included comfortable upholstered seating, a bright, spacious interior design, separate driver's cabs, entrance and exit doors, air brakes and up to date electrical equipment. The one luxury feature that impressed all observers and pulled in the punters during the winter months was the

provision of heaters. Passengers were invited to savour their journeys in a warm and cosy environment, so unlike that offered by other forms of public conveyance on London's streets. The new vehicles even inspired the LCC to start the process which led to the production of their state of the art tramcar – Bluebird car 1 of 1932.

The advent of the Felthams on the MET and LUT sections promised a future for the tram network. A booklet was produced for the general public, politicians and transport professionals. In an effort to avoid accidents the following safety devices were described:

On the near side of each dash panel is a FRONT EXIT cautionary notice with a bullseye centre. The application of the brakes automatically switches on a red light in the rear bullseye, as a warning to oncoming traffic, whilst the action of opening the front exit door causes a similar light at this end to indicate CAUTION to traffic approaching in this direction.

One would have thought there could be no mistaking when a Feltham wished to pick up and set down passengers, but some folk were still not satisfied. On 26th March 1931, Francis Curzon, 5th Earl Howe, prominent racing driver, past winner of the 24 hours Le Mans race and former Tory MP for Battersea South pointed out *a new difficulty is arising on the roads of this country* in a House of Lords debate on the Highway Code. Like many of his fellow peers he championed the right of the motorist not to give way to potential tram passengers. Furthermore, as a member of the committee of the RAC, he wanted the government to intervene to vet any new tram designs. Although hardly an objective witness, he trusted his powers of observation:

The new vehicles have windows all round,

and the passengers alight from the front end and not from the back. They are flush on the side, and you get no warning of the intention of anybody to alight.

Obviously, the warning signs and red lights had not made an impact on him or his chauffeur! Such deliberate anti-tram propaganda from the noble lords was to be expected, but a diminution of political support for London's tramways was also apparent in the lower house.

Herbert Morrison, the new Minister of Transport, now had wider national responsibilities for the movement of goods and people around the country. An extensive highway construction programme was being carried out as part of an unemployment relief scheme. Morrison was a motorist. He had discovered the joys of motoring in 1925, when Alderman Emil Davies of the LCC had presented him with a car to be used on Labour Party business. Lacking the sight in one eye, Morrison was the first to admit that he was an indifferent driver. Some of his passengers complained that a trip through the capital with Herbert at the wheel was positively hair raising. His new found transport freedom came at the expense of travelling by public transport. His attitude to the trams began to change.

On 25th September 1929, the Cabinet met to consider Morrison's draft proposals for a unified scheme of public transport within a radius of 25 miles (40km) from Charing Cross. Of the three models for the new traffic

Luxury car 1 was the prototype of a new series of LCC tramcars that never left the drawing board. Still wearing its attractive blue and white livery, it now displays the LONDON TRANSPORT fleet name on the side of the vehicle. Car 1 has been captured on film in Pemberton Gardens on the approach track to Holloway Depot.
Dave Jones Collection

authority – a joint municipal authority, an authority consisting of representatives of various interests, a business board – the latter won the day. In the words of Morrison and his colleagues in Cabinet:

In the interests of efficient operation, we favour the third alternative, namely, a *small board of business men of proved capacity.*

The minister explicitly stated that, as regards the composition of the new board: *there would seem to be no reason for giving* special representation to local authorities *qua tramway owners.*

In short, he doubted whether they would be up to the job.

The Minister further bolstered his case by quoting the following financial situation, in which only the indebtedness of London's municipal tramways was highlighted:

The total nominal capital of the companies is about £92,000,000, of which the Underground Common Fund Companies represent £62,500,000, the Tramway Companies £4,500,000 and the Metropolitan Railway Company £25,000,000. The total capital raised in respect of local authorities' tramways is over £23,000,000 and the outstanding debt on these tramways not redeemed or provided for is £11,000,000.

No doubt those listening round the Cabinet table gasped, when it was revealed that the trams were in hock to the tune of 11 million pounds. Ironically, bearing in mind the government of the day was a Labour one – socialists to a man – no mention was made of the fact that the trams provided a vital service for those on low incomes by offering cheap transport and workmen's fares. Within the confines of 10 Downing Street counter arguments detailing the rates and taxes paid by the trams, together with their contribution to the maintenance of the trunk roads were conspicuous by their absence.

Assuredly, the firebrand anti-Combine campaigner had mellowed somewhat in the few months since he took office. On 8th November 1929, Herbert Morrison was the guest of honour at the Underground Administrative Staff Dinner, which was held at the Café Royal. He was being wined and dined by the opposition and appeared to be enjoying himself. In his speech proposing the toast of 'The Companies' he praised Lord Ashfield:

I and Lord Ashfield can meet as we have before in every spirit of friendship and goodwill ... I recognise that Lord Ashfield, although the trustee of millions of pounds subscribed by shareholders, has taken a broad and, to a great extent, a public conception of his responsibilities.

Morrison went on to commend the noble Lord's progressive business spirit. In reply, Ashfield flattered his guest by congratulating him on achieving the post of Minister of Transport. Frank Pick reiterated this theme in his toast to 'The Guests', before everyone enjoyed an excellent cabaret in the ballroom, which was followed by dancing – a social activity particularly favoured by the new Minister.

Those rank and file members of the London Labour Party, who worked as platform staff and drivers on the buses and trams were excluded from this gathering,

Aside from the main trunk routes terminating in the centre of town, there were many suburban services providing important local links for communities. One such was the East Ham service from Royal Albert Dock to Wanstead Park. We observe the terminus at Wanstead Park Avenue, Aldersbrook Road. This section perished in 1936, to be replaced by buses; however, the buildings remain to this day. G. N. Southerden

When the Kingsway Subway reopened for double deck operation, cars of the new E/3 class found employment as the workhorses of services 31, 33 and 35. Car 1964 is depicted on its way from Battersea to Hackney. The three Kingsway Subway routes provided essential connections across London. They also attracted visitors to the capital, who wished to experience the novelty of an underground trip by tramcar. G. N. Southerden

During the planning stages of the LPTB the opportunity was taken to survey the congestion 'hot spots' of the capital. Inevitably, the Elephant and Castle intersection was the subject of much debate and controversy. In a far from ideal situation several policemen on point duty endeavour to maintain order.
We are looking towards London Road, where a car on Kingsway Subway route 35 heads the queue. On the right of the picture traffic in Newington Causeway awaits its turn. On the left a tram on route 2 turns southwards in the direction of Newington Butts, while car 1023 on route 66 is about to veer left towards Walworth Road.
London Transport Museum

as were all their other fellow workers on the Underground. One wonders how they felt, when their champion, Herbert Morrison, dyed-in-the-wool socialist, appeared to be hobnobbing with the management. Was this an indication that his support for the municipal tramways was ebbing away?

The thorny issue of traffic congestion was never far from the Minister's in tray. A particular black spot was at the Elephant and Castle junction in south London. A grand total of six tramway bearing roads met at this location. The solution favoured by the motoring lobby and several politicians was to dispense with the trams, but this would have crippled the system. One vast gyratory roundabout was one of the ideas debated in the London County Council (Improvements) Bill on 19th November 1930. Herbert Morrison stressed the economic importance in building a new layout suitable for 'modern conditions' and he reflected on the continued existence of the trams:

The tramway problem is by no means the principal incentive behind this project. I imagine that if the general manager of the tramways had been asked whether he would like to lead an agitation in favour of clearing up the Elephant and Castle, he would say: 'No, it is not an ideal place for circular tramway traffic. We get through and I am content to leave things as they are.'

Primarily, this is needed not on tramway grounds, but on general traffic grounds.

If the Bill goes through, the tramway position will, of course, be improved, and the tramways will not present the same difficulty to other forms of traffic as they do at present.

The implication that trams were a problem and a difficulty for other traffic was not a new one, but the idea was more surprising coming from the lips of one of their erstwhile staunchest supporters. As we shall see, the congestion at the Elephant and Castle would later be the subject of a speech by Lord Ashfield. During his time at the Ministry Herbert Morrison developed a new relationship with Ashfield. Both men were shrewd political operators, who needed one another. After the demise of two traffic coordination Bills, it became imperative for Morrison to consult with all interested parties in order to draft new legislation.

It has been said, and the minutes of the September 1929 Cabinet meeting support the idea, that the Minister shifted his position away from municipal socialism to state capitalism in the formulation of the new London Passenger Transport Bill, which was published on 13th March 1931. At a speech at Transport House on 17th April, Herbert Morrison described the Combine *as a very fine organisation*. Labour colleagues, who had a vision of advocating workers' control, were politely shown the door. It was anathema to Morrison that his enemy, Ernie Bevin, or indeed any of the union bosses, should be pulling the strings of the

new transport board. According to Morrison himself, he met Ashfield and:

I converted him to the London Passenger Transport Board by having three afternoons with him on our own.

In fact, a deal was hammered out between Morrison and Ashfield on three Saturday afternoons at the Ministry of Transport. Frank Pick was employed as Ashfield's advance guard. He played the role of hard negotiator with all the facts and figures at his finger tips. His boss, on the other hand, was more conciliatory and considerably more gracious, when it came to finalising a settlement.

As a result of these three post prandial sessions the trap began to close on London's tramways. There was still support in the House of Commons for preserving the system, but this was all but wiped out in the General Election of 27th October 1931. The formation of a new National Government in response to the Great Depression had resulted in the Labour Party losing 231 seats. Among the casualties were many of the London tram stalwarts, who had spoken up in favour of the LCC and the other municipal operators. One of the high profile candidates to be rejected by the electorate was the Minister of Transport. Herbert Morrison left office and devoted himself for the time being to local authority matters. The political sea change was manna from heaven for the Combine. It meant that Lord Ashfield and Frank Pick now had the prize firmly in their sights.

HERBERT MORRISON's LPTB Bill, introduced in March 1931, was classified as a 'hybrid', and as such, it was treated as a public Bill of national importance, which affected private interests – the shareholders of the Combine and others with a financial stake in the transport industry. The transport industry itself, in the shape of one of its influential trade magazines, THE COMMERCIAL MOTOR, was quick to point out in the issue dated 24th March 1931, one clause in the proposed legislation, which was of particular interest to its readers:

Whilst it is felt that tramways in the dense traffic areas cannot be condemned so long as they carry heavy loads from those areas, the case for tramways in the outer suburbs, where traffic is light, is weakened. The Bill, therefore, gives the Board power to deal with the abandonment of tramways where desirable.

It is fair to state that, almost since its inception in 1905, THE COMMERCIAL MOTOR had taken every opportunity to vilify street tramways, and now it seemed its voice was being heard loud and clear.

After the Labour debacle at the General Election the Bill was carried forward by the new National Government. Although Morrison took most of the credit for the eventual success of the Bill, it was Lord Ashfield, ably aided by Frank Pick, who nursed the project through to the statute book.

Indeed, it was the Combine that seemed to be taking the initiative. They had introduced modern vehicles in the form of the Feltham type trams and Frank Pick, putting aside for a moment his busman's cap, was credited with securing a new deal with Middlesex County Council in respect of leases granted to the MET network of routes. However, the management duo's next joint enterprise was to have catastrophic consequences for London's tramways. The project of modernising the semi moribund LUT system started in a small way. C. J. Spencer, the General Manager, suggested to Ashfield that the Kingston area routes be replaced by trolleybuses. This form of transport was variously dubbed trackless trolleys, trackless trams or just plain trolley omnibuses by promoters, who included vehicle and tyre manufacturers, electrical component suppliers, town planners and civic dignitaries anxious to rid their towns of the antiquated trams.

The trolleybus proposals found favour with the local authorities and the resulting Parliamentary Bill slipped through with a minimum of delay. In fact, it provoked very little debate. In legal terms the trolleybuses were treated very much as trackless trams and therefore obliged to offer workmen's fares. AEC, one of the affiliated companies to the Combine, supplied the chassis of the

rolling stock for the new venture, which commenced operation on 16th May 1931. A budget of £230,000 was allocated to the scheme, of which some £66,500 was to paid for the reinstatement of roads after the tram rails were removed. Tram route 69 from Twickenham to Kingston had the 'honour' of being the first line to be converted. Other services soon followed and by the autumn of 1931 trolleybuses had reached Wimbledon and had ousted trams on the Kingston town routes.

The locals were impressed. No longer did they have to suffer a ragbag of ramshackle tramcars on their streets. Many of the LUT vehicles, described rather unkindly as 'Victorian relics' by their critics, were so draughty and prone to shipping water during inclement weather that they earned the nickname 'influenza cars'! Passengers could now travel in comfort and, of course, motorists were mightily relieved after roadworks had removed the hated tramlines. All appeared sweetness and light. The only fly in the ointment was the cost of the whole project, still labelled 'experimental' by the Combine. What can only be described as 'creative accounting' solved the problem. A hire purchase deal and transfer of funds within the group took care of the paperwork.

In May 1932, General Manager Spencer gave a lecture to the Annual Congress of the Tramways, Light Railways and Transport Association, a prestigious gathering of transport bosses from the UK and the Continent of Europe. It is worth quoting his assessment of the financial results of his new trolleybuses:

Revenue from the routes converted to trolleybus operation has increased by approximately 26 per cent over the tramcar earnings in the corresponding period in the previous year, although the revenue per car mile is not very different from that of the tramcars. In order to provide adequate accommodation for the peak load periods it has been found necessary to run about 24 per cent more trolleybus miles, due to the smaller passenger carrying capacity of the vehicles as compared with tramcars. The extra miles have to some extent offset the gain in revenue. In fact, the result is that the total cost of trolleybus operation is rather more than that of the replaced tramcars, but fortunately the trolleybuses are earning, as stated, more revenue, and consequently there is a substantial improvement in the operating results.

This statement appeared to confirm to inveterate tram haters the wisdom of the conversion scheme, although doubts remained as to the viability of a Londonwide replacement programme. Those transport professionals not wedded to the trackless

scenario felt that Spencer was making generalised conclusions from a specific case. They remained to be convinced.

The main tram routes in the capital were safe for the moment. Trolleybuses just did not possess the carrying capacity to match their railbound predecessors. In fairness to C. J. Spencer and his vision for the future, he still favoured tramway modernisation on trunk services. Frank Pick, on the other hand, was

The Luxor Cinema, Twickenham provides the backdrop for a lone LUT tram on route 67 from Hampton Court to Hammersmith. Also noteworthy in this view is the way in which the London United Company cut costs in stringing trolleybus overhead wires. Wherever possible they used the existing tramway poles to support the new installation. One of the constants in life is change – the trams ceased in 1935, the replacing trolleybuses in 1962 and the Luxor was demolished in 1986 – such is progress!
Dave Jones Collection

known to be sceptical of the merits of trolleybus replacement of tramways, he reckoned his buses could do a better job. Pick, who had valuable contacts within the motor industry, was well aware of the latest advances in bus technology. These included improved chassis and bodywork construction allied to the more efficient Diesel engine (buses so equipped at the time were often called 'oilers', due to residual anti-German feeling!).

In a post luncheon speech at the opening ceremony of the LUT trolleybuses Frank Pick rather let the cat out of the bag:

Having purchased these trackless trolley vehicles with the expectation that we might profit, they are to be taken from us by a board set up by the government and all profits are to go to the same authority. We have this satisfaction in connection with this transfer: we have not paid for them yet. The new board may inherit our debts as well as our trackless trolleys. I do not think we of the London United will be very depressed at our immediate prospects.

Maybe this was a case of 'in vino veritas', but it was still rather tactless of Pick to

assert that the new legislation was already a done deal, with the implication that the state would cover the company's debts. The statement also confirms that the real cost of trolleybuses, bought on hire purchase instalments, may not have been quite the bargain originally claimed. The Combine's investors no doubt felt they were in a win-win situation; plans were being actively considered to include the trolleybus network to include several of South Metropolitan Company's lines radiating from Croydon. Trams working these services were outdated with a high proportion of four wheel, open top cars operating over single track and loops layouts. All in all, the senior management of the Combine must have been rather pleased with the comparative ease with which the LUT conversion had been achieved.

Frank Pick was confident in repeating the success by securing enough Parliamentary support for the LPTB Bill. The crux of the debate centred on financial matters concerning compensation and compulsory purchase of transport operators. Some Members of the House of Commons felt that the nation's taxpayers were being asked unfairly to stump up the cash to pay off debts incurred by the municipal tramways. The redoubtable John Jones MP kept up the opposition to the Bill. His was almost a lone voice in a last ditch attempt to keep his beloved West Ham Corporation Tramways out of the clutches of the new board. When he sat down at the end of the debate on 1st December 1932, he was defeated man.

The Parliamentary mood was summed up by Sir George Gillett MP for Finsbury in a debate on 14th February 1933:

The two systems, of tramways and omnibuses, the one private and the other municipal, competed for our custom. At last an arrangement was made to cut down to a certain extent the losses of both parties. I believe it is essential to have one service. I think the experience of London has proved that you have changing traffic conditions. The fact that the London County Council have, rightly or wrongly, expended a large amount of money in order to purchase their tramway system naturally inclines them to adhere to that system. But there are many towns where the tramways have been pulled up, and, in many parts of the country, it may have been a wise thing to do. . . The time may come when those responsible for the traffic problem of London may see that the day of the tramway is over. They may find some millions of money still unpaid, but it may be quite possible for them to divert the stream of traffic into the new tube or omnibus systems, so that they will be able to refund the tramway debt out of their income.

It was now widely accepted at Westminster that the trams would have to go. This position was strengthened by the findings of the Royal Commission on Transport, which had sat from October 1928 to December 1930. The august body of 11 citizens, which included the Marquess of Northampton and the Earl of Clarendon, published their report in 1931. It was quite concise in its recommendations. Although acknowledging the role played by tramways in urban transport, the report advised that no new tramways should be built and that existing systems should be gradually phased out, to be replaced by more modern forms of public transport.

Bearing in mind the well funded anti-tram lobby, these conclusions were to be expected. It was pointed out at the time that, as the members of the Commission were taken away from the Palace of Westminster in their chauffeur driven cars, the least of their worries concerned cheap fares and the transport needs of millions of tram passengers on low incomes. In real terms the Combine had now been given carte blanche to follow the national trend and dispense with London's tramways.

At a speech given to the Royal Society on 24th March 1933, Lord Ashfield gave a firm outline of his opinions on traffic congestion and its causes. Unsurprisingly, he singled out one form of transport for particular criticism. Ashfield's views would continue to dictate official policy:

At many points in London, as for example at the Elephant and Castle, the existence of tramways constitutes a special aspect of the problem, for tramways are undoubtedly a cause of congestion. They occupy the middle of the road, and following traffic has to be held up while passengers are picked up and set down; while those

Scene of many intense debates on the future of London's tramways, the Houses of Parliament overlook Westminster Bridge. The time by Big Ben is 10.37am, as car 798 makes its way towards Wimbledon on service 14. This tram route via Haydons Road was one of the earliest casualties of the new LPTB regime. Note the splendid array of motor vehicles; the opposition buses are out in force. Tradition and common sense dictated that nearly all non-tramway traffic kept clear of the tracks on Westminster and Blackfriars bridges.
London County Council

tramway terminals which are located at important junctions, occupy valuable road space just at those points where it is most required. The solution of the tramway problem appears to lie in the direction of producing a trackless trolley vehicle of equal capacity to that of the tramcar, free from the rigidity imposed upon it by the necessity of running upon rails. Where vehicles of this type have been operated in London it is satisfactory to note that there has been operated a distinct reduction of traffic congestion, and a greater fluidity of traffic movement as a whole has resulted.

Again, as in Morrison's 1930 Parliamentary speech, the vexed question of the road layout at the Elephant and Castle brought the tram 'problem' into the political spotlight. In truth, what the debate does highlight, is the single minded desire of contemporary highway engineers to refuse to contemplate any solution which incorporated the tramways into a modern road layout.

Traffic lights had first appeared at Ludgate Circus in July 1931. In this respect the Metropolitan authorities lagged way behind other great cities of the globe, where transport planners were investigating the possibilities of traffic signals favouring trams, thus speeding up the service. In connection with safety zones and passenger refuges this approach also enhanced general road safety. As far as London was concerned, the authorities were very worried about fatalities averaging four people a day. The trams were unfairly blamed, but in a three month period in 1930 buses were involved in 32 fatal accidents and trams in eight.

Persons unfortunate enough to fall in front of a tramcar had at least a sporting chance of survival. Each vehicle was equipped with a lifeguard gate which automatically tripped a tray to scoop up an obstruction from the roadway before it engaged with the wheels. Of course no such safety devices existed throughout the bus fleet.

In many countries it was acknowledged that trams, which pursued a fixed, predictable course through the streets, were inherently safer than other 'more flexible' modes of motor traffic. Indeed, it was maintained that the railbound vehicles imposed a form of lane discipline on other road users. Such arguments failed to register with Lord Ashfield and his associates.

Ashfield had decided on trolleybuses and his growing passion was bolstered by alleged disappointing news from routes equipped with the new Feltham tramcars. In fact the waters had been muddied by two different sets of results. On the MET trunk routes operated by Finchley and Wood Green depots the Type UCC vehicles were immediately popular with the travelling public, their

THE 74-SEATER TROLLEYBUS

ON March 27th, the largest capacity trolleybus in Great Britain was put into service by the L.U.T. between Hampton Court and Wimbledon.

This new trolleybus is an experimental A.E.C.—English Electric vehicle, the body of which was designed by a committee comprising A.E.C., Tramways, Railway and Omnibus engineers of the T.O.T. Group of Companies, and built by the L.G.O.C. at Chiswick. The driver's cab is built in the main body and in general appearance the vehicle resembles the "Q" type bus.

The more notable features of the new trolleybus are :—

A six-wheel chassis.

An overall length of 30 feet.

Weight fully laden, under 13 tons.

Power from an 80 h.p. motor, mounted in the centre of the chassis, and linked to the rear axle by one short driving shaft.

Trolley poles and base of a new lightweight type.

A central entrance with a low, wide platform, made possible by a dropped chassis-frame. Sliding doors, pneumatically operated, controlled by the driver.

Seating accommodation for 74 passengers

—34 in the lower and 40 in the upper saloon. (The existing L.U.T. trolleybuses seat 56 passengers.)

Longititudinal and crosswise seats, fitted with rubber cushions and upholstered in moquette.

Emergency exits at the rear of upper and lower saloons.

A Courageous Tramwayman

Mr. J. Ward, District Inspector, L.U.T., has been congratulated by the Directors of the Isleworth Brewery, on the courage he displayed in stopping two of their horses, which were attached to a dray, when they bolted from outside the "Coach and Horses," London Road, Hounslow. Mr. Ward, who showed great presence of mind, seized the bridle of the offside horse and, although dragged along for about forty yards, managed to bring the animals to a standstill before any serious damage was done.

progress only being hampered by slower LCC cars working the joint services. Passenger levels remained healthy on these routes between the northern suburbs and central London. On the Uxbridge Road, on route 7 of the London United, the story was more complicated. Whether by design or accident, the Combine had made three crucial errors in respect of rolling stock, power distribution and track layout.

The service was maintained by a combination of the old and new, consequently, intending passengers never knew if they were going to get a comfortable Feltham or a draughty survivor from the first decade of the century. This uncertainty affected ridership levels. Maintenance of an efficient power supply also determined the level of service on the route. The electrical infrastructure, as originally put in place by the LUT in the early 1900s, was now beginning to show its age. Although updated sub station equipment was installed at Southall and Hayes, the power requirements of the new tramcars were only partially met, thus causing inevitable delays and slow running during peak load times.

However, the main problem lay in the track layout. Beyond the canal bridge at Southall the line was basically single track and passing loops until the outskirts of Uxbridge. This antiquated arrangement caused delays especially in the rush hours. Reconstruction of the main road to dual carriageway standards had been started by Middlesex County Council. This left the way open for the tram tracks to be positioned on the central reservation, provided agreement could be reached with the Combine. It is worth noting that, when the same local authority offered a similar chance to rebuild roads in the MET operating area in the 1920s, the idea was firmly kicked into the long grass. Apparently Frank Pick had neither the vision nor the cash to snap up the offer.

In fact, pro-tram supporters accused Frank Pick of being remarkably two faced. At the Combine's Annual Tramways Staff Dinner, held on 24th January 1930, at the Trocadero Restaurant, the guest of honour was the Deputy Chairman himself. A staff reporter at the event noted:

Mr Pick went on to say that the chief trouble

above The Feltham type luxury trams breathed new life into Uxbridge Road route 7. Whilst a lady is boarding at the rear of the car, another passenger makes an exit at the front. One assumes the gentleman with the briefcase and brolly does not want to miss his tram home. It was the operation of these vehicles at tram stops that so mystified and annoyed Lord Howe. London Transport Museum

left The last LCC line to be built was here on Westhorne Avenue, Eltham. The council houses on the nearby estate were constructed to a pleasing design with adjacent spaces for gardens and trees. Residents were supplied with quality public transport in the shape of tram route 72. For a few pennies a ride could be taken to the heart of the capital or to the shopping centres of Lewisham and Woolwich. This location has changed considerably in the intervening years and now forms part of the interchange between the South Circular Road and the A2 Rochester Way Relief Road. D. A. Thompson/LCCT Trust

with tramways in the early days was that insufficient space was allowed for them on the highway. He declared that, had a wider space been left, our tramways would be bigger and better today.

The Chairman [sic] then touched for a moment upon the question of finance. He said that tramways had in the past been greatly handicapped by lack of money but, he was glad to say, things were now taking a turn for the better.

Pick used the 'lack of space' argument as a stick to beat the tramways and yet, when given the opportunity to modernise the layout, he demurred.

The LCC had taken advantage of Government funds in the form of unemployment relief grants to push through construction of the Westhorne Avenue extension. This begs the question why the London United and Middlesex County Council were unsuccessful in tapping the same source of investment capital in order to upgrade the route. The reality was that journey times from Shepherds Bush terminus to Uxbridge were hardly altered by the introduction of the new rolling stock and therefore it could be stated that the performance of modern vehicles on route 7 did not live up to expectations.

Another more pressing reality occurred on 13th April 1933, when the LPTB Bill received the Royal Assent. Appointments to the new board were announced on 18th May. Lord Ashfield was chairman and Frank Pick his vice-chairman. The other members were John Cliff, assistant general secretary of the TGWU; Patrick Ashley Cooper, former director of the Bank of England; Sir John Gilbert, former chairman of the LCC; Sir Edward Holland, alderman of Surrey County Council; Sir Henry Maybury, highway engineer and roads adviser to the Ministry of Transport.

If we take a moment to look at the names on the list, the most obvious omission is Morrison himself. One would have thought this assembly of the great and the good might have found space for the former Minister of Transport, who lost his Parliamentary seat in 1931. However, the gentleman concerned was far too busy organising the London Labour Party for their campaign to gain control of the LCC. As for the other members of the board, some names stand out. John Cliff of the TGWU had started his career in July 1900 as a tram conductor in Leeds. He later acted as assistant to Ernie Bevin and was principally concerned in representing the interests of London Transport staff. Sir Henry Maybury was the subject of an interesting tale told to their Lordships on 3rd March 1932. Lord Conway of Allington, who admitted to having somewhat of an obsession with tram scrapping, related the story:

Mr Maybury, then road surveyor to Kent, decided to make the road between Eltham and Lewisham the finest road in the world. ... He reckoned without the London County Council. No sooner was the road done (or very shortly afterwards) then along comes the County Council, takes it all up, and lays down trams, which nobody wanted, and utterly destroyed that piece of road which had been built at so great a price.

Aside from Mr Cliff there appeared to be no potential tram supporters on the board. Indeed the opposite was probably the case. No place could be found for a representative from one of the handful of municipal tramways absorbed by the LPTB. A diehard like John Jones MP could not have realistically expected to be included in the decision making process.

Thus the appointees took up their positions. A new day had dawned for London's public transport and, although the occupants of the managerial chairs were unaware of the future, the reign of the LPTB was to last from 1st July 1933 until 31st December 1947.

July, 1933   T.O.T. STAFF MAGAZINE   221

LONDON PASSENGER TRANSPORT BOARD
1ST JULY, 1933.

MR. JOHN CLIFF; MR. PATRICK ASHLEY-COOPER; MR. FRANK PICK; SIR EDWARD JOHN HOLLAND;
(Vice-Chairman)

SIR JOHN WILLIAM GILBERT,   THE RT. HON. LORD ASHFIELD   SIR HENRY MAYBURY,
K.B.E.   (Chairman)   G.B.E., K.C.M.G.

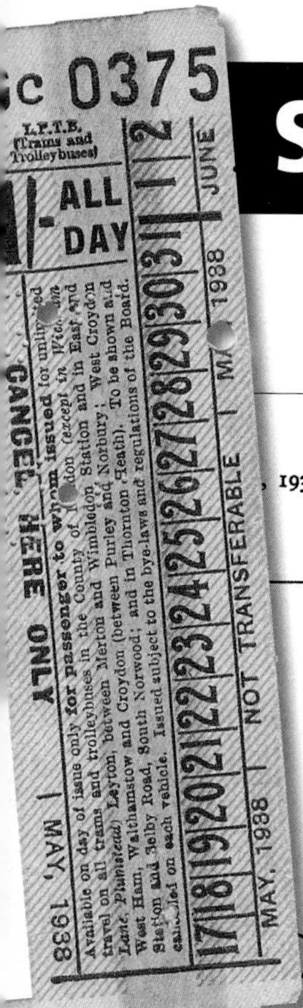

SHILLING ALL DAY

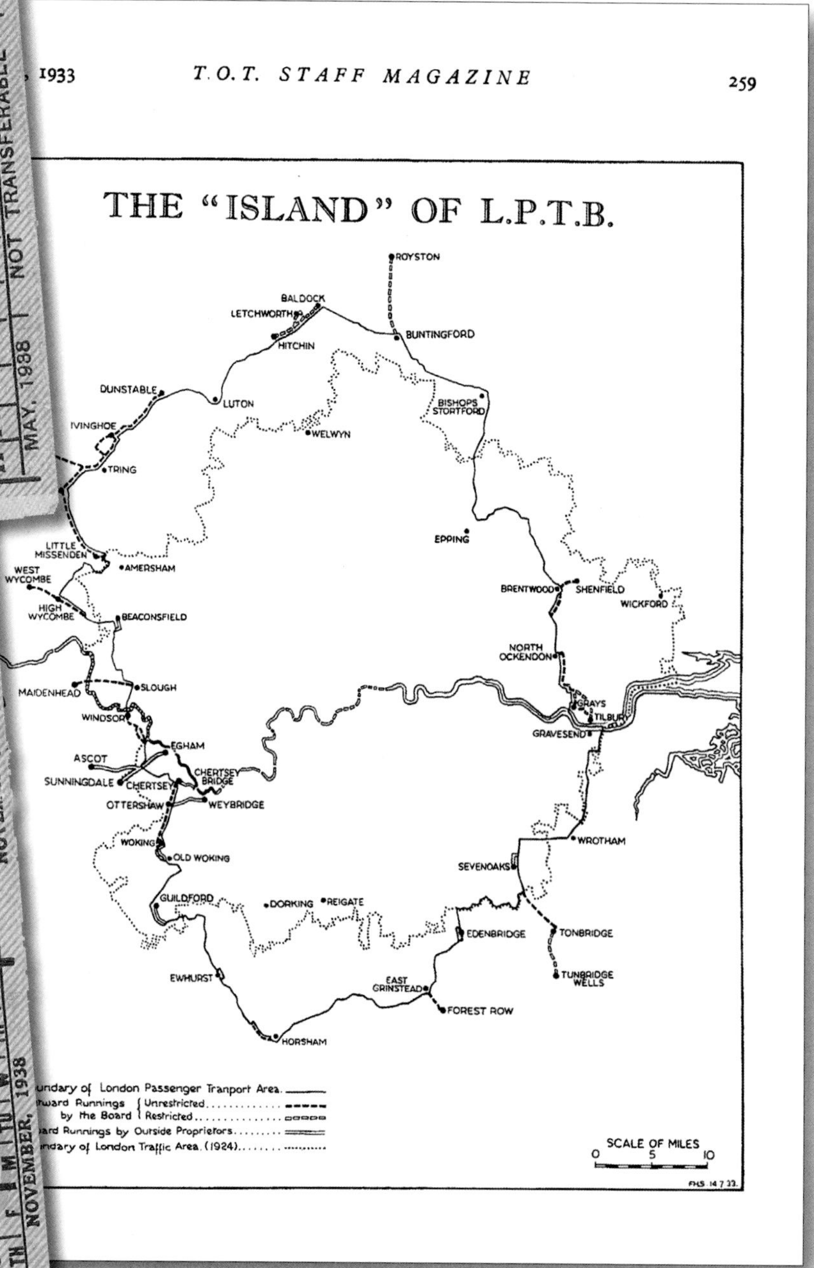

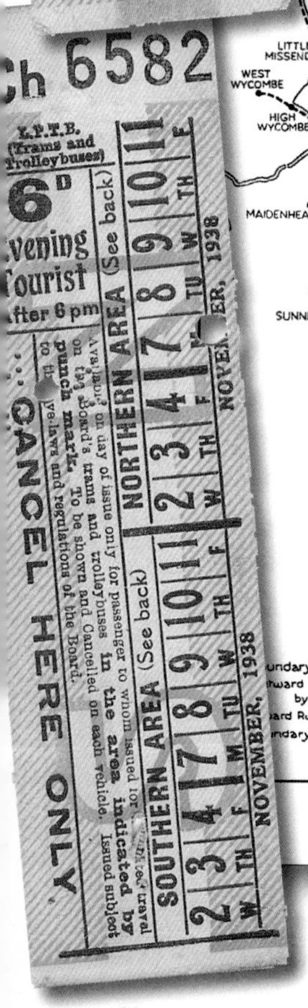

T.O.T. STAFF MAGAZINE   259

THE "ISLAND" OF L.P.T.B.

Boundary of London Passenger Transport Area.
Inward Runnings { Unrestricted / Restricted } by the Board
Inward Runnings by Outside Proprietors
Boundary of London Traffic Area. (1924)

SCALE OF MILES
0   5   10

FHS 14.7.33

I N THE summer of 1933 the idea that all London's tramways were on or nearing their last legs is a gross distortion of the truth. Travel costs were cheap; the Shilling (5p) All Day ticket, which gave unlimited travel over most of the system, was greatly appreciated, especially by folk of limited financial means. Cheap midday fares, ordinary returns and the wide possibilities of transfer journeys on the same ticket added to the attractiveness of tram travel. Unfortunately, others with a different agenda ensured that the anti-tram propaganda of the period was so ingrained it developed a vocabulary of its own. Trams never went anywhere, they crawled, clanked, clattered or crashed their way through the landscape. This was in complete contrast the almost noiseless trolleybuses, which managed to glide to their destinations.

Obviously, critics were unaware that many members of the London Transport tram fleet could show their internal combustion engine competitors a clean pair of heels. Aided by fast acceleration, the ex-Walthamstow cars, together with the four motor HR/2 vehicles and the UCC Felthams, regularly matched or exceeded the 30 mph urban speed limit, introduced by the Ministry of Transport in 1934. In an era before radar speed traps Metropolitan Police personnel in patrol vehicles were issued with instructions to keep an eye out for tramcars being driven in excess of the permitted 30 miles per hour (48km/h) on such well known 'race tracks' as Southbury Road, Woodford New Road, Downham Way, Westhorne Avenue and Brighton Road, South Croydon. Late night journeys back to the depot could be particularly exhilarating for many tram passengers!

However, some commentators persisted in clinging to the tram dilapidation fiction in an effort to justify the abandonment programme. The network inherited by the new board on 1st July 1933 certainly had its detractors, but the tram system was still vitally important for the economic wellbeing of the capital. Just under 18 months before vesting day trams had carried almost 30 per cent of the annual total passenger traffic in London. Route mileage was calculated at 328 (528km). The constituent tram systems of London Transport, as the LPTB was known colloquially, were inspected by engineers, enabling decisions to be made on the condition of track and rolling stock. Future policy was going to be influenced by these reports. Contrary to rumours circulating at the time, none of the operators was in such a state of disrepair that public safety was endangered.

In the top category of efficiency can be placed the LCC and the MET trunk routes. The London County Council network of 158

route miles (254km) operated by 1,663 trams formed the centre of operations. Some 123 route miles (198km) were conduit equipped; the rest of the system used overhead wires. Passengers were encouraged to avail themselves of the best fare bargain in the capital. The purchase of a Shilling All Day ticket allowed unlimited travel over the whole LCC network and many of the joint services with other operators.

Through running with the MET was an important feature of daily operation. The Metropolitan Electric worked over 53 route miles (85km) with a fleet of 316 tramcars. The municipal systems of east London accommodated a mixed fleet of vehicles with the more up-to-date versions being employed on joint services with the LCC. The 'back street' routes saw intensive service catering for some of the poorest inhabitants of the

metropolitan area. The odd man out in the east was Ilford, which pretty much kept itself to itself and claimed to be the only tramway in London to run consistently at a profit!

The County Borough of Croydon lay south of the River Thames and maintained a main line connection with the LCC at Norbury. It also possessed a compact tram system, worked, jointly in some cases, by the Corporation and the South Metropolitan Company. The latter company operated as far as Sutton and had a connection with the LCC at Tooting. Open top, four wheel trams were a common sight and gave the area a distinctly 'period' feel.

The remaining three operators included the London United, whose route mileage had

above Out on the A23 Brighton Road motormen could occasionally indulge in some strictly illegal speeding. The favoured time was late in the evening, when there was less traffic about. Even in broad daylight, as illustrated in this picture, there was plenty of opportunity to demonstrate the swiftness of electric traction without the encumbrance of other vehicles. The Croydon tracks were usually well maintained and lent themselves to fast running. D. A. Thompson/LCCT Trust

left The former MET tracks in Southbury Road were the setting for some swift journeys between Enfield and Ponders End. Towards the end of the tramway era at this location car 2172 pauses to allow passengers to alight. One very modern feature ahead of the road junction was a 'skate' in the overhead wire. This was activated by the trolley wheel and alerted the nearby traffic lights to the tram's presence. D. A. Thompson/LCCT Trust

been curtailed by trolleybus replacements, and the municipal pair of Erith and Bexley. The Uxbridge Road route of the LUT was still regarded by some as having star performer potential and had been partly equipped with Feltham type tramcars. No such modern rolling stock was available for Bexley and Erith. These two were cast in the roles of lame ducks of the network, and thus were obvious candidates for early abandonment.

As regards the management structure of the new set up, T. E. Thomas, former General Manager of the LCC Tramways, was appointed to head the Central, South and East divisions, while C. J. Spencer of the Combine retained control of the North and West divisions. This arrangement was short lived, because Spencer left the LPTB in October 1933. There were rumours of personality differences between him and Lord Ashfield. Thereafter, Thomas remained in sole charge, and it was he who decided on action, when the various reports reached his desk. His offices were situated at the former LCC headquarters in Belvedere Road by County Hall.

Reporting to the General Manager were his rolling stock assessors. They were allotted the task of casting a critical eye over their inheritance. The LPTB took charge of 2,615 double deck and a mere 15 single deck tramcars. Thomas's department was also responsible for 61 double deck trolleybuses – one assumes that Messrs Pick and Ashfield had now arranged for them to be fully paid up members of the fleet! To get some idea of the scale of the London Transport organisation, the motor bus totals included 4,104 double deck and 977 single deck vehicles.

Although electric tramcars were, and are still, built to last with a service life in excess of that of the average motor bus, the missives reaching Thomas's desk must have given him food for thought. Aside from obvious disaster zones, such as the 'boneyard' in the grounds of Fulwell Depot, where numbers of the former London United fleet were quietly mouldering away, the continued use of open top vehicles was unacceptable and needed urgent attention. Many of these cars dated from the turn of the century. On the other side of the coin, representing a substantial investment for the future, there were around

450 vehicles constructed in the late 1920s and early 1930s.

A report dated 26th May 1934 crossed T. E. Thomas's desk. He had asked for the latest cost analysis pertaining to his Tram & Trolleybus Department. The document noted that the average number of tramcars in service was 2,476 and that in the financial year 1932/1933 the maintenance costs of trackwork, paving and road surfaces amounted to £252,000. In this context the average cost per tramcar was £102 per annum. It was stated that a 73 seater trolleybus was taxed £106–16s–0d in licence duty. The document concluded:

Having regard to the relative capacity of the vehicles employed it would seem that there would be no difference in the annual costs to the Board from the substitution of trolley buses for tramcars.

Aside from its passenger carrying responsibilities, the new board became one of the capital's major land owners. A considerable acreage of prime sites was occupied by tram tracks, yards, outbuildings and, in several cases, ornamental small gardens, reflecting municipal pride in their transport system. Often forgotten, but cherished by the animal loving British, were the sundry felines on the staff in the time honoured role of depot cats keeping down the local rodent population.

Vehicles were housed in 36 depots, varying in size from the small set up, situated off the charmingly named Walnut Tree Road, Erith, which housed 16 trams under cover, to one of the largest establishments of its type in Europe at New Cross, which could accommodate 314 vehicles. Repair and maintenance facilities were available at the former LCC Central Repair Depot at Charlton, and at Hendon Works in north

London, Fulwell in west London and West Ham in the East End. Stores of permanent way materials were kept at Rye Lane Yard, Deptford Wharf, Battersea Wharf, Leven Road Wharf, Poplar and Brentford PW Yard.

All properties had been visited by the new owners with a view to their potential for conversion to bus or trolleybus operation. Even before a detailed inspection took place, it was immediately obvious to the survey teams that some sites were completely unsuitable for further development. It was not just a case of giving premises the odd lick of paint. In some establishments time had stood still since the first decade of the twentieth century – earlier than that in the case of former horse tramway buildings converted to electric traction. Demolition and reconstruction to 1930s standards with modern canteen and crew facilities was just not feasible and it was no surprise that the LPTB condemned a number of sites. First to go, on 16th August 1933, was the former municipal tramways depot in Nelson Street, East Ham. Vehicles were transferred to the much larger facility at Greengate Street, West Ham. All in all, out of the 36 starters in the LT tram depot race, only 26 completed the course and were deemed suitable for long term use by replacement buses or trolleybuses.

It might have been thought in this rush for efficiency that the route structure would have been rationalised to fit in with the other modes of transport inherited by the LPTB. Coordination of public transport services to avoid wasteful competition appeared a common sense way forward. There was a strong argument in favour of curtailing bus routes which served the same roads as trams on trunk services. Savings could be made on

fuel, rubber and other precious commodities, as well as ensuring that the electrically powered, environmentally friendly tramcars took the main load. However, almost no progress was achieved in this sphere. One was left with the impression that the buses and trams were two different competing organisations. On the Barking Road and Commercial Road there were 10 bus routes shadowing the trams; the story was the same all over the capital. On the Bow Road, tram services 61 and 63 were accompanied by

nine motor bus routes. Trunk services from Croydon to Streatham started with four bus 'companions' and ended up with seven. On the Uxbridge Road the bus presence multiplied from three to seven routes on the approaches to Shepherds Bush.

At the latter location there had been a very early attempt at transport coordination. In 1899 the board of the London United Tramways had begun the process of integrating their proposed new electric tram service with that offered by the new

Central London Railway tube line from Shepherds Bush to central London and the City. Through fares were later introduced, but an interchange station away from the street, where passengers could transfer from the trams to Underground trains by means of moving staircases, never left the drawing board. The project was resurrected after the First World War, but the Combine was unwilling to supply the requisite funds.

The prevailing philosophy coming from 55 Broadway, SW1, headquarters of the new board, indicated that the principle of employing buses (or tube trains) as feeders to the trams was not one they wished to adopt. In fact, an uncharacteristic air of sloppiness crept into proceedings, when it came to sorting out tram route numbers. Part logical, part haphazard, the LCC service numbers and those pertaining to joint operations terminating in central London were retained. However, the situation was far from ideal with duplication of route numbers. Route 7 ran from Parliament

One the depots inherited by the London Passenger Transport Board was situated at Abbey Wood. As can be seen, the interior was strictly utilitarian. In common with many ex-LCC establishments the place was equipped with a traverser to move trams sideways to the various stabling roads. The three standard E/1 class vehicles in the picture will probably leave the building in time for the evening peak period.
London Transport Museum

Hill Fields to Holborn; it also joined Sutton to West Croydon, and for good measure, it appeared on the Felthams travelling from Shepherds Bush to Uxbridge! To add insult to injury, long after this mess should have been sorted, the official timetable for March 1935 listed no less than two number 10s, two 55s, two 57s, two 60s, two 62s, two 66s and two route 68s. It was patently obvious that someone in the planning department had a horror of easing the numerical pressure by exceeding the century mark, consequently, there never were any tram services numbered in the hundreds. A somewhat lame official explanation for the chaos cited the fact that many of these tram routes were not long for this world and that any renumbering might confuse the passengers!

Plans for the abandonment of part of the tramway network focused initially on those short sections of track, which were covered by existing bus routes or could be operated more economically by motor vehicles. In fairness, estimates were prepared for tramway reconstruction, but one is left with the impression that this process was a cursory one and was never intended to be a serious statement of policy. On 23rd November 1933, it was announced that London Transport was promoting legislation to substitute trolleybuses for trams on 90 route miles (145km). On the previous day a press release was distributed, which contained a map of the new trolleybus routes. This was unwelcome news for the dwindling number of tram supporters. Trolleybuses with a seating capacity equal to that of the average

tramcar were touted as the solution to traffic congestion. All the main tramways leading to central London were now vulnerable.

However, before the main trolleybus thrust, certain tidying up of tram routes took place. In every case motor buses were the preferred form of replacement. The first two casualties were tracks formerly owned by the South Metropolitan Company. On 7th December 1933, service 4 from Penge to the Robin Hood junction with Anerley Road disappeared, together with a service 6 curtailment, resulting in abandonment of track between Mitcham Fair Green and Cricket Green. Not too far way, on 16th May 1934, ex-LUT rails in Haydons Road, Wimbledon and in Plough Lane became redundant, leaving only a short spur to serve the Summerstown Stadium.

The only other abandonment of note took place outside the central bus area. The Kentish market town of Dartford had been served by trams since 14th February 1906. Almost three decades of public service were cut short, when the local single track and loops route to Wilmington bowed out on 17th April 1934, to be replaced by additional vehicles on country bus service 401. Track was retained to Dartford Station at the northern end of the Wilmington Branch. Here in north Kent, as in the Wimbledon, Mitcham and Penge areas, arrangements were made by the LPTB to deal with the redundant tramway infrastructure.

According to the strict letter of the law – the Tramways Act 1870 – when a tramway was abandoned, the roadway had to be rest-

ored to its previous condition, before tracks were laid. Obviously, leaving the highway in the same condition as existed in horse tram days was a complete nonsense, bearing in mind the requirements of 1930s motor traffic. The situation required some tact and diplomacy; delicate negotiations were commenced with local authorities to solve this particular problem. Needless to say, there was much haggling over money. Rails were sometimes lifted, but often they were just covered with a layer of asphalt in the knowledge that the roadway would be thereby reinforced by their continued presence. Traction standards, now bereft of overhead wires, were often retained for street lighting purposes. Those in Lowfield Street, Dartford on the abandoned Wilmington branch lasted into the 1950s, while in many other locations disused tramlines have endured, undisturbed and unseen, into the present century as mute reminders of a bygone era.

Now, seemingly at the eleventh hour, a ray of hope appeared for the beleaguered tram supporters. An article was published in the February 1934 issue of PENNYFARE, the staff magazine of the LPTB. As such, one assumes it carried the official stamp of approval. Under the title *Cinderella Speaks Her Mind* it praised the service rendered by the trams:

Most readers of 'Pennyfare' are, no doubt, aware that a tramway authority, besides paying rates on its track, is required to maintain the road surface between the rails, together with a border, eighteen inches wide, on either side. This means that the Borough Councils through whose streets tramways operate are saved the cost of upkeep of an average considerably exceeding one half the width of those streets. In round figures this saving is estimated at £250,000 per annum in the LCC area alone; the rates on track in the same area amount to a further £31,000 per annum.

It is true that, like Cinderella, the tramways have performed an enormous amount of valuable work, but unlike her, they have received no visit from a fairy godmother. Tramwaymen, however, are the very soul of patience, and they can be relied on to give ungrudging service to the travelling public. . . Cheap fares, an important item in the passengers' eyes, are made possible on tramways because of their comparatively low operating costs . . .

The up-to-date tramcar is unsurpassed for comfort and safety. On a foggy night the tram way is often the only way. The fact that trams are looked on with disfavour by some other road users as being the cause of congestion, is more than counterbalanced by their special usefulness in dealing with large masses of passengers during rush periods.

London has reason to be proud of its tramways, and as part of London Transport they are likely to remain indispensable for many years to come.

Truly, the powers that be at 55 Broadway were giving out mixed messages. Positive terms such as 'low operating costs, comfort, safety, usefulness and indispensable' seem totally at odds with the general ethos of tramway abandonment. Was this article a final desperate plea from one of the last friends of the tramcar?

Hope springs eternal. Even from the mouth of the Chairman himself, there appeared to be some straws of comfort for tramway supporters. In a lecture delivered at the London School of Economics on 5th March 1934, Lord Ashfield attempted to present an overview of the finances of the LPTB:

So far as can be estimated, the whole of the Underground and Tube Railways earn sufficient money to pay their working expenses, to set aside reasonable sums to meet depreciation and to provide for the renewal of their equipment, and after

meeting the interest upon those of their securities which have a prior charge upon their revenues, have left a sum of money sufficient to pay little more than 1 per cent upon the balance of the capital employed.

The average return upon the whole capital is only 3¼ per cent, and no provision is made for the redemption of the capital invested in these railways.

If I turn to the tramways, the position is a little better. The combined tramway under-takings in London, after meeting working expenses, and making adequate provision for the renewal of the equipment employed, earn upon the capital invested in them a rate of interest of just over 4 per cent.

If I turn to the omnibuses, of the 220 million car miles which the omnibuses run in a year, roundly 25 per cent are run which do not earn a revenue sufficient to meet in full the costs of their provision which the Board must make for the service of London in the discharge of its duty as a public utility undertaking, and on the other hand, it shows how slender are the resources which the Board have at their disposal for development and expansion . . .

The highlighted section devoted to tramways only serves to deepen the mystery. On the face of it the much maligned trams seem to be in a better position financially than other forms of transport in the organisation. There certainly appears to be no indication from the noble lord's speech that the 'slender resources of the Board' are about to expand to encompass the millions of pounds needed to junk the tram system.

Hopes were eventually dashed when the

main legislation did materialise, in the form of the London Passenger Transport Board Act 1934. There was to be no fairy godmother to rescue Cinderella. The Act confirmed that the board were seeking powers to introduce a staged withdrawal of trams in favour of their trackless counterparts. Contracts were let as part of a vast procurement programme, however, there were some who still harboured doubts about the wisdom of the whole scheme. Whilst the replacement of trams by trolleybuses in the Kingston and Wimbledon areas had been hailed as a success, it was an altogether more complicated situation nearer to the heart of the metropolis. Putting poles and wires, where none had previously existed, in streets served by former LCC conduit equipped lines, was bound to attract unwanted criticism.

As for world famous vistas, such as the view across Westminster Bridge to the Houses of Parliament, a barrage of protest could be expected. The thought of the alleged visual disfigurement caused by ugly overhead wires roused the ire of many campaigners. One detects a certain naivety in London Transport's planning, if they expected the hostility of the affluent and influential anti-tram lobby to be placated by the appearance of trolleybuses in the City or the West End, or indeed in any of the previous tramless areas of fashionable London.

Lord Ashfield and his staff had a fight ahead of them, but they appeared determined to see the back of the trams within the decade. If further evidence were needed of the Chairman's intent, then the guests at the Auxiliary Omnibus Companies Association annual dinner, held on 23rd October 1934, were left in no doubt as to future priorities:

Lord Ashfield said that approximately £115,000,000 was invested in London Transport, while an annual wages bill of £15,000,000 was paid out of the gross earnings of £27,000,000. London Transport vehicles carried 9,500,000 passengers daily, an annual total of 3,500 million people; and each one of the 75,000 employees should feel the pride and satisfaction of belonging to this magnificent organisation . . . More money was needed to provide better omnibuses, develop the trolleybus and continue the Underground extensions, each mile of which cost nearly £800,000.

The London tramway system was now well and truly left out in the cold.

Car 1871 belongs to the HR/2 class. These powerful vehicles were employed on services traversing Dog Kennel Hill in south London. They were built to last several life times. They had a good turn of speed and could be relied upon in all weathers.
D. A. Thompson/LCCT Trust

MISSED OPPORTUNITIES

ROUND CHARLTON DEPÔT

From Donkey-Days to Pullman Ways

THE days when tramcars were drawn along the Walworth Road by three donkeys were recalled, when we paid a visit to the Central Repair Depot, Tramways, at Charlton.

Mr. W. H. Baverstock, the foreman of the saw mills, has seen the evolution of the tramcar from those donkey-drawn car days to the present day, with its luxurious pullman car, distinguished by its blue and white finish and streamline effect. Although 69 years of age, Mr. Baverstock has a remarkable memory, and his faculty for remembering dates is surprising. His tramway career goes back to 1887.

One of his assistants, leading-hand F. S. C. Searle, can go back even further, to 1886, when he joined the North Metropolitan Tramway Company.

The Charlton Depot covers about seven acres and is built on reclaimed land, at one time a marsh. The foundations of the shops are laid on a concrete raft and piles.

Through the Shops

The overhaul of cars at Charlton is on the progressive system. As one enters the South end, on the left is the Mechanical Section while on the right are the Bodywood, Wiring and Painting Sections.

In the latter sections four tracks are equipped with continuously moving ropeways, two of which are in the body repair shop and two in the paint shop. Each ropeway is about 370 ft. long and travels at a uniform speed of 3 inches per minute, and output can be regulated by the number of units on them. Extensive body repairs are dealt with on a stationary road.

When a car arrives for complete overhaul, the body is lifted by an electric hoist, the trucks are removed to the truck shop in the Mechanical Section and replaced by already overhauled trucks. The car is then connected with the body-shop ropeway, in which shop the seat cushions are removed, together with any fittings and

furniture needing attention, and the structure of the car body overhauled. Controllers are re-coppered or replaced and power and lighting cables tested.

The car is then ready for the paint shop, but before being connected to this shop's ropeway, trucks and lifeguards are sprayed-painted with low-pressure spray-guns.

Quick Work

On entering the shop, the car is attached to the ropeway and the process of washing down the body, giving one coat of colour, fixing transfers and one coat of varnish is completed in 15½ working hours, the paint and varnish being applied by brush. Meanwhile, the trucks removed to the truck shop are dismantled on another ropeway, consisting of two tracks in the Mechanical Section, which is about 270 ft.

LONG-SERVICE CHARLTON MEN
Mr. W. H. Baverstock, Foreman, saw mills, 47 years', and Leading Hand F. S. C. Searle, 48 years' service.

THE OLDEST AND THE YOUNGEST
Mr. H. Perry (69), and Boy A. Durrant (14), standing beside a 14-inch Gap-bed face-plate lathe

long, where motors are removed and trucks completely dismantled on one track, while on the other track the trucks are reassembled and equipped with motors which have been renovated on another section of the ropeway in the motor shop.

In the plough shop we met Mr. A. Birch, the foreman, who has been associated with tramways for over 31 years. Mr. Birch showed us several specimens of early ploughs which, in service and utility, compare unfavourably with those in use to-day. Roughly, we were told, 1,000 ploughs per week are re-conditioned.

Tyre Grinding

The tramcar wheel tyres are in most cases corrected for shape of the tread by grinding in machines for that purpose. Very badly worn and flatted tyres are turned and the flange is formed in wheel lathes. In order that shrinking-on of tyres should not affect the mechanical properties obtained by heat treatment on the 70-80 ton

per square inch tensile tyre, use is made of an electric tyre-heating transformer that prevents the tyres being raised above safe temperature.

In the machine shop, we found a 14-in. Gap-bed face-plate lathe being operated by Mr. H. Perry, who has been working on this type of machine for 27 years. He is 69 and the oldest member of the Charlton staff.

We also stopped for a while to watch Mr. H. Corderey operating a capstan machine, which at the time was turning rocker-lever bolts. The multi-coloured shavings, which peel off in concertina fashion, would delight the hearts of youngsters.

In the foundry, much of the tramways standard equipment is cast, and the use of an elevator and conveyors has made it possible to have the moulding boxes broken out over a grid and the sand elevated, milled and returned to the storage bins for use. The bins are right over a duplex-pneumatic ramming machine, and, in consequence, output is expedited and waste eliminated.

A further item of interest was the mechanical stokers in the boiler house to where the wood shavings are conveyed through ducts from the saw-mill and mixed with the coal. There is very little avoidable waste at Charlton.

British Standards Institution Class B insulation for traction motors has been adopted for armature and field coils, magnetic coils and controller windings. The windings derive increased life from the higher temperatures permissible with this class of asbestos insulation, compared with cotton-covered conductors. The armature coils are machine-wound and passed to women operatives, who form them in hot and cold presses and insulate the coils with mica cloth sheets.

Craftsmanship

The foregoing is just a brief description of part of the work undertaken at "Charlton." The staff approximates 1,000 workpeople, and although only renovation and repair of tramcars is generally carried out, when necessary a complete tramcar

---

AN OBJECTIVE observer of London's transport scene in the early 1930s might have concluded that it was a reasonable policy to abandon certain 'time expired' tramways. It was also reasonable to assert that the type of replacement vehicle, be it with electric traction in the form of trolleybuses, was a matter for the planners at 55 Broadway. Piecemeal curtailments of the tram system imparted a deceptive sense of permanence. The threat to the continued existence of the major trunk routes did

not appear so immediate as to cause great concern. Two pieces from the staff magazine PENNYFARE illustrate this lull before the mass abandonments in the second half of the decade.

An article, dated August 1934, detailing life at Charlton Central Repair Depot, gave the impression that well motivated personnel, including many craftsmen, were intent on maintaining the highest standards. Of note is the optimistic tone of the account, coupled with picture of 'constructing a tram

body on modern lines'. All of which gave a thoroughly positive view of the role of the tramcar. The second article appeared in October 1935; it imparted the impression that the tram fleet, or at least an important part of same, was being actively modernised. It did contain a hint of the future by stating 'their appearance at first will be mainly on the south side of the river', thereby implying (correctly) that the south London routes would benefit longest from the presence of 'rehabs' (rehabilitated tramcars).

PENNYFARE was never narrowly parochial in its outlook. Articles were published on transport subjects from all four corners of the globe. In October 1934 a three page illustrated account described the new PCC (Presidents' Conference Committee) trams being introduced in Chicago. These vehicles represented a quantum leap in tramcar design and they heralded a new era in passenger comfort and technical

CONSTRUCTING A TRAM BODY ON MODERN LINES

be built. In , the original e and white pull- n car (a model of ch can be seen in entrance hall, east g, at 55 Broad-), was made e and we found J. McGrail, gen- l foreman, and S. Sheppard, rman, body shop, nly examining a ncar which was ng reconstructed modern lines. . Sheppard told that he had been tymaking since 6, while Mr. Grail proudly nted to the car der construction the type of work the depot turned out. The major portion of the materials used he renovation and repairing of tramcars ers the depot in a rough state, and any t of a car can be made by a Charlton rkman at short notice.

Much of the work is highly skilled and ds for the highest class of craftsmanship. ny tools, of a special nature and only ble for individual work, are made by erienced workmen. There is little of mass-production atmosphere about, l mishaps are few. Generally, the pression gathered from a visit to the air depot is one of " getting on with the job," and, if it were possible to identify any particular sound above the rhythmic humming of the machines, one might hear snatches of the latest popular song, giving a true harmony of the smooth-running of the depot and a contented staff.

And as we leave the depot we find a well-equipped canteen where, in addition to good meals at reasonable charge, concerts, boxing matches (Charlton Depot has many excellent exponents of the art), whist drives and dances are held, while indoor games are played, the whole being under the auspices of the L.T. (Tramways Central) Social and Athletic Association.   G.F.

THE END OF THE DAY

innovation. In short they were about as far distant from London Transport's rehabs, as regards design and efficiency, as you could get. Lightweight in construction, featuring bodywork of aluminium and a corrosion resistant steel alloy, each single deck PCC car seated 58 passengers. Although the Chicago versions had two men crews, it was perfectly possible to dispense with the conductor and entrust the motorman with fare checking responsibilities.

Real improvements in design had been

A STREAMLINED ALUMINIUM TROLLEY-CAR

CHICAGO'S NEW STREET CARS

The Chicago Surface Lines are pioneering in street car design to determine the best type of equipment to meet modern traffic conditions in Chicago. Through the courtesy of The Chicago Surface Lines we are enabled to give the following details (taken from the " Surface Service Magazine") of two of the three cars of advanced type recently constructed.

CHICAGO has had on view recently its third example of what the street car of the future may be like. The car, of new design, and constructed by the Pullman Car and Manufacturing Corporation on specifications prepared by Dr. C. F. Hirshfeld, director of the Electric Railway Presidents' Conference Committee, has been operated on the Chicago Surface Lines for about a month, together with two streamlined cars recently constructed for the Surface Lines.

These three cars form a sort of family. They represent the views of different individuals with respect to the proper method of embodying in metal the results obtained by the Committee. Steel has been used in the car first constructed, aluminium in the second, and corrosion-resisting steel alloy in the third, the latest car. Although these cars differ in design and construction, they aim at these objectives : quiet operation ; smooth but rapid starting and stopping ; pleasing exterior and interior construction ; greater comfort for passengers in seating, ventilation and illumination ; lighter weight and sturdier construction.

Built of Aluminium

In the second of these new type cars, aluminium has been used extensively in the body and trucks. The car weighs 29,600 pounds, and is approximately 40 per cent. lighter than standard street cars of the type used in Chicago. It differs radically from the first new car built of steel, although both have streamlined bodies and newly developed equipment throughout. The dimensions of the two cars are practically the same and both seat 58 passengers in comfortable upholstered seats. Both have indirect illumination and are ventilated by forced draught systems. But in their equipment and design there is a wide difference.

This second car has four 60-horse power, 300-volt high speed motors, providing ample power for quick pick-up. The brakes

effected in the running gear, as readers are informed:

The third experimental car is extremely quiet in operation. This is attained by use of wheels built of alternate layers of rubber and steel, by a welded car body in which all squeaks and rattles are eliminated, and by use of rubber to deaden sound in the trucks and springs.

It was also suggested that PCC technology, in the form of advanced truck design, could have benefited the tube in London.

In the month previous to the publication of the article T. E. Thomas and G. F. Sinclair had begun a study tour of North America. George Flett Sinclair was Chief Rolling Stock Engineer to the London County Council and as such he was instrumental in the creation of LCC prototype car 1. His brief for the LPTB also included trolleybus technical matters. The trolleybus side came to dominate his thinking, as it did with his travelling companion. Further evidence for this emphasis came in the pair's conversion to the idea of building trolleybuses with chassisless construction – a technique they witnessed being perfected in the USA.

An account of the adventures of Messrs Thomas and Sinclair appeared in PENNYFARE for February 1935. They had the chance of observing traffic conditions at first hand in the cities of the New World. They were introduced to the new tramcar technology offered by the PCC, as they remark in the summary to their article:

The tramcar in America has held its ground in spite of low petrol costs, because of its high capacity and the effective steps taken to secure the safety of its passengers. It is impossible to overstate the importance of safety zones in retaining traffic for the tramways in busy streets.

The summary of their opinions begs the

Motorman's quarters on the aluminium car

are a combination of air brakes, braking by using the motors to generate electric current, and braking by magnetic shoes sliding on the rail. These braking systems are combined and controlled automatically by a newly developed device known as a retardation controller. The brakes are

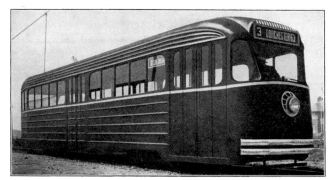
THE THIRD OF THE IMPROVED MODEL CARS
A newly developed alloy corrosion-resisting steel has been used in the construction of the body

equipped to maintain uniformly any desired rate of braking up to a maximum of $4\frac{3}{4}$ miles per hour per second.

Graceful Lines

Automatic acceleration is attained by a new type of controller which steps the car up after the power is applied at rates varying from $1\frac{1}{2}$ to $4\frac{3}{4}$ miles per hour per second, according to the speed required by traffic conditions.

The exterior of the car has graceful lines in keeping with the modern trend toward streamlining, and is finished in a light royal blue colour combined with aluminium and black striping.

The interior finish is of sheet aluminium, including the ceiling, which is of special arched shape meeting in the centre with a duct for circulation of air. The doors, built of extruded aluminium sections and sheets, are of the folding type, electro-magnetically controlled and operated.

Ventilation

The ventilating duct, along the centre line of the ceiling, draws off the air from the car by means of an exhaust fan located at one end. During the winter months fresh air

Interior view, looking to rear. (The Conductor can be seen seated in the centre (left), by the entrance doors)

is drawn in at one end of the car near the roof and blown over electric heaters. It is then carried by ducts along the floor line and discharged into the car to provide uniform heat. The same system is used in the summer to provide fresh, but unheated air, for ventilating purposes.

The indirect lighting trough along the ceiling provides illumination of the soft glow type with an extremely high intensity.

The seats are constructed of aluminium and upholstered in leather. The windows are in fixed position, as sufficient circulation

of air is obtained by the forced draught systems. The floor is constructed of cork material, top surfaced with linoleum.

Rubber and Steel Wheels

The third car, the most recently constructed, is extremely quiet in operation. This is attained by use of wheels built of alternate layers of rubber and steel, by a welded car body in which all squeaks and rattles are eliminated, and by the use of rubber to deaden sound in the trucks and springs.

Ventilation is obtained by a forced draught system, which circulates over heating coils, in winter. Indirect lighting is used, and windows can be raised or lowered by turning a crank.

While the car body is not streamlined, it presents a pleasing effect because all of its parts have been pressed into shape and then welded into place. The newly designed starting and stopping equipment enables the car to accelerate and decelerate at speeds practically twice as great as those in standard street cars, but without any discomfort to standing or walking passengers.

The car weighs 31,000 pounds, as compared with weights of 40,000 to more than

50,000 pounds in standard equipment.

From the experience gained with these cars in the actual transportation of passengers, the designers of the industry will be able to evaluate the advantages and disadvantages of the different designs to the end that greatly improved street cars can be made available to the industry and the public.

An interior view

---

question why the pair lacked the courage of their convictions and missed the opportunity to introduce American good practice to the streets of London. The case for safety zones or pedestrian refuges at tram stops was unanswerable and they were a regular feature in many other developed countries. However, the main issue revolved around the fact that Thomas and Sinclair singularly failed to appreciate the potential of the revolutionary PCC. As representatives of an internationally respected organisation, they were in a unique position to acquire British and European patents and manufacturing rights. At the American Transit Convention in Cleveland, Ohio the two senior managers from London Transport were taken aback by the advanced engineering of the PCC car. However, their ardour had cooled somewhat after their return home and they injected a note of caution by stating:

The lowest cost of producing cars of this type in quantities was given as £4,500, a price

which would be prohibitive for a vehicle in competition with buses.

In order to place this figure in context, New double deck bogie cars were being supplied to Leeds from English Electric at Preston and from Brush at Loughborough at a price between £2,600 and £2,800 each. It was assumed that PCC cars would have to be imported from the States, thus adding shipping costs to the bill.

In retrospect it is perhaps too easy to accept the validity of the economic argument. Allegedly London Transport was not in a position to shell out money for new tramcars, however innovative they might have been. The fact that restrictive business practices and price fixing cartels among bus manufacturers and suppliers of electrical equipment had caused large sums of money to be earmarked for the trolleybus conversion programme was considered a price worth paying for modernity. As for loading islands, their cost, shared between

local authorities and the LPTB, would have been insignificant, compared to the amounts expended on the buses and tubes.

When production in the United States did get going, the unit price of the PCC fell. There is no doubt Messrs Thomas and Sinclair looked a gift horse in the mouth; there was a deal to be made. It would have been a prestige sale for the Americans. History would later prove that the new trams would outlive several generations of buses. Production of modern vehicles even extended to producing a version of the PCC that was equipped for conduit operation on the boulevards and streets of central Washington. Thus, the peculiar operating arrangements of the London tramways could have been satisfied, but it was not to be.

A final irony was that the chairman of the Melbourne Metropolitan Tramways Board, H. H. Bell, also issued a statement on viewing the new PCC vehicles:

Many will welcome the introduction of the

wonderful American PCC car to the continent of Australia, a few, no doubt, will have a feeling of disappointment that an English manufacturer should not have had the pride of introducing 'a revolution in trams'. It is a significant fact that the [Melbourne] Board have thought it worth acquiring the sole manufacturing rights for the production in Australia of the PCC tram, which they propose to manufacture in a form suitable to Australian conditions.

Luckily for the citizens of Melbourne, they saw no reason to heed any advice coming from 55 Broadway. On this occasion they did not defer to the 'mother country'! At the time of writing (2012) Melbourne has the largest street tramway system in the world.

If further evidence were needed of the way the wind was blowing in the capital of the British Empire and Commonwealth,

the announcement of the Chancellor of the Exchequer, Neville Chamberlain MP, in the House of Commons on 5th June 1935, dispelled any lingering doubts:

As a result of negotiations which have lasted over many months, arrangements have just been concluded between the Government and the Standing Joint Committee of the London Passenger Transport Board and of the main line railways under which, subject to the necessary Parliamentary sanctions, the Transport Board, the London and North Eastern Railway and the Great Western Railway, will enter at once upon a programme of great improvements and extensions of London transport . . .

The programme involves the building of about 12 miles of new tube railways, the electrification of approximately 44 miles

of suburban railway, the doubling and electrification of about 12½ miles of further suburban railways, and the substitution of trolleybuses for tramcars on 148 route miles. The total cost of the works included in the programme is in the region of £35million.

The Chancellor also stated it was hoped that all the projected works would be completed within five years.

It hardly seems fair to compare LPTB car 1373 with the latest offering from across the Atlantic – the American PCC tramcar. This photograph dates from April 1934 and shows that the new regime at 55 Broadway was still very much wedded to traditional concepts of tramcar construction. Note the old fashioned trucks and running gear, plus the centrally mounted plough carrier for operation over conduit equipped tracks.
London Transport Museum

DISMANTLING ROBINSON'S EMPIRE

SIR JAMES Clifton Robinson was once General Manager of the London United Electric Tramways Company. Edwardian entrepreneur and larger than life personality, he presided over the construction of a network of tram routes in Middlesex and Surrey. His empire stretched from Wimbledon in the east to Uxbridge in the west. However, by the time of the formation of the LPTB in 1933, Robinson's transport legacy was beginning to crumble.

Not that this outcome was inevitable. A plan hatched by General Manager, C. J. Spencer, could have altered the situation. In the late 1920s he proposed upgrading part of the LUT network with the introduction of 126 new trams. Track reconstruction was included in the total package, which was costed at just above the half a million pounds mark. An application was made to the Treasury for a Government grant, but this came to nothing and the proposals never received the green light.

Only the trolleybus scheme was implemented with the result that workmen employed by various civil engineering firms had already commenced track lifting operations in the Kingston area. Partial conversion of the large 5½ acre (2.2ha) Fulwell Depot had also been effected, with just under half the building being allocated to the maintenance and storage of the new trackless vehicles. Logically for the planners at the LPTB this site provided a suitable base for an extension of operations, which would entail the complete expulsion of the remaining tramcars on services from Hampton Court and Hounslow to Hammersmith and Shepherds Bush.

The 1934 Act spelled out the steps needed to alter the public transport network. Tram routes 57, 63 and 67 were in the firing line. Double track predominated, except for the terminal arrangements at Hammersmith.

These involved one way working in an enlarged terminal loop encompassing Studland Street, Glenthorne Road and King Street. Maintenance of the permanent way was deemed satisfactory, the only new work being the relaying of certain crossovers. This form of layout occurred with great frequency in the narrow section of Brentford High Street. Delivery vehicles and other sundry horse drawn traffic often inhibited the flow of tramcars at this location. So obstructive was the chaos that a by-pass, the Great West Road, was opened by King George V and Queen Mary on 30th May 1925. Unfortunately the financial distress of the LUT prevented the company from taking advantage of the opportunity offered by the new highway. Relocation of tracks on to private right of way would have cost too much. This 'what might have been' theme runs through much of the history of the London United. Missed opportunities to modernise the tramway contributed to its ultimate demise and it can be argued that this scenario was played out all over the capital, as the trolleybus bandwagon started to roll.

The remaining network in the area totalled some 29 miles (46km), operated by a mixed batch of 150 cars. Aside from 46 Felthams, the rest of the fleet was pretty well past retirement age. Unkind commentators talked about Fulwell Depot and its 'collection of museum pieces', which were ripe for the scrap heap. Hounslow Depot was not much better off in the rolling stock stakes. The only exception was car 350, nicknamed Poppy; this was an experimental vehicle constructed in 1926. Destined for the breakers' yard in spite of its relatively young age, Poppy regularly did the 40 minute journey on route 57. At Shepherds Bush it met up with Felthams on the Uxbridge Road line. Disappointingly for local tram enthusiasts, type UCC cars were never used for regular service on routes 57 and 67. Their length caused them to ground on a dip in the track in the Brentford area.

A further reason for the non-appearance of the Felthams owed its origin to the chronic underinvestment by the previous owners, the London United Company. Power supply problems coupled with the antiquated state of the electrical infrastructure had contributed to an unsatisfactory state of affairs. Concern was expressed by General Manager Thomas that all former LUT tram services were now

A foreign observer, Dr Friedrich Gruenwald from Germany, once observed that the former LUT cars were built like battleships and perpetuated the British eccentricity in vehicle design. Perhaps the good doctor was on a spying mission? Car 2389 rests at Hampton Court before the return journey on route 67 to Hammersmith. LCCT Trust

vulnerable to failures and service interruptions. Obviously, since official policy had now set its face firmly against tramway modernisation, the only investment permitted would be in connection with implementation of the trolleybus alternative. Thus in the first months of 1934 the conversion programme acquired added impetus.

A positive reaction by the local press and general public to the imminent introduction of trolleybuses was assisted by the publicity coming from 55 Broadway. Noise emanating from building work in connection with depot reconstruction ruffled a few feathers, but apart from the odd complaint about trolleybus traction standards being put in the wrong place, the work in the summer and autumn of 1935 appears to have caused little complaint. On the night of 26th October, the trams were expelled from Hounslow and Fulwell depots. The replacement trolleybus routes 657 and 667 started the next day. Also withdrawn in this first stage of the conversion programme was the Kew Bridge to Hammersmith section of route 26.

Lord Ashfield headed a distinguished cast on hand for the inaugural celebrations, which were held at Hounslow Depot and afterwards at the Clarendon Restaurant, Hammersmith. Among the official party were several representatives of AEC, who had constructed the new trolleybuses. They included a director of the company, Colonel J. T. Moore-Brabazon MP, an aviation pioneer and later Minister of Transport in Winston Churchill's wartime cabinet. He was a noted opponent of tramways. The Associated Equipment Company, previously part of the Combine, would, together with Leyland Motors, benefit enormously from the conversion programme.

When the trams went, so did their quirky eccentricities. In the December 1934 TRAFFIC CIRCULAR, issued by London Transport and prominently marked

PRIVATE: NOT FOR PUBLICATION,

there occurs the following instruction:

SERVICE No. 26 –
KEW BRIDGE TERMINUS.

Motormen are instructed that when standing at Kew Bridge Terminus the hand brake must be applied to the fullest extent and secured by the retaining hook.

The prospect of a runaway tramcar having to be fished out of the nearby Thames was not one to be contemplated by the top brass in 55 Broadway!

In the same Traffic Circular is a reminder that there was a particular disadvantage to tramway abandonment. Trolleybus staff operating out of Fulwell Depot were told how to handle their vehicles in dense fog. Conductors were sometimes required to act as pilots for their drivers. Equipped with a flare or a sufficiently powerful lamp, conductors were expected to proceed at walking pace in front of each trolleybus. Of course, the much maligned tramcar on its fixed track was a much better bet and safer option in restricted visibility.

Car 2381 has received a complete repaint in London Transport colours, but the new décor cannot mask its antiquity. Already trolleybuses have replaced trams on the direct connection to Kingston-upon-Thames, and route 67 will be an early candidate for conversion.
Note the use of advertising on this tram – Manns Brown Ale, Boyd Pianos, OXO and a poster promoting the Boat Race. *LCCT Trust*

Although the trams had now departed from these west London thoroughfares, the rails remained. Along most of the abandoned sections there seemed to be no hurry on the part of the local authorities to expedite their removal. London Transport failed to set a good example by omitting to resurface the depot yard at Fulwell, where an interesting variety of tram track remained intact, including a scissors crossover near the Wellington Road entrance. Ironically, the double track on London Road, Twickenham survived to outlive the replacing trolleybuses, when they themselves took their leave in May 1962.

However, tracks along Chiswick High Road were lifted. Most of the work was done the hard way by workmen wielding picks and shovels. Trolleybus drivers were instructed to proceed with caution past these roadworks. The local authority took the opportunity of remodelling the junction between the Great West Road and the High Road. A new roundabout opened on Sunday, 6th September 1936. The cost totalled £5,415; it was not charged to London Transport!

The demise of the 67 left tram service 89 as the sole occupant of the one way system at Hammersmith. The mixing of trams and trolleybuses over common sections of route was not an ideal arrangement, but the travelling public were expected to cope with what was termed officially as a 'transitional situation'. Of course, the trams only used one of the replacement trolleybus wires. Just in case motormen or conductors were in any doubt over the new status quo, the November 1935 TRAFFIC CIRCULAR offered this helpful advice:

STUDLAND STREET.
The frog on Pole No. 49 in King Street will be set for trolleybuses – Conductors on trams to Acton to pull frog on journey to Acton.

Almost the same instructions were for Beadon Road at the Metropolitan Station, where conductors on Hammersmith bound 89s had to descend from their trams in the middle of the street to reach the nearest traction standard in order to set the overhead points (pull frog) so that they could proceed. One would have thought, since the latest form of electric vehicle could pull over to the kerb, it would have made more sense from a road safety point of view to have allotted this task to trolleybus conductors rather than their tramway colleagues.

The whole affair was regularised on 5th April 1936, when tram route 89 ceased to operate from Acton to Hammersmith. On Saturday afternoons route 55 cars had also used the tracks in Askew Road and Paddenswick Road to gain access to the Hammersmith one way loop terminal. Trolleybus route 660 now fulfilled these functions, the replacement vehicles having

taken up temporary residence in the former LUT depot at Acton. The use of this location prompted a general reshuffle of trams away from Hanwell Depot, whilst it was being rebuilt to receive trolleybuses.

Service 7 trams continued to operate from Uxbridge to Shepherds Bush, but their days were numbered as new traction standards and overhead wiring made an appearance. Highway realignment was taking place with the result that the original tram route in Park Road, Hayes End was bypassed entirely by the trolleybuses on replacement route 607. On Sunday, 15th November, the type T 'Palace' cars and the Felthams were officially declared *hors de combat* as far as the Uxbridge road was concerned. Thus perished the last major London United service, on which so many hopes had been pinned.

Whilst the older vehicles went for scrap, the newer Felthams were too precious to waste. In the weeks leading up to the conversion, individual cars had been sent over to Hampstead Depot to be fitted with plough gear, so that they could operate over conduit equipped lines in south London. At the end of service in the western suburbs they were despatched via a rather circuitous route to Streatham, Telford Avenue and Brixton Hill depots. Only tram route 55 from Hanwell to Brentford now remained and it lasted until 13th December 1936, when the process of dismantling Robinson's Empire was brought to a conclusion.

T. E. Thomas, buoyed up by initial success in west London, expressed guarded optimism for the future in his January 1936, New Year's Message to his staff:
The Board has to assume that trolleybuses will be more successful in their operation

than the trams. It has some grounds for that assumption and so far it has been justified. About 40 miles of tramway have been abandoned this year in favour of trolleybuses, and many more will be abandoned in 1936. This is expensive in the first instance. Tram depots have to be reconstructed or new depots built. New substations and electrical equipment are being provided. New vehicles are being supplied, and a contribution has to be paid to the road authorities for the removal of the rails and reinstatement of the carriageway. On the other hand, the Board is relieved of the expense of road maintenance, although that is offset by a heavy tax upon each trolleybus, amounting to over £100 a year. Speeds are higher and the newest type of vehicle should be more attractive than the old. The Board seeks to attract new traffic and not merely to win passengers from its railway and omnibus systems.

Assuredly, new traffic was being attracted to the metropolis, but it was not always in the form London Transport envisaged. In an eight year period from 1931 the population of Greater London grew by half a million to 8,728,000. Much of this expansion occurred in semi-detached suburbia, where green fields

Car 2320 is working service 89 in its last months of existence. The tram is passing a horse drawn tower wagon with a wiring crew aloft. The overhead infrastructure for trolleybuses is being erected. The workmen obviously needed a head for heights and a belief in the equable temperament of the horse! Just in case, wooden chocks have been placed under several wheels of the wagon.

disappeared under new housing estates. The upshot of all this was an inevitable increase in car ownership. The annual report of the London Traffic Advisory Committee notes that from a slow start there were 689 traffic light installations, as at 30th September 1936. This was a certain indication of mounting congestion on the capital's streets.

Dense traffic conditions negated the much vaunted mobility of the new trolleybuses. They had to take their chances in a maelstrom of vehicles, many of which were still horse drawn. At least the trams provided some kind of lane discipline on their fellow road users. When this aid to traffic control disappeared, the ensuing free-for-all only served to accentuate the problem of too many vehicles trying to compete for too little space. Ford's new Dagenham plant and other British companies, such as Austin, Vauxhall

and Morris, ensured a reliable supply of cars priced around the £100 mark. In just five years since the founding of the LPTB in 1933 the number of private cars licensed in the London Transport area rose from 292,000 to 475,000.

According to the September 1936 issue of PENNYFARE the problem appeared to have worsened:

The remarkable growth of private car ownership is, of course, a contributory factor to the burden upon the streets; in England the number of current licences issued during the last nine years has increased by 117 per cent, while for London and five Home Counties the increase amounted to 130 per cent, exceeded in certain individual instances, such as Middlesex, where the County Council report an increase of 195 per cent.

Luxury Feltham car 2137 is depicted on the Uxbridge Road outside the Red Lion at Hillingdon. Space exists up to the property line on the right of the picture for the enlargement of the highway. The trams were unfairly blamed for holding up the project. The modern tramcar's progress is hampered by the fact that it is waiting at a loop for a tram coming in the opposite direction to clear the right of way over the next section of single track. Note the fare stage 23 number affixed to the traction standard. After tramway abandonment a dual carriageway road was constructed at this location. Dave Jones Collection

Against this background of traffic filled streets, the outlook for surface public transport in the capital certainly did not appear as assured as had been promised by the founding fathers of the LPTB. Abandonment of London's tramways was not the panacea for a congestion free future.

SOCIAL SERVICES ON A SHOESTRING

THE BEXLEY Urban District Council Tramways & Dartford Light Railways Joint Committee had been in operation since 1917. It formed an interesting network with the Erith U. D. C. Tramways. Reports reaching the desk of T. E. Thomas painted a disturbing picture of the condition of the tramways in this area of north Kent. Eye witness statements from London Transport engineers and surveyors only served to intensify the gloom. Options for the new owners included straightforward abandonment or an expensive reconstruction of track and overhead, together with a thorough overhaul of the antiquated rolling stock. Bearing in mind the official policy of trolleybus substitution would take some months to implement, the powers that be settled on a regime of make do and mend. The local tramways were living on borrowed time. In fairness to the Board estimates were prepared for a complete renewal of the network. A figure of just under £200,000 was

quoted. This did not include the section east of Dartford to the terminus at Horns Cross.

Somehow in this flurry of paperwork the mandarins at 55 Broadway overlooked the human dimension. The trams working the streets of north Kent might have been rickety and slow, but they had a loyal local following. Staff were well known to their regular passengers and would often go out of their way to assist. However, this friendly atmosphere could not hide the root cause of Erith's malaise. It had never succeeded in opening through running with the LCC at Abbey Wood. Indeed, it had overstretched itself before the First World War and poor financial results had contributed to the closure of the Northend route on 31st August 1910. This was the first significant loss of electric tramway mileage in the metropolitan area.

The territory of Erith Urban District Council encompassed a mixture of small Thames side industries and the somewhat larger establishment, where Vickers manu-

factured armaments and ammunition. In short there was a marked provincial air about the place, completely different in character from the fashionable hustle and bustle at the heart of the metropolis. Erith had more in common with the industrial towns of north Kent, such as Gravesend, Swanscombe and Northfleet. With a population of 32,780 in 1931, ribbon development along suburban roads promised to bring more traffic to the tramways.

Staff morale was always high at Erith. The council was regarded as a good employer, in spite of the fact that wages were the lowest in London. In 1933 the LCC was paying drivers and conductors £3–13s–0d (£3.65) a week, while their Erith colleagues only received £3–5s–0d (£3.25). Although tram crews were unionised, their TGWU representatives realised that money was very tight and that the whole organisation from management downwards worked on a shoestring. Upkeep of the fleet was kept to

The old tram depot was situated just off Bexleyheath Broadway. It was deemed totally unsuitable for the replacing trolleybuses. In the middle of this assembly of the Bexley fleet is the PW department's flat truck, which was normally towed behind a service car. On one occasion in pre-LPTB days it was commandeered by the youthful guests at a birthday party. Decked out with balloons and streamers, it transported the kids along the Erith Road to Barnehurst. Such high jinks would never be tolerated by the new regime at 55 Broadway.
H. Wightman/A.J.Watkins

The Wilmington shuttle was one of those leisurely affairs that appealed to tram enthusiasts and locals alike. Alas, the LPTB did not think much of it. Shortly before the end of tramway operation car 20C of the former Bexley fleet waits to leave the terminus. Somehow, the 401 replacement bus will be poor recompense for this charming scene.

a bare minimum. The livery of the vehicles, once an attractive apple green and primrose, had been changed to a more serviceable dark brown, which had now weathered to a good approximation of black!

The one device to brighten the exterior of every tramcar was the council crest and coat of arms. On Bexley Gala day, held at Danson Park at the end of July, Erith and Bexley cars handled the traffic. Erith crews, who regarded their Bexley counterparts as a less politicised and more conservative bunch, delighted in pointing out the words *LABOUR OVERCOMES ALL THINGS* under the Erith council crest. This overtly socialist message was treated in good spirit by all concerned, as was the shunting of trams backwards and forwards on the single track and loops outside Danson Park to let service cars have right of way.

Trams belonging to Bexley Council were to be seen on the main route from Woolwich, Beresford Square to Dartford, Horns Cross. Lines originally owned by Dartford Council Tramways were operated by Bexley after a disastrous depot fire in August 1917 wiped out the Dartford fleet. Thirty-three vehicles now serviced 11 route miles (18km), which included a branch from Dartford Station to

Wilmington. As at Erith, the condition of the rolling stock gave LT engineers cause for concern.

The arrival of surveyors and technical experts aroused much speculation among local tramwaymen. When looking at large scale modernisation programmes, it is all too easy to overlook the genuine concerns of the workers affected. At a time of continued economic uncertainty in the early 1930s, the imposition of substantial change from a large, powerful organisation such as London Transport, provoked worries about job security among the former Erith and Bexley tramwaymen. In order to quell wild rumours and to allay real fears in the workforce, George Tapp, the resident TGWU representative, was granted a meeting at County Hall with the boss, General Manager Thomas. George had been enjoined by his colleagues at the two local depots to impress on management that the trams provided a service for the community.

What would now be called a 'focus group' had been set up by several former employees of Bexley and Erith municipal tramways. The rather rudimentary resources of this purely unofficial body consisted of a clipboard plus sundry pencils, supplemented by old school

exercise books, all of which had to be ferried to points of interest in an antiquated motor cycle and sidecar unit, that had apparently done service with His Majesty's forces on the Western Front! Thus equipped, the amateur survey team began its task. One of its first objectives was to study the impact of the replacement of trams by trolleybuses. Logically they should have started with the LUT set up in west London, but it was felt this might provoke disciplinary measures from the higher ups at the LPTB. Therefore, clandestine visits were made to Maidstone, Southend-on-Sea and to Hastings. Soundings were also taken as to working conditions on the new trackless vehicles. The findings of the team were then communicated to George, who had to assess the points raised before his interview with senior management.

George later recalled that Mr Thomas did not seem particularly pleased to see him. On hearing about the concerns of the local tramwaymen, the boss was dismissive and remarked that he was not interested in trivia. Not unnaturally George was annoyed and defended the cause of his colleagues, only to be told in no uncertain terms that, whilst workers ran the show in the Soviet Union, the set up at 55 Broadway was on entirely different lines! George was further informed that powers were being sought to convert to trolleybuses. He was told that the new vehicles would be of a similar type to those already working on the former LUT routes. A sum of £30,000 was mentioned as being necessary to effect remedial work on the existing tramways in the north Kent area, until the trolleybus scheme could be implemented. This investment involved transfer of rolling stock, patching up of the permanent way and renewal of the overhead wiring. George was somewhat offended by his boss's remarks that the track was 'appalling with bits missing' and that 'the overhead was hung like washing line' and therefore totally unsuited for continued use. Although T. E. Thomas did concede that the Erith overhead was better than that at Bexley and that it had at least some scrap value!

One thing was certain to George and all his colleagues – the new regime had no intentions of working on a shoestring. At the end of June 1933, in the week before the official takeover, 12 surplus LCC M class trams started arriving to begin the replacement of the older members of the Bexley and Erith fleets. The veterans were then despatched first via Welling and Plumstead to Abbey Wood Depot, and from there to Brixton Hill Depot in south London for scrapping. A suggestion that the service from Woolwich to Bexleyheath Clock Tower should be augmented by standard ex-LCC bogie cars, as had been the case in a short lived jointly operated route just before the First World War, was one of the 'local proposals' rejected by T. E. Thomas.

On 18th December 1933, as a practical measure to improve access, a single track connection was inserted at Knee Hill, Abbey Wood, to link the former Erith System with the main ex-LCC route to Woolwich and central London. It was also now easier to transfer rolling stock in and out of Abbey Wood Depot. This location could house vehicles previously stabled at the small depot in Walnut Tree Road, Erith. The building ceased to operate trams on 28th December 1933; it was eventually returned to local council ownership and it survived intact, complete with track layout, until the 1970s.

The London Transport public relations team, actively encouraged by Ashfield and Pick during their Combine years, now had the task of issuing press releases. In the autumn of 1933 they went into overdrive. The Kentish Independent (1843–1984) was typical of the many local newspapers in the metropolitan area, which promoted the LPTB party line. Under the heading of *Definite News At Last* an editorial informed readers of the brave new world to come:

From the offices of the London Transport Board a statement has been issued which amplifies the announcement made a few weeks ago, and will dispel all the doubts which have existed as to the Board's intentions regarding passenger transport facilities in the Bexleyheath and Erith districts.

The much abused trams, which have been in use for over thirty years, are to be abolished. As soon as a bill is passed in Parliament, the Board will substitute trolley buses for the trams from Beresford Square, Woolwich, through Plumstead, to Abbey Wood, linking up with the Erith tram route, and carrying on through Belvedere and Erith, over Northumberland Heath to Bexleyheath.

On the more important route – Woolwich to Dartford – trolley buses will run from Beresford Square, via Plumstead, Welling, Bexleyheath, and Crayford, to Dartford.

It will be seen that this provides the circular service – Woolwich, Erith, Bexleyheath, and back to Woolwich – which has been advocated in the Kentish Independent several times in recent years.

The most satisfactory part of the announcement is that once the powers have been obtained, the provision of additional overhead wires and the construction of new buses will not take more than a few months. The change-over may be effected early in 1934, if the powers are obtained during the present Session of Parliament.

Existing tramway lines will be removed.

Workmen and officials have been busy during the last few weeks measuring and taking particulars as to the tram standards in the Bexley district.

The optimistic tone of this editorial must have pleased the folk at 55 Broadway. Perhaps it was all a little too optimistic, because deadlines slipped and events did not move as quickly as predicted. Undaunted, the Kentish Independent later took it upon itself to give its readership a blow by blow account of the conversion process. However, before the trolleybus circus came to town, the two local tram services received route numbers. On 3rd October 1934, the Woolwich to Horns Cross service became tram route 96; Abbey Wood to Bexleyheath was numbered 98.

A little of the original Erith ambiance survived on route 98 with the arrival of a trio of 'foreigners' in the shape of ex-East Ham open balcony, covered top cars 53 and 58; the third new arrival was former Croydon Corporation open top car 349. At the time it was suggested, rather unkindly, that these three tramcars had been foisted on Erith because no one else would have them! Needless to say, the locals had got out of the open top habit and passengers and crews objected to car 349, when the rains came. During spells of inclement weather this particular tram subsequently demonstrated a mysterious tendency to develop minor faults, thus preventing it from leaving the depot.

In the spring of 1935 construction crews descended on the area. The tram standards

The date is 15th February 1935, and the official LPTB photographer has arrived to record the brand new bus shelter at Bexleyheath Clock Tower. Green Line coach routes A1 and A2 (later renumbered 701, 702) served this location. Of tramway interest is a standard M class car on route 98 to Abbey Wood. Perhaps the LPTB should have paid heed to the gloomy expressions of the two old men. In a few months the local authority will institute a one way traffic scheme, which will ensure that the new shelter is on the wrong side of the road for passengers boarding or alighting. The structure was then demolished!
London Transport Museum

The line from Dartford to Horns Cross at the extremity of route 96 ran through an interesting landscape. Part rural, part industrial, the area was the furthest east you could travel by London tram. In the distance one of the former Bexley Council B class cars, acquired from the LCC during World War I, is occupying the single track in the middle of the highway.

mentioned in the newspaper article were deemed too decrepit for trolleybus use and consequently new traction poles had to be planted along the doomed tram routes, with almost all of the overhead construction on the span wire principle. Little of the paraphernalia inherited from the tramway era was of any practical use. Bracket arms, installed in the Edwardian era and adorned with fancy tracery, were found to be weakened with corrosion. Feeder cables had to be renewed and new substations built. Provision had to be made for dual working of trams and trolleybuses from Market Hill, Woolwich to Abbey Wood; this arrangement was expected to endure until tram routes 36, 38 and 40 could be phased out at some later date.

Old bus chassis, reborn as motorised tower wagons, acted as platforms for the workmen employed on overhead wire construction. At the junction of Wickham Lane and Plumstead High Street and at Bexleyheath Clock Tower crews laboured through the night. Tensioning of new span wires occurred during the daylight hours. Temporary wiring for the trams appeared outside Plumstead Station, at Welling Corner, along the road from the Nag's Head, Welling to Crook Log, and in the centre of Erith. The situation was particularly acute in Bexley Road, Erith, where the tram track was laid towards one side of the carriageway. Some ingenuity was required to ensure that the trolley poles of the railbound vehicles remained in contact with the power source.

In the month of August 1935, the local press was issuing regular updates on progress. The construction of London Transport's one and only purpose built trolleybus depot was drawing onlookers to the site on the east side of Erith Road. New traction standards and span wires were noted in Welling and in Bexleyheath. The KENTISH INDEPENDENT for Friday, 9th August, remarked that new trolleybuses were on order and that workmen had now reached Plumstead High Street in the erection of trolleybus overhead wires. In the edition of a week later we are informed that 100 men, formerly employed by Bexley and Erith, had been retained to work on the new vehicles. The excitement mounted until the edition of Friday, 6th September 1935, announced:

Two of Erith's new trolley buses were given a trial trip on Wednesday. The overhead was completed for the trial trip from Erith to Bexleyheath. The new buses resemble the petrol buses which ply between Erith and Woolwich.

In fact one of the first trips was made by George Tapp, who had received three days training within the confines of the new depot before being let out on to the public highway. He remembered thinking back ruefully to his life as an Erith Council motorman. Protected from the elements, encapsulated in his trolleybus cab, he missed 'the lack of family atmosphere' and he felt that working for London Transport 'the human element was not the same'. On the other hand he had

to acknowledge that his conditions of service, his wages and the associated fringe benefits were better with his new employers.

Life on the open platform of a tramcar was never dull. As befitted its poverty stricken status, Erith had to rely on second hand purchases to maintain the service. Four open top vehicles, acquired from the London United company, had an annoying tendency of derailing in West Street at the level crossing of the industrial railway leading to Cory's Wharf on the River Thames. The speed of the trams at this location was usually walking pace, so it was normally a straightforward manoeuvre to reverse the tram and rerail one of errant bogies. Adult male passengers often lent a hand to the crew, while the level crossing keeper and the driver and fireman of one of the industrial steam locomotives occasionally joined in the fun. The use of a tow rope plus sundry metal wedges, placed in the rails, would normally solve the problem.

With everything fixed, the journey would resume. It was all part of a day's work for George and his fellow tramwaymen.

Modernity, in the shape of trolleybus route 698, came to Erith on 10th November 1935. Most of the local tram fleet was then driven away to be scrapped. Another exodus followed after 23rd November, when trolleybuses on route 696 ousted trams from the Woolwich to Dartford via Welling section. Based on an internal LPTB traffic report taken over three days in January 1934, it was considered more economic to abandon track from Dartford to Horns Cross and to let motor buses take over the service. Official observers had noted that from St Vincent Road loop, Dartford to Horns Cross in the morning peak period the five trams an hour transported a meagre total of 18 passengers.

While it is true that the tramways operated by the urban district councils of Bexley and Erith could be described as being

TRAM TERMINUS. ABBEY WOOD.

NO: 3930

in a distressed state, it is also true that the *esprit de corps* among the workers was very high. The very nature of the slow and steady service appealed to many of the locals. The pace of life was more measured and the trams were part of the landscape.

It was perhaps inevitable that 1930s suburban house building, coupled with the revitalisation of the armaments industry, increased the need for a modern system of public transport. The tramway from Woolwich to Dartford constituted a natural traffic route, but it never received the investment needed to instal double track and new rolling stock. In its antiquated condition the system could not cope with the demands of a rapidly changing world.

WOOLWICH – DARTFORD AREA TROLLEYBUSES.

Trolleybus operation from 10·11·35 ▪▪▪▪
　　　　　　　　　　　　24·11·35 ▭▭▭▭

Tramway operation..................... ▭▭▭▭▭▭
Tramway route to be abandoned.. ╫╫╫╫╫╫

· SCALE ·

HORNS CROSS

Trolleybus routes. This map, which originally appeared in the December 1935 issue of PENNYFARE, traces trolleybus routes 696 and 698 which would shortly be introduced to replace trams in the area. The tram routes to be withdrawn, with their short lived numbers, were 96 Woolwich – Bexley Heath – Dartford – Horns Cross and 98 Abbey Wood – Erith – Bexley Heath.

left Abbey Wood terminus is the setting for an encounter between car 1101 and a sparkling new trolleybus (CGF 102). The county boundary between Kent and London separates the two vehicles. Behind the tram a turning circle has been erected for the trolleybuses. Apparently the roadway was wide enough to counter any objections the Metropolitan Police might have had to buses obstructing other traffic. Abbey Wood was served exclusively by electric traction until route 38 was abandoned in July 1952. Trolleybus route 698 lasted until March 1959.

right Erith Council Tramways car 13 has been repainted in LT colours, but has not been renumbered in the main fleet. It is depicted on the new December 1933 connecting track by the Harrow Inn on the corner of Knee Hill and Abbey Road. Today this scene is dominated by the flyover carrying Harrow Manor Way. G. N. Southerden

47

UP HILL AND DOWN DALE

MANY NATIVES of Croydon were proud to assert that their home town rightfully belonged in Surrey and definitely not in south London! With a population of around 233,000 in the early 1930s, the area was described in an official guide book as:

A great county borough and market town, which regards itself as a detached municipality outside the metropolitan area!

In terms of the local tramway system an effort was being made to counteract this isolationism. Connecting tracks to the larger neighbour over the boundary in the London County Council domain had been installed in February 1926. Intensive service on main trunk routes 16/18 linked Purley with Croydon, Streatham, Brixton and the Victoria Embankment. The tram service from central Croydon to Thornton Heath,

originally route 2, was a purely local affair with single track and loops along Brigstock Road. A similar form of track layout was traversed by services 4 and 5 from West Croydon to the county boundary at Selby Road. Double track then took the trams over Kentish territory to their respective termini at Crystal Palace and Thicket Road, Penge. A depot with capacity for 25 SMET vehicles existed off Oak Grove Road, Penge.

On the western side of the borough routes extended to Sutton and to Tooting, where a change pit was installed in August 1926, so that trams could continue their journeys over LCC conduit equipped tracks. The western lines were almost exclusively double track. They had been laid out by the old South Metropolitan Company as conventional street tramways; at the turn of the century the opportunity had been missed to provide the trams with reserved tracks across Mitcham Common and through the farmland of Carshalton. The inauguration of services in November 1906 started a trend and new suburban housing development followed the tramlines west of Wallington to the centre of Sutton. A depot situated at Westmead

Road, Sutton put out a mixed fleet of tramcars, both of the single truck and bogie variety, all of which to London Transport eyes were decidedly antique in appearance. The statistics show that the inheritance from the corporation alone amounted to 55 trams, one works car, one tower wagon; 118 staff were due to be assimilated by the new organisation. As regards the outlying SMET lines, the economic situation had become more acute since the sale in July 1932 of the company's very lucrative electricity supply business. It was therefore no great surprise when all the former South Metropolitan lines came under scrutiny. The priority for trolleybus conversion was the Sutton to Crystal Palace service, which on the eastern side of Croydon included the climb up Anerley Hill, at a gradient of 1 in 9.

Clearly, the whole network centred on Croydon demanded expert analysis from the LPTB's planning department. Unlike the former LUT lines to the west of the capital and the Bexley/Erith enclave, where the trolleybus conquest was over in a few months, there was a strong case in Croydon to retain the major north to south tramway route, which terminated at Purley. This former corporation main line had been relaid in the mid-1920s and was to all intents and purposes an important part of the south London network. Transferring tram services en masse throughout the area to trolleybus operation had its attractions, especially in view of the stated LPTB policy to avoid dual working of trams and trolleybuses over the same roads. However, the practical decision was taken to make the transition over a period of six years and to avoid putting all London Transport's electric traction eggs in one basket.

In the initial stages of formulating strategy on the ex-SMET routes the planners at 55 Broadway had to hand an earlier report commissioned by the Combine on 16th September 1930. In the section devoted to the South Metropolitan Electric Tramways And Lighting Company Limited the following recommendations are made:

Subject to certain highway improvements taking place it has been agreed to extend tramways from Mitcham to the St Helier (Morden) Estate, a distance of

At the junction of Benhill Avenue and Sutton High Street trams from West Croydon terminated. Two gentlemen descend the open staircase of car 2401, while open top car 4S waits to depart. The time is 7:30pm on 21st August 1935. *O. J. Morris/F. Merton Atkins*

Car 2396 was an ex-LUT veteran, one of the so called 'influenza cars'. In spite of its poor reputation it makes a dignified turn from Ruskin Road on to Park Lane, Carshalton. The roads hereabouts were built new for the SMET tramcars. The area was and still is very much semi-detached suburbia.

approximately 1 mile. It is also possible that the two routes to the west of Croydon may be converted to a trackless trolley system. Further, if the Croydon Corporation will also convert their relatively short length of intervening track, this system may be extended to the remaining two routes. The cost of these works is estimated to be as follows:-

(1) 50 new trackless trolley cars at £2,100 each £105,000
(2) Abandonment of 13 miles of tramways at £4,500 per mile £58,500
(3) Conversion of overhead cables to trolley car System at £1,000 per mile £13,000
(4) Extension of track to Morden Estate £30,000

Although the 1930 report suggests that trolleybus conversion of the SMET lines was a viable proposition, it is interesting to speculate that an extension of the tramway from Mitcham, Cricket Green to the LCC St Helier Estate might have netted real dividends for the company. As things turned out, the total cost of £206,500 was too much for Messrs Ashfield and Pick. The SMET trams were fated to soldier on, no new rolling stock was built and joint services with the LCC to potentially lucrative housing developments never materialised. In the event Frank Pick's LGOC buses were deployed, with the consequence that the Cricket Green tramway spur withered on the vine and a valuable opportunity for tramway expansion was lost.

Not all past suggestions were discounted by the LPTB. A previous proposal from the now defunct SMET management to hand over the Croydon to Mitcham section to the LCC resurfaced on 6th December 1933, when former LCC service 30 was extended to run from Harrow Road, Scrubs Lane to West Croydon. Operated by some of the

Former Croydon Corporation car 347 presses on towards the Crystal Palace terminus at the summit of Anerley Hill. Electric traction was more than capable of tackling one of the steepest gradients in the metropolitan area. In spite of its hill climbing prowess car 347 looks distinctly old fashioned and definitely would not have impressed T. E. Thomas at headquarters. A vehicle designed at the beginning of the Edwardian era appeared out of place in the streamlined 1930s.

Single track with passing loops characterised the local Croydon service along Brigstock Road, Thornton Heath. Although subject to an outdated layout, the tram service worked very well and reputedly it was one of the most remunerative on the LPTB system. Route 42 flourished despite the criticism by Mr Doran MP. G. N. Southerden

slowest cars on the system, passengers riding London's longest tram route had the prospect of enjoying a through journey time of 81 minutes. Vehicles working route 30 changed from trolley to conduit at Putney Bridge Road, Wandsworth and back again at Mitcham Road, Tooting Junction.

However sedate the progress, at least fare paying travellers on the three through routes from Croydon into London did not have to suffer the dubious pleasure of exposing themselves to the elements on an open top tram to Crystal Palace or enduring a draughty, damp experience in the upper saloon of one of the ex-LUT 'influenza' cars, now resident at Sutton Depot. The publicity department at 55 Broadway had an easy task in persuading people of the merits of the new, comfortable trolleybuses. The conversion process got under way, but not without its eccentric side. Ushering in the streamlined trolleybus era were horse drawn tower wagons, employed in the erection of the latest, up-to-date overhead equipment.

This apparent mismatch of ancient and modern caused some comment, especially from animal loving locals who petted the patient steeds attached to each wagon.

Everything seemed to be on course for a successful outcome, but then the planners hit two snags. It was a straightforward process to rebuild the depot in Westmead Road, but finding a suitable terminal in the centre of Sutton caused a few headaches, until it was decided to extend the trolleybus overhead wires to a new turning circle in Bushey Road. The trams, being double ended, had reversed quite happily for almost three decades outside the Grapes public house in Benhill Street. The end came on 7th December 1935, when tram route 7 – journey time 31 minutes, through fare sixpence (2½p) – was replaced by trolleybus route 654. Most of the trams went for scrap at Brixton Hill Depot.

A second cause for concern was Anerley Hill. The South Metropolitan had never suffered an accident on the slope of Anerley Road, but London Transport were not so fortunate. On 25th October 1935, a tram crew went for a 'comfort break' at the terminus, only to find their charge missing when they returned. Luckily, a brave passenger, Leonard Tofield of Elmers End, was sufficiently *au fait* with the mechanics of the tramcar to apply the handbrake before the inevitable downward plunge, derailment and possible demolition of other vehicles, roadside properties and sundry pedestrians.

Obviously, trolleybuses tackling the same gradient needed to be made sufficiently safe to avoid further embarrassment. In contrast to the contretemps a few weeks earlier, the official unveiling to the press of an enhanced bus braking system on 20th January 1936 convinced the doubters. With this final obstacle out of the way, tram route 5 from Crystal Palace (High Level) to West Croydon perished on 8th February 1936. The redundant fleet was driven back to Penge Depot, where George Cohen & Sons (1883–1967), the well known demolition contractors, reduced the former pride of the SMET to matchwood and twisted metal.

In a matter of a few months tram services to Penge, Crystal Palace and Sutton had ceased to exist. The spotlight now fell on the Thornton Heath branch. Route 2 was renumbered 42 in October 1934; the journey time from Croydon (Greyhound) to Thornton Heath was 16 minutes, with a through fare of only 2d (0.8p). Tramcars maintained a service interval of three to five minutes, which reflected the popularity of the route. However, not all locals supported the trams; one particular VIP thought them 'very antiquated'. The subscriber to this point of view was Edward Doran, Conservative MP for Tottenham North. He lived at 63 Beverstone Road, Thornton Heath, and he tabled a question in a House of Commons debate on 18th July 1935:

Mr Doran asked the Minister of Transport whether he can give any indication of when it is proposed to abolish the tramway system between Thornton Heath tramway terminus High Street and the Greyhound, Croydon, via the Brigstock Road; and whether, in view of the inefficiency and obsolescence of this route, he will urge the traffic commissioners to expedite the hearing of proposals for an omnibus service between these points?

Mr Hore-Belisha: I am informed by the London Passenger Transport Board that they do not at present contemplate the discontinuance of the tramway service between Thornton Heath tramway terminus and Croydon, and that consequently there is no present intention of providing an omnibus service between these places.

It has to be said that Edward Doran MP was a strong supporter of Nazi Germany, and as an anti-Semite he particularly disliked Mr Hore-Belisha. Although only a matter of speculation, one wonders whether the Minister had a quiet word in Lord Ashfield's ear to urge him to maintain route 42 just to annoy Doran! As it turned out, the Brigstock Road trams outlived their fiercest critic by some six years.

It was hardly surprising that Croydonians found the upholstered seats of modern trolleybuses to their liking and the LPTB responded by promising an early conversion of route 30. Surrey County Council jumped the gun somewhat by insisting on the complete reconstruction of the Blue House Bridge on Commonside West, Mitcham. Work began in

the spring of 1936 and involved a temporary single tram track during the reconstruction of the bridge over the railway. It is to London Transport's credit that they maintained the through tram service rather than taking the option of employing replacement buses.

The roadworks on Mitcham Common were not the only cause for concern. The LPTB had inherited a depot at Aurelia Road just off Mitcham Road. This establishment with a capacity of 20 trams had been moribund since the mid-1920s. On an inspection visit before the 1926 closure, Victor Matterface, a senior tramway engineer in the Combine, had described the place as chaotic with poor standards of vehicle maintenance. Moreover, a member of staff living nearby had arranged to have the traction current 'diverted' for his domestic use. Unfortunately such largesse from the tramway company did not figure in his job description and he was given the sack.

In spite of this woeful reputation the depot plus its potential storage capacity remained a useful asset, but the place appeared to exert an almost supernatural ability to cause mischief. In what can truthfully be described as a policy mix up, on 8th December 1935, the single track leading to the depot was disconnected from the main line, only to be reinstated on 2nd June in the following year. To be fair to all parties, a rearrangement of the rolling stock demolition programme dictated that Brixton Hill Depot had to be vacated quickly by the scrappers, because of extra work needed to

receive the Felthams. Accordingly, Aurelia Road was returned to active duty post haste. Thereafter, a dismal procession of doomed tramcars was dispatched to the newly renamed Croydon Depot for scrapping. The funereal atmosphere was enhanced by the fact that Croydon Corporation had used the building as a mortuary in the late 1920s. Lurid tales of the haunted tram depot spread among the workforce and those of a nervous disposition were probably relieved, when the building was closed on 22nd November 1937.

The clearing of Aurelia Road Depot was in response to the introduction of trolleybus route 630 on 12th September 1937. It was noted with approval that the new vehicles made good time crossing Mitcham Common, but then had to slow down to negotiate the narrow bottleneck of the junction between Pitlake and Tamworth Road in Croydon, which was controlled by signal lights.

Outside the confines of the borough tram routes 12, 14, 26, 28, 6 and 31 were affected, when Hammersmith Depot lost its railbound fleet. Wandsworth Depot went over to mixed operation to supply trolleybuses for route 612 from Battersea, Princes Head to Mitcham

At the change pit in Putney Bridge Road in 1937 shortly before the introduction of trolleybuses, we observe the conductor of a northbound route 30 tramcar. He is standing on the fender (known to crews as the 'bumper') in order to manipulate the trolley rope, so that the pole can make contact with the overhead wire. In a few days this scene will belong to history. J. Bonell/LCCT Trust

Fair Green. In many ways this conversion represented an attempt to join existing trolleybus routes to the rest of the network in the north and west of the capital.

Tracks linking Harlesden with Hammersmith, Fulham, Putney and Wandsworth were abandoned, as was the predominantly conduit equipped section along Garratt Lane in the direction of Tooting. Here, connection was maintained to the Plough Lane Stadium in Summerstown. The effect of all this was not just to deny Croydon an alternate tramway connection to the south London network, but also through journeys were disrupted in a route slicing exercise. Clapham Junction and York Road, Wandsworth became transfer points from tram to trolleybus. The rationale behind the September 1937 conversions was that links would be restored in due time, when the rest of the south London lines went over to trolleybuses.

The withdrawal of tram route 30 created spare capacity at Thornton Heath Depot to receive trams formerly housed at Purley Depot. Officially the car sheds on Brighton Road, Purley, which could hold around 20 vehicles, were then designated as a store and last resting place for tramcars facing the scrap man. The LPTB retained ownership of the building. Purley took on the mantle of Aurelia Road in the matter of disposing of surplus rolling stock. It was now a wise policy of senior management to keep redundant depots. Increasingly the international political situation focused minds on the terrible possibilities of aerial attacks. In the event of another war fleet distribution at different locations would minimise the risk of wholesale loss of vehicles in a bombing raid.

In 1937 Parliamentary authority was obtained for the full conversion of the remaining routes of the south London system. Croydon would then lose services 16/18 and with them the Feltham type vehicles now operating from Streatham and Brixton Hill depots. These relatively modern trams were perceived in a totally different light to the old relics locals had been forced to use on the former SMET lines. When the public became aware of the threat, reservations were expressed as to pace of the conversion process. It was clear from letters to the press that some folk actually preferred trams and wanted them to stay. Doubts were also voiced as to the need for back streets to accommodate proposed trolleybus turning circles. Residents objected to their suburban view of the heavens being obscured by overhead wires.

Croydonians were not the only people debating the transport policy of the LPTB. In THE COMMERCIAL MOTOR for 12th February 1937 a leading article, entitled *Is the Trolleybus a Passing Phase?*, included a London Transport photo of a trolleybus on

In suburban areas shops and houses followed the tramlines. Here in Brighton Road, South Croydon commercial development was given a boost by the inauguration of reliable electric traction. Through services to central London, as witnessed here by the presence of a standard LCC tramcar, added to the attractions of this part of town.

Brighton Road South Croydon. 20053B

the Uxbridge Road. One wonders whether the experts quoted in the article were working for Frank Pick or did the great man himself have a hand in stirring the pot? At any rate it is very likely that a source at 55 Broadway briefed the magazine with the following statements:

Many experts are inclined to look upon this vehicle as a hybrid, which might be employed in what may be termed the transitional stage of the move from tram to bus . . . As the London Passenger Transport Board is likely soon to be the largest user of the trolleybus, we were anxious to obtain its opinion upon this matter, and we find that the Board is not fully wedded to the type and cannot make a final decision upon the subject for some years . . . All things being equal, there is little doubt that the Board would have decided to add oil engined buses to its present fleet to make up for the loss of trams . . .

Lord Ashfield, regarded as the leading advocate of the trolleybus, was probably not amused!

The article does contain the usual rhetoric about trams as being 'a source of congestion and unsuited to modern traffic conditions'. In fairness to the trolleybus the unnamed author does refer to it as 'an excellent machine which has created new traffic'.

Back in metropolitan Surrey the supporters of the main line from Purley to central London would eventually be granted at least part of their wishes. Those who had pressed the case for a policy review in 1937, could not have known at the time that the centre of Croydon would continue to echo to the sound of tramcars for another 14 years. In an interesting postscript during wartime, the CROYDON ADVERTISER for 16th April 1943 made reference to the LPTB proposal to run trolleybuses on the Thornton Heath route. On the occasion of the relaying of track on the said route, the editorial concluded:

The question of tramcar versus trolleybus is too big a one to be dealt with in a brief note, but I think it is one of those problems that should be decided by the people themselves. Incidentally, it is worth mentioning in passing that many towns that scrapped their tramways have lived to regret the act.

As events unfolded in the immediate post war era, THE COMMERCIAL MOTOR was proved right, trolleybuses were regarded as distinctly passé by the LPTB and diesel buses were in the ascendant. Perhaps the most remarkable realisation of the power of the Croydon folk memory was the rebirth of tramways in the town right at the end of the twentieth century.

The Purley terminus was the furthest south you could reach on the London tram network. Car 1211 will shortly reverse over the scissors crossover to begin its return journey to Victoria Embankment. Although it was a lot quicker to go by train to central London, the trams were cheaper.

There was a suspicion that the LPTB management deliberately kept some of the oldest members of the fleet, such as car 2405, in service so as to highlight the difference between the trams and the modern trolleybuses. Certainly there were concerns in west London over the reliability of trams. Here at Craven Park the motorman must be blessing the fine weather, as he is totally exposed to the elements, if the skies darken. Driving one of the replacing trolleybuses will be a pleasanter experience for him. *D. W. K.Jones/ National Tramway Museum*

TRAMS HAD been a feature of north London life for six decades before the arrival of the LPTB. Apart from a brief experiment with steam traction, horses had supplied the motive power, until the opening of the first Metropolitan Electric Tramways Company route in July 1904 heralded the start of a comprehensive electrification scheme. Lines would eventually radiate from the County of London throughout Middlesex and into neighbouring Hertfordshire. Within the territory administered by the LCC a complex network of conduit equipped tramways served the local populus. Through running agreements had been concluded by the MET and the LCC, with the effect that joint services crossed connecting tracks at six separate locations.

In the early 1930s regular passengers on the system were confronted with a choice of rolling stock, which can only be described as eclectic. If travellers were fortunate to live in the Finchley and Wood Green areas they could expect to ride on modern Feltham type vehicles. Elsewhere the picture was rather mixed. Looking distinctly old fashioned. there were even some open toppers still doing the rounds. Adding to the array of body styles, trim little four wheel single deckers catered for bank holiday crowds and the occasional off season visitor to Alexandra Palace.

Lord Ashfield was well aware of the potential of the system, but as Frank Pick pointed out, on the other side of the coin nobody in senior management was blind to the MET's faults. Pick had often been cast as the chief negotiator with Middlesex County Council in an increasingly tough task of balancing the books. Both men had previously gained access to a damning report by Sir Ernest Clark, which was dated 16th September 1930. Headed FINANCES OF THE TRAMWAY GROUP, Sir Ernest did not pull any punches. On the prospects of new investment he stated bluntly:

It is very doubtful indeed whether investments in this group will be remunerative, and they must be regarded as undertaken (a) to prevent further depreciation and obsolescence of the existing capital assets, and (b) to fulfil the obligation falling upon this group of companies to provide London Transport facilities.

In spite of this gloomy prediction, the distinguished accountant did cost out a development scheme, which would have included improvements to the tramway infrastructure plus the acquisition of 54 new vehicles. Sir Ernest estimated an immediate injection of cash totalling £366,500, plus a possible further £156,000 to keep the MET ship afloat and to guide it into a safe harbour. At some stage in the proceedings, another potential course of action must have been suggested. Sir Ernest writes:

Alternatively, it may be decided to convert certain routes to a trackless trolley system, and if, for example, it is ultimately decided to convert, say half the existing tramways to such a system the cost of conversion, including the abandonment of track, conversion of overhead cables, and provision of new rolling stock would be roundly . . . £400,000.

Interestingly, it was calculated that the sale of the assets of the MET Omnibus Company, including 315 buses, plus the disposal of other investments, could realise a profit of £611,000. All of which painted a much brighter picture for the railbound side of the company. Bearing in mind the Metropolitan Electric was in the unique position of being a public/private partnership with the county council contributing finance to maintain the tracks, the whole report would have raised some eyebrows among the elected representatives of Middlesex, where opinions were divided as to the future of the whole enterprise.

Paradoxically, Sir Ernest's depressing report did not herald the immediate demise of the MET. In fact money was found to effect improvements. In 1931 permanent way renewals targeted four miles of double track in the Tottenham, Edmonton and Lordship Lane areas. Of the total cost amounting to £112,745, Middlesex County Council paid £47,745. The highways concerned were surfaced with asphalt to modern standards, thus benefiting all traffic. Further track relaying, including two and a half miles on the Great North Road, continued into the London Transport era.

Three projects then caught the imagination of the travelling public and were widely praised in the local and technical press. When the Piccadilly tube line was extended northwards from Finsbury Park, the opportunity was seized to construct tramway interchange stations at Manor House and Turnpike Lane. Loading islands with stairways gave tram passengers direct access to the Underground booking halls of the Piccadilly Line.

At North Finchley, Tally Ho Corner, another farsighted idea was taking shape. Although instigated by the MET, the scheme was completed by the LPTB. It involved a gyratory system of tramways, which included a tram station situated adjacent to Nether Street, out of the main traffic stream. It was calculated around 16,000 passengers a day could now board and alight in complete safety. This latest facility opened on 24th

February 1935. Middlesex County Council contributed £12,715 to the cost. They must have thought it was money well spent, but, incredibly, after a working life of only 36 months the whole lot was junked! The fate of the other two prestigious projects was not much better. Trams ceased using Turnpike Lane interchange in 1938 and the Manor House tracks fell silent a year later. It would appear London Transport was wedded to financial profligacy; however, we are getting ahead of our story.

Unsurprisingly, Sir Ernest's report was eventually to have fatal consequences for the local tramways. The January 1934 issue of PENNYFARE included a map of routes to be included in a Bill presented to the current session of Parliament. First in the firing line were the western services of the MET. Citizens living in the Cricklewood, Edgware, Harlesden, Wembley, Sudbury, Willesden and Paddington areas were going to be treated to the invasion of the trackless. In many

The Manor House loading islands, which gave direct access to the booking hall of the Piccadilly Line, represented a substantial investment in the tramways. Unfortunately the arrival of the LPTB in 1933 effectively stifled a comprehensive programme of modernisation. The bright future of the trams as part of an integrated transport network faded quickly with the new regime.
London Transport Museum

North Finchley tram station is the setting for two trams going in different directions. Ex-LCC car 882 will take the direct route to the centre of town, whilst ex-MET car 2280 will go the long way round through the western suburbs of the capital. Passengers can board and alight here in relative safety; however, they had to be aware of trams arriving and departing at frequent intervals. The double track approach, illustrated here, became a potential bottleneck of a single line exit from the tram station.

ways the whole programme of trolleybus substitution for trams constituted a logical progression northwards from the former London United territory boundary on the Uxbridge Road.

Detached from the main proposals, but no less threatening to the structural integrity of the old MET, was the published intention of scrapping the routes from North Finchley and Enfield to Wood Green, Finsbury Park, Camden Town and Euston. These were two trunk services into the capital, operated jointly by the MET and the LCC until the formation of the LPTB. It has been suggested that Lord Ashfield wanted to strike while the iron was hot. The anti-tram lobby in Parliament was in the ascendant; thus the impression was created in some quarters that trolleybuses might be welcomed into previously tramless districts. However, in a House of Commons debate on 18th December 1933, Sir Alfred Beit, wealthy owner of a mansion in Kensington Palace Gardens and Conservative MP for St Pancras South East, set the alarm bells ringing:

Sir Alfred Beit asked the Minister of Transport in which districts the proposed conversion of certain tramway routes to trolley-omnibus in London will involve the erection of overhead wires where at present no such wires exist?

The Parliamentary Secretary to the Ministry of Transport (Lieut.-Colonel Headlam): I am informed by the London Passenger Transport Board that their proposals for the conversion of certain tramway routes to trolley vehicle working would involve the erection of overhead wires in the Metropolitan boroughs of Holborn, St Pancras, Islington and St Marylebone, where such wires do not at present exist for traction purposes.

Sir A. Beit: Is the hon and gallant Gentleman prepared to say what would be the mileage of wires involved?

Lieut-Colonel Headlam: I could not possibly say that, but, of course, any proposals would have to be put in legislative form and would be submitted to the House by way of a Private Bill, so that the matter would be open to criticism.

And criticism there certainly was! The

Car 2319 was a former LUT type T vehicle, once called a 'Palace Car' because of its luxurious Edwardian style fixtures and fittings. Those days are now long gone and the tram is nearing the end of its working life on route 62. It was scrapped in August 1936.

prospect of the new vehicles traversing Tottenham Court Road to serve the fashionable shopping areas of the West End met with fierce local resistance. As it turned out, this rebuff signalled concerted opposition from politicians and influential local citizens to Lord Ashfield's plans for operation in central London. The trolleybus became 'machina non grata' in affluent circles.

The lack of enthusiasm for the Board's plans also spread to informed members of the public such as Henry Watson of Chiswick, who wrote to the TRANSPORT WORLD magazine on 15th January 1935. Mr Watson was the author of a standard text book entitled STREET TRAFFIC FLOW. In many respects he was a lone voice arguing against tramway abandonment and for an increase in investment in modern track layouts and passenger loading islands. He was particularly critical of the LPTB's intention to run trolleybuses in central areas:

I deplore the conversion of the Hampstead Road route. On the Board's own admission it is unsound, for it is a heavy traffic line and the extension of a few hundred yards is of no use to anyone. It ought never to have been sanctioned.

There is, moreover, no doubt that the trolleybus is more likely to entail fatal accidents than tramways. In the last three autumn months in London two pedestrians were killed by trolleybuses and two by tramcars, the latter being 44 times the number of the former. One does not, of course, see any reference to this in the newspapers and technical journals. Had the results been reversed, there would have been plenty of publicity.

One wonders which individual or group

The conductor of car 2497 looks back at the photographer, as he adjusts the trolley rope at Canons Park terminus. It is the summer of 1936 and the powers-that-be are deciding whether this section of track north of Edgware merits conversion to trolleybuses. Historically speaking, the MET wanted to run trams as far as Watford, but powerful local opposition sabotaged the plans. Therefore, the rails ended at Canons Park, which was hardly the most satisfactory of traffic objectives.
A. D. Packer Collection

within the organisation was casting doubt on official policy and characterising it as 'unsound', as implied by Mr Watson's letter. Not that internal dissent would have any effect on the course of events. Whatever the waves being created, Lord Ashfield appeared determined not only to ride out the storm, but to accelerate the tramway abandonment programme. Indeed, it could be said that caution was thrown to the winds later in at least two instances, in Edmonton and Walthamstow, when the dash to get rid of the hated trams went ahead, in spite of serious problems with vehicle supply and lack of electrical infrastructure for the replacing trolleybuses.

Out in the suburbs the management at 55 Broadway were having better luck. Here the adding of extra overhead wires to an already existing set for the local trams was unlikely to provoke opposition. Indeed a positive reaction could be expected from the travelling public, when it was announced that the motley collection of rolling stock used on the former western routes of the MET would be retired as quickly as possible. What can only be described as vehicle failures began to dog local tram services. There is no proof that the LPTB indulged in a deliberate policy of neglecting vital maintenance to their railbound fleet, but there is a suspicion that, since the trams were not long for this world, standards slipped. Inevitably the service suffered, as Samuel Viant, Labour MP for Willesden West, noted in a Commons debate on 4th March 1936:

It is the intention of the board to run trolley buses in certain parts of London. Trams are running at the present time, but the service is grossly inadequate. In the main Harrow Road which runs through Willesden it is not an uncommon thing, between the hours of 10 in the morning and 4 in the afternoon, to have to wait as long as 10 and 12 minutes for a tram.

Prior to the board taking the service over you could get a tram in three or four minutes. But even worse still, between the hours of 5. 30 and 7 o'clock in the evening, when factories and offices are closing down, trams from Edgware Road, from Hammersmith and from Acton come only as far as the junction, dump their passengers out there and return to Acton, Hammersmith and the Edgware Road. These passengers have to continue the remaining portion of their journey as best they can. It is true that another tram service, supplemented by an omnibus service, does continue towards the Willesden Green area, but so limited is the service that numbers of men prefer to walk rather than compete with women and girls to get on a tram or omnibus.

That members of the male working population were so gallant to their female counterparts was a sign of the times. London Transport promised better things on the timekeeping front, when, as from 5th July 1936, tramcars were withdrawn from routes 66 and 68. Cars on route 66 took 62 minutes to complete the journey from Canons Park to Acton; they covered part of the same ground as route 68, which worked only from Acton to Craven Park via Harlesden. Further loss of tramway mileage occurred on 2nd August, when routes 45 and 60 breathed their last. Three weeks later, on 23rd August 1936, officials probably hoped the local MP was not out with his stopwatch, as trolleybuses replaced trams on services 62 and 64.

Thus in the short space of seven weeks the routes of the old MET working from Finchley to Harlesden and along the Harrow and Edgware roads had been erased from the London tramway map. As a last reminder of past glories, the connecting tracks to Hendon Depot, which housed facilities for the repair and the scrapping of vehicles, were decommissioned on 24th October 1936.

With the passing of the trams some quaint old habits also ceased, as explained in the November 1934 TRAFFIC CIRCULAR:

WILLESDEN GREEN INTERLACING TRACK.

Staff are reminded that during fog an Official is on duty at the above point to give right-of-way whistle signals which are as follows:– One blast for UP cars to Paddington. Two blasts for DOWN cars to Cricklewood, Cars must not proceed over the interlacing without the whistle signal from the Official or the Conductor, sent ahead, who must use the same signals.

And as a final farewell to the Harrow Road tramwaymen, one hopes that the owner of the Jubilee Garage could now rest more peacefully at night, since the end of tramway operation in the street outside:

CROSS-OVER NEAR JUBILEE CLOCK.

Damage has been caused to a sign outside the Jubilee Garage, High Street, Harlesden, allegedly due to the trolley of a car turning on the cross-over at this point. Motormen and Conductors are instructed that when turning from the DOWN to the UP road, the car must up to the stopping place at Pole No. 185 before the trolley is turned so as top avoid risk of damage.

This map was drawn for the October 1937 edition of PENNYFARE.

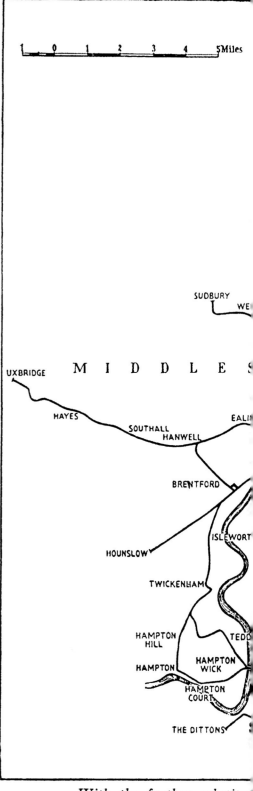

With the further substitut

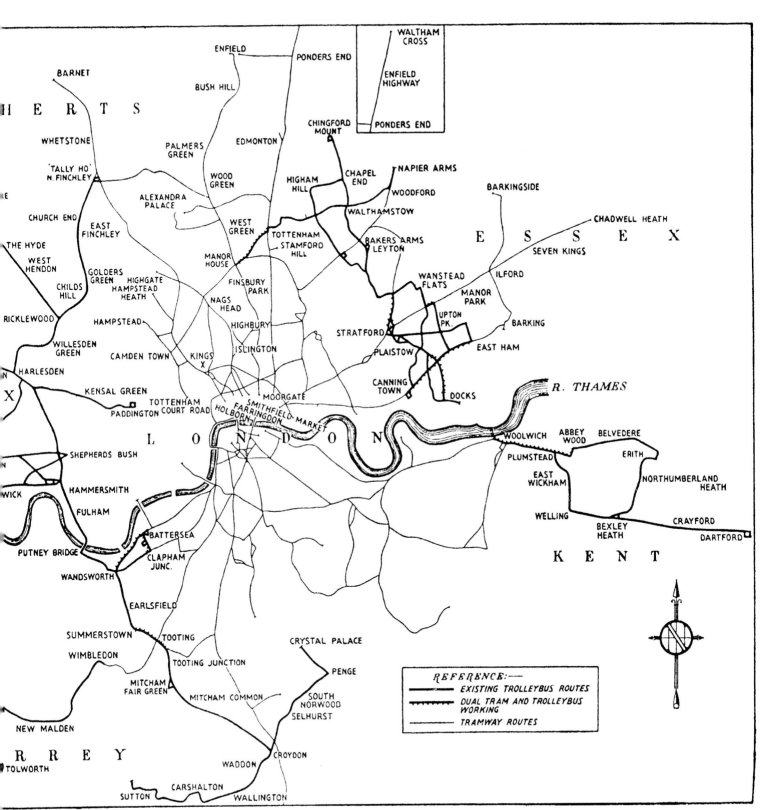

trolleybuses for trams on September 12, London's trolleybuses are now operated over 147 route miles

LONG DAY'S JOURNEY

Acts of Parliament promoted by London Transport in the years from 1934 to 1937 had a depressing familiarity for tramway supporters. On 20th July 1937, the Royal Assent was given to legislation which administered the coup-de-grace to the remaining tram routes both north and south of the River Thames. Since the formation of the LPTB in the summer of 1933, aside from the odd letter to the press, there had been no organised opposition to the London conversion scheme or, indeed, to scrapping proposals in other British towns and cities. This situation was about to change.

In December 1936 a trio of tramway supporters met to discuss future courses of action. S. G. Jackman was well known for his pro-tram stance in the letters columns of the newspapers. J. W. Fowler owned a printing works in Cricklewood Broadway, and Dr Hugh Nicol, a respected scientist and contributor to the famous Pelican paperback books series, had been photographing trams and street scenes since the late 1920s. The name the three fixed for the new organisation was the Light Railway and Transport League (LRTL). Note there was no mention of tramways in the title. One assumes the word had gained such a toxic connotation that it was deemed more politic to avoid it altogether.

The laudable aims of the LRTL included the retention and modernisation of existing systems. However, the path of true love for the tramcar did not run smooth. Personality differences in the embryonic organisation led to the formation of a breakaway group, later to adopt the title of the Tramway & Light Railway Society (TLRS). In spite of this early schism in the movement, sufficient members had joined the LRTL by the end of 1937, to merit the publication of a monthly journal THE MODERN TRAMWAY, with the first issue appearing in January 1938. In the intervening weeks wiser counsels had prevailed and the word 'tramway' had been

reinstated. Of immediate concern to many League members was the imminent demise of the rest of the former MET network. Trams still ran from Barnet, Enfield and Waltham Cross to central London, but their days were numbered. Also on the condemned list and somewhat nearer to extinction were the lines serving Alexandra Palace. The EVENING STANDARD attempted to influence the situation in December 1937 by declaring:

The two tram routes which serve the Alexandra Palace were described today by Mr Ernest Cawdron, Chairman of the Alexandra Palace Trustees, as a very primitive form of transport. He was speaking at a Ministry of Health inquiry at the Palace which was considering a £15,458 scheme for a new road through the grounds of Alexandra Palace to link up the Hornsey and Wood Green entrances. The road is to be used by a bus service to serve the Palace in place of the tramway services.

Correspondents of THE MODERN TRAMWAY, who submitted eye witness observations on the situation were obliged to concede:

These routes were opened 1904–5. The single truck one deck cars built in 1904 for these routes are still in operation with practically no alteration whatsoever from

when they first entered service. The wicker basket longitudinal seats with which they were then fitted are still being sat on. The track has been allowed to fall into very bad condition.

It was a fact of life that lack of investment had taken its toll on the Alexandra Palace trams. The combination of hard seats and rough riding over steadily disintegrating track acted as a powerful disincentive to potential passengers. The night of 22nd February 1938 saw the end of the 'Ally Pally Bang-Bangs' as they were known locally. The final journey by car 2311 was given a good send off by the assembled crowd, one of whom had written a valedictory ode on the side of the vehicle:

I am only a tram yet even I have a heart.
After 33 years I now have to part.
Loyally I have served and given of my best,
But many there are who would not have me rest.
The decision is made and who dare hinder.
Farewell dear public, I am doomed to a cinder.

London's last single deck tramcars in passenger service were then towed away to

Car 2302 stands in splendid isolation at Alexandra Palace. Aside from high days and holidays lack of passengers was an occupational hazard for route 37 to Wood Green. As such, this route and its companion route 39 to the western side of the Palace were an easy target for the advocates of the motor bus.

On the Great North Road by High Barnet Station tramcar 2201 ascends the gradient towards Barnet Church. Although its days are numbered, this tram car still looks good for a few more years. Car 2201 is using the positive wire of the trolleybus overhead; however, route 19 never received a direct trolleybus replacement. J. Bonell/LCCT Trust

the scrap yard behind Walthamstow Depot. In their final years they had transported the staff of the new BBC television service, which began broadcasting from studios at Alexandra Palace on 2nd November 1936. Anecdotal evidence suggests that the open driving platforms of the trams were employed to test the first outside broadcast cameras of the BBC. The rather secluded nature of the private right of way used by the single deckers must have added an air of mystery to the proceedings.

There was no such romanticism, when Frank Pick officially opened the reconstructed road through the Palace grounds on 28th May. As Pick remarked in his speech, the rickety trams had been ousted by modern motor buses. Passengers could now travel in comfort, sitting on upholstered seats. There was no room for sentiment, a new era of efficiency had arrived. And if people were in any doubt as to the veracity of this last statement, they only had to look at the teams of contractors now installing new traction standards along local tram routes. Trolleybuses were about to make a large scale entry into their lives.

The invasion of the trackless finally materialised on 6th March 1938, when routes 9, 13, 17, 19, 21 and 51 were retired. Conversion work had been going on for some months at Finchley and Wood Green, where depots had to be altered to accommodate the trolleybuses. It was pointed out that the car sheds at Finchley had a knack for absorbing cash, since they were extensively rebuilt in 1930–31 in preparation for the Felthams. Now the site had undergone yet another upheaval with the Felthams being evicted to pastures new in south London.

Trolleybuses had now gained a foothold in central London and rather predictably PENNYFARE also went to town on the event. In the April issue readers were left in no doubt as to the success of the project. In a

On 11th March 1936, the morning commute to work was enlivened somewhat by this scene in Palmers Green. There was a whiff of panic in the air; however, a threatened transport strike failed to materialise in this part of London. Just over a year later during the 'Coronation' bus strike scenes like this would be commonplace. The trams just carried on and shifted crowds of passengers. Getty Images 3274544

three page article slightly dubious facts and figures were quoted about the superiority of the trolleybus over the tramcar in respect of service speeds and journey times. It was stated that trams in north London would be a memory by the end of 1939. As regards the cost of the whole matter, a sum between seven and eight million pounds was cited.

The funeral wake attracted much attention and a procession of motorists and cyclists accompanied the last car from Barnet. On board were Driver W. Lowe and Conductor F. Mardell, who had crewed the first tram to Barnet 31 years previously. A total of 93 trams were withdrawn first to Holloway Depot, where they were relieved of any useful fixtures and fittings, such as destination boards and route blinds. They were then driven to Hampstead Depot, there to await the wreckers with their sledge hammers and gas torches.

Although Finchley was now tramless, the railbound vehicles operating routes 29

and 41 hung on for another two months. Wood Green Depot was still operating trams when on Saturday, 23rd April 1938, a visit was made by members of the LRTL. As THE MODERN TRAMWAY noted:

The cars inspected all previously belonged to the Metropolitan Electric Tramways Company and consisted of the following types: C, G, F, H and Feltham. All cars have BTH electrical equipment and, with the exception of the Felthams, were all fitted not many years back with two new 60 hp 509 type motors and new controllers, consequently they are very fast cars. The experimental car No. 2167 (MET 330) took the party from Wood Green to Edmonton with our hard working Treasurer (J. W. Fowler) perched on the front with his ciné camera. It is a real joy to all old MET friends to know that a lasting moving record will always remain of what were at one time undoubtedly some of the most interesting tramcars London possessed.

The technical details in this report rather give the lie to London Transport claims in the PENNYFARE article that trolleybuses had 50 per cent better acceleration than their railbound counterparts. Similar propaganda statements emanating from 55 Broadway found a receptive audience in local newspapers and among the ranks of the tram haters. Errors of judgement were also made in the premature scrapping of perfectly serviceable ex-MET rolling stock. A modernisation programme 1928–30 had resulted in improved upholstered, traverse seating in the lower saloons, plus a brighter décor with improved lighting. Drivers' windscreens had also been fitted to some vehicles. In the opinion of the LRTL many former members of the MET fleet were in a better state of preservation than LCC and east London trams, which had been selected to see out the remaining years of the system.

The word must have got round concerning the very limited life span of the

---

TROLLEYBUSES IN THE CITY
North London's Trams Almost Gone

TRAMS in North London will be just a memory in less than two years' time.

Their death-knell was sounded by the introduction of the trolleybus, which has quickly become popular because of its faster and smoother riding, and more comfortable seating. Almost silent as it glides along, it reduces the noise in the streets, particularly at points where there were tram track cross-overs, while it makes for greater safety by drawing onto the kerb. Its chief advantage, however, is that its power of acceleration, being 50 per cent. better than that of a tram, gives it a higher average speed. By offering this better service the trolleybus has already attracted increased traffic, for more passengers are using it for pleasure travel as well as for business journeys.

Plans for the elimination of all trams north of the river have been perfected, and the change-over will be made in twelve stages, at intervals of approximately two months. The entire conversion scheme, which includes certain parts of South London where trolleybuses have already superseded trams, will be completed by the end of 1939 at a cost of between £7,000,000 and £8,000,000.

Initial operations in Stage 1 of the change-over began on February 23 with the withdrawal of certain tram routes, and the stage was completed on March 6, when six new trolleybus routes were opened and trolleybuses were operated in the City of London for the first time.

New Trolleybus Routes

This huge conversion, the largest of its kind ever undertaken in one day, brought into service 93 new vehicles, which are supplied with power from twelve sub-stations. In erecting the poles and fixing the 95 miles of wire for the 23½ miles of new route the Board's engineers carried out their task expeditiously, for most of the work has been done since December last. Incidentally, every effort is made to reduce the number of new poles by using existing ones or attaching the wires to suitable buildings when the necessary permission is given.

Four of the new services run from North Finchley to Holborn Circus, where a loop has been built to avoid any congestion which would

be caused if trolleybuses turned at the City terminal. Vehicles on routes No. 517 (via Highgate) and No. 521 (via Wood Green) proceed from Kings Cross to the City via Gray's Inn Road and Holborn, and return via Charterhouse Street and Farringdon Road; those on No. 617 (via Highgate) and No. 621 (via Wood Green) are diverted at Kings Cross and traverse the loop in the opposite direction.

With a six-minute headway on each of the four services, 40 trolleybuses an hour operate between North Finchley and Holborn Circus during the peak period, while from the Nags Head, where the routes converge, there is a

The new and the old in Gray's Inn Road   [Planet News]

three-minute service both to Farringdon Road and Gray's Inn Road. The new services save interchanging by connecting East Finchley and Highgate with Gray's Inn Road and Holborn (517), North Finchley with Central London (617), Bounds Green, Wood Green

[Keystone]
IT JUST LOOKS THIS WAY
The Prince Consort raised his hat many years before trolleybuses came to Holborn Circus, but that, we think, was only because he lived in a previous era

and Finsbury Park with Farringdon Road (621). An early journey is made on Route No. 621, for the first trolleybus leaves North Finchley for Holborn Circus at 3.10 a.m.

The two other new routes are No. 609 (Barnet Church to Moorgate) and No. 651 (Barnet Church to Golders Green and Cricklewood). During this conversion the following tram routes were withdrawn:—9 (Whetstone and Moorgate), 13 (Highgate and Aldersgate), 17 (East Finchley and Farringdon Street), 19 (Barnet and Euston Road), 21 (North Finchley and Holborn), 51 (Wood Green and Aldersgate), 39A (between Enfield and Wood Green), 71 (between Wood Green and Aldersgate).

The Test Run

A test run over the Holborn loop was made on March 3, when some of the advantages of the trolleybus were demonstrated. The vehicle used was one built to a standard first introduced some three years ago, but with certain modifications, and its speed and riding qualities compared with those of a private car.

In a statement after the run, Mr. T. E. Thomas said that trolleybuses were no longer a new feature in the London area; but now, thanks to the broadmindedness of the City Corporation, who were represented at the test run by Sir Hugh Turnbull and Mr. Davidson,

they had penetrated into the heart of the Ci[ty] Trolleybuses were now an integral part [of] London Transport, and with the introduct[ion] of those on the six new routes there would [be] more than 700 operating in the London are[a.] They were carrying 400,000,000 passengers [a] year, of whom 60,000,000 were issued w[ith] workmen's tickets. With seating capacity [for] 70 passengers, they were able to replace [the] trams without increasing the number of vehicl[es] and they reduced traffic congestion by th[e] greater speed and mobility.

Referring to the silence of the trolleyb[us] Mr. Thomas said that perhaps this was [the] only criticism which had been made agai[nst] them, but it would teach people to use ot[her] senses besides hearing alone. He pointed [out] that there had been no increase in the numb[er] of road accidents since the ban on motor c[ar] hooters at night. He mentioned that the driv[ers] of the new trolleybuses were specially trai[ned] tram drivers, who had been taught in dep[ot] and on the road. Some of them were inclin[ed] to be excessively careful in the early stag[es] but they quickly gained confidence and usua[lly] settled down within a month.

The latest trolleybus development, he sa[id] was the introduction of what might be call[ed] the "chassisless" vehicle, for some of [the] component parts of the chassis were includ[ed]

[Planet N[ews]]
Conductor F. Mardell and Driver W. Lowe with [Mr.] Herbert Bee. Together they made a little bit of tr[am] history. See next page

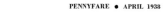

remaining former Metropolitan Electric trams. Members of the public travelling on the last tram from Enfield on 8th May 1938, added a wholly unwanted dimension to the scrapping process. Self appointed souvenir hunters fairly wrecked parts of the vehicle, with the result that what began as a sentimental farewell, ended with the local constabulary being called out to arrest the hooligans. London Transport took note to liaise with the police on future conversion nights, which were now happening at two monthly intervals. However, as we shall see, this strategy would later fail spectacularly. Rather perversely, the stricken last night tramcar of type H was repaired and then sent to the scrap yard!

The demise of routes 29 and 41 in May emptied Wood Green Depot of trams. The last of the north London Felthams departed for the south; the rest of the erstwhile inhabitants of the depot made the one way journey to oblivion. Edmonton Depot serving

the Hertford Road services remained in commission, but there seemed to be no stopping the mandarins at 55 Broadway in their desire to speed up the conversion process. T. E. Thomas and his colleagues risked not having enough new trolleybuses for the job in hand.

In the spring of 1938, even the most optimistic of tram supporters had to face unpalatable facts. It appeared London Transport were well on track to rid the capital of its trams by 1943 at the latest. In the normal course of events this target was perfectly achievable. However a chance meeting with a small group of Austrian refugees on a tram in Stamford Hill, caused at least one young member of the LRTL to ponder what might happen if Great Britain were drawn into another European conflict. The Austrians were forced to flee their homeland in March after the Nazis invaded.

Headquarters were also aware of events on the Continent. An LPTB TRAFFIC CIRCULAR

for Friday, 22nd April 1938, included a section marked

AIR RAID PRECAUTIONS.

Published in response to enquiries from the staff, the advice was practical: The Board do not wish to discourage members of the staff from co-operating in any local authority's scheme for organization of passive defence against air raids. It must be appreciated, however, that the Board's services may become of such national importance that, in time of war, no personnel can be spared from their normal duties or from the Board's own emergency organisation.

Pride of the fleet, luxury car 1, has completed its journey from Waltham Cross in Hertfordshire to Purley in Surrey. Rather symbolically it finds itself being hemmed in by motor buses, but its streamlined design stands in contrast to the angularity of its internal combustion engined competitors. One assumes the tram load of LRTL members is now slaking its collective thirst at a nearby hostelry before the return to central London.

PENNYFARE ● APRIL 1938   Page 65

...ody. This led to a reduction in weight and ...and an improvement in the riding qualities. ...onclusion, Mr. Thomas said he noticed ...e Prince Consort was raising his hat ...e first trolleybus passed his statue in ...n Circus on the test run. This might ...en as a good omen for the future.

Withdrawing the Trams

...ough it involved 300 separate movements ...ng the new trolleybuses to their depots ...t rid of the obsolete trams, the big change-...as completed in less than six hours.

...st of the 93 trams withdrawn from service ...run into Holloway depot, where they were ...ed of their destination boards, route ...rs and blinds, and other fittings before ...transferred to Hampstead depot to be ...up.

...enty-eight modern trams, known as the ...m type, were taken from Wood Green ...eatham depot for further service, while ...rs were moved from Finchley to Wood ... depot, so that the work of converting ...ey depot into a trolleybus shed could be ...eted.

...antime, 50 trolleybuses from HOUNSLOW, ...n and other north-western depots were ...erred to Finchley, which now accom-...es a fleet of 84. Fifty-four vehicles had ...usly been transferred to Holloway, which ...ouse 230 trolleybuses and be the largest ... of its kind in this part of London when ...econstructed.

*   *   *   *

...nd how do you like driving a trolleybus ? " ...ked a 53-year-old driver.

...have been driving all types of trams for the ...wenty-eight years," he replied, " but after ...x on the trolleybuses the latter are much ...preferred.

...first I wanted to keep to the middle ...e road, but that soon wore off. Yes, ...buses are a great improvement, and I ...iate the comfort and cleanliness of the ...s cabin. The tram took me along— ...can take a trolleybus where *I* want to go ! " ...hat about the cross-overs ? " we enquired. ...es, they did puzzle me at first. On a tram ...so used to ' rushing ' them that I wanted ...the same thing with my trolleybus. ...ver, the careful coaching of my instructor ...e over this difficulty. Now I automatically ...e speed."

Cheering the last car home   [*Planet News*]

A Rousing Farewell

When the last tram left Barnet for Tallyho Corner on March 5, so many people gathered to bid it farewell that special police had to control the crowds. Crowded with passengers, some of whom hung on the footboard or sat on the buffer, it was escorted to Wood Green depot by a cavalcade of motorists and cyclists, who played a fanfare on their horns and bells whenever it stopped. As it entered the depot the crowds of people sang "Auld Lang Syne."

Driver W. Lowe and Conductor F. Mardell, of Finchley depot, who took the first tram to Barnet thirty-one years ago, were in charge of the last tram, and the last passenger to leave the car was Mr. Herbert Bee, who travelled on the first tram with the driver and conductor. He still has the first ticket issued on this route —and now he has the last.

*   *   *   *

Tailpiece. A correspondent has written to the Board that, since the withdrawal of trams in North London, he and other residents have been unable to sleep.

" It is so unnaturally quiet at night," he writes.

left When car 1 was hired for its record breaking trip, there was no Sunday service on the section from Waltham Cross to Ponders End. This view of the Hertford Road shows the initial stages of the journey south to Purley. Car 2170 is working route 79, which operated on Sundays every six to eight minutes between Enfield and Smithfield. W. A. Camwell/National Tramway Museum

below Car 2214, working service 59, is pictured at Edmonton. It was originally MET type H car 282. In spite of its decent overall condition this vehicle will be scrapped in a few months time. It met its end in October 1938. A. V. Mace

covered the spectacle, generally reported positively. It was indeed a long day's journey, which participants were right in thinking would never be repeated. The message of the LRTL that tramways had a future in the metropolitan area also found itself in the columns of the newspapers. PENNYFARE printed a brief note, expressing the opinion that the five shilling (25p) ticket, specially issued for the trip, would become a collector's item. Other than this there was no official response. In fact on the same page of PENNYFARE was a statement that the trolleybus conversion scheme, costing £10,000,000, had reached the halfway mark and that the fleet now totalled 812 vehicles. The LRTL's message of tramway retention had obviously fallen on deaf ears.

The former MET tracks used by car 1 lasted until 16th October 1938, when routes 59, 79 and 49A were withdrawn. Tram route 49 lost its northern section to find itself cut back to Stamford Hill. An interesting casualty of this conversion stage was route 49A, which joined Enfield with Ponders End

Clearly moves were afoot to create some form of civil defence against aerial attacks. If war were declared, then it was probable that all the LPTB's expansion plans would be put on hold, including the tramway abandonment programme.

The sombre mood of tramway enthusiasts was lightened by a remarkable event. It was remarkable in the sense that it had never been attempted before. An idea mooted at a committee meeting of the LRTL on 28th December 1937, came to fruition, when former LCC luxury car 1 was hired for a marathon tram journey. The issue of THE MODERN TRAMWAY of June 1938 takes up the story, headed

OUR SIXTY MILE ODYSSEY:

On the 15th May 1938, District Inspector Baker, an official of the London Passenger Transport Board, seated comfortably at the controls of the first L. C. C. electric luxury tramcar, drove it from Waltham Cross in Herts to Purley in Surrey, and back again. Once again an historic event was recorded.

Yes, at 2. 0 precisely, the familiar streamline design of London Transport's Number One Luxury Tramcar, slowed to a standstill in the narrow main street of Waltham Cross, Hertfordshire . . . A battery of press photographers demanded our attention before the departure . . . The stretch of track that lies between Ponders End and Waltham Cross, and which has never seen a tramcar on a Sunday for many years, was taken full advantage of. We literally flew. Down the road we skimmed, with

the wind whistling past the ears of those members who stood on the platform . . .

The piece continues in similar vein. It was a write up which tended towards sentimental romanticism, as the merits of the tramcar on its journey across the capital were eulogised. But then, who can blame the adherents of the beleaguered League from savouring their moment in the sun.

The whole outing was deemed a great success and the national press, which

60-MILE JOY RIDE

Grand Tour Was First—and Last

"**S**ORRY, lady," said the conductor of a tramcar that pulled up at Savoy Street on the Embankment yesterday, " but the minimum fare on this car's five shillings."

" Where're yer going—China ? " asked the man who was selling pea nuts, all fresh-roasted, a penny.

The trip this tramcar was about to begin was well worth five shillings because it had never been done before and it will never be done again.

When the conductor rang the bell and we started off up the Kingsway tunnel he was performing the first act of an historic

Cheery passengers leaving for the tram-ride

ceremony, akin to the part of the man who pulls the string at an unveiling function. This ceremony might be called " The Tram Lover's Farewell to His Tram."

We were off on the longest all-urban tram journey in the world—up to Waltham Cross in Herts and from there more than 30 miles down to Purley in Surrey (writes a News Chronicle reporter).

Waltham Cross has no trams on a Sunday, but in view of the way in which trolley buses are pushing the trams right off the rails, the members of the Light Railway Transport League decided to make a grand gesture before it was too late.

They decided on a splendid ride lasting hours over 60 miles of lines.

For the 5s. we passed through 14 boroughs and had tea en route. They were hazarding, too, that the highest-priced tram ticket ever issued in England may be worth something to collectors.

STRICTLY UTILITARIAN

My fellow passengers, members of the League, declared that there was nothing of the fanatic about them. Their interest in trams is strictly utilitarian.

They said trams carried more people, lasted longer, and caused less congestion. They drank to the health of trams at tea.

Cutting from the News Chronicle newspaper of Monday May 16, 1938.

Cars 1076 and 2242 are depicted in Southbury Road, Ponders End. It is a Saturday afternoon in the summer of 1938 and route 49 drivers have permission to take their charges from the usual terminus at Edmonton right the way through to Enfield. The decision has already been taken not to replace this section by trolleybuses. *Henry Priestley/National Tramway Museum*

Activity at Highgate change pit in 1938 sees car 2201 making the transition from the conduit to the overhead. This particular manoeuvre appears to have attracted the attention of several London Transport inspectors. The conductor has already raised the trolley pole for the journey north to Barnet.

via Southbury Road. Worked at an interval between trams of six to eight minutes, the journey lasted six minutes at an adult fare of only one penny. It was noted by enthusiasts that this stretch of track was one where drivers would push their charges to achieve higher speeds than usual. Of course, this practice was frowned on officially, but with the end in sight, crews attempted to demonstrate that sitting in an accelerating tramcar over the humped back railway bridge at the eastern end of Southbury Road was indeed a thrill to savour. It was an experience not to be maintained by the newer form of electric traction, because it was decided that the road would be better served by motor buses. Only a short section from Hertford Road to the forecourt of Ponders End Garage was wired for trolleybuses.

The replacing trolleybuses, which did reach Waltham Cross, had to be extended from the old tramway stub terminal to a newly constructed turning circle in Eleanor Cross Road. It is worth quoting an account of

the last night 'celebrations', as witnessed by a youthful LRTL member, John Barrie:

The 49's were curtailed at Stamford Hill, although the section of track between Amhurst Park and Wards Corner, Tottenham, was left open for depot workings on the 71's. The last car from Waltham Cross was H type 2231. Unfortunately, the car was absolutely wrecked by hooligans and police had to turn everybody off the car at Ponders End, making several arrests. This meant that I had to walk home from Ponders End, which did not exactly please me, particularly in view of the fact that I was pretty browned off with the conversion . . .

Sadly for young John the euphoria of his mammoth trip on car 1 had now evaporated completely. His distress was further compounded on 5th November, when car 2261 closed the 27 route from Edmonton. The aptly named Tramway Avenue, Edmonton witnessed the final procession of tramcars from the depot on their way to either Purley or Hampstead for scrapping. This conversion stage saw the end of former Metropolitan Electric Tramways vehicles working from an ex-MET depot.

The demise of the MET came on 5th February 1939, when route 71 from Wood Green to Holborn was replaced. John Barrie was again on hand to note in his diary:

We were waiting at Wood Green for the last

car to arrive, when to our horror we heard the approach of car 1269, which was the last of the MET-motored cars left at Holloway. We were horrified to think that this car was going to meet the same fate as the previous last cars, and get wrecked. Fortunately, I don't know if the fate of the other hooligans from the Waltham Cross car at the Courts had had a deterring effect on the would-be wreckers, or whether it was that by now the novelty of last cars had worn off, but hardly anybody turned up to welcome 1269. Any rate this was a ride of rides. The controller handle of this fine car was pulled round and left there for the whole of the journey back to Holloway Depot and this was by far the fastest ride I have ever had on an E/1.*

In the space of a few years the tramway network built up in the counties of Middlesex and Hertfordshire had been dismantled. Smoke had risen from the funeral pyres of unwanted tramcars. Many of them could have given further service to the travelling public, but the official policy of tramway abandonment was paramount.

right This scene proves that the imposition of trolleybus overhead wires along thoroughfares equipped with conduit tramways did not always result in an eyesore, as the critics claimed. Car 2225 is pictured crossing the railway bridge in Hampstead Road near the famous art deco factory building, formerly used by Carreras Cigarettes.
A. V. Mace

below The date is 10th April 1938. Car 1153 stands in Lordship Lane, Wood Green. Made to measure suits were retailing at John Maxwell's shop between thirty and fifty shillings (£1.50 – £2.50). The tram driver is about to start on his 62 minute journey to Aldgate. Route 71 was another tram route never replaced on a like for like basis.
W. A. Camwell/National Tramway Museum

OLD ROUTES, NEW WIRES

THE LONDON County Council had bequeathed a unique legacy to the LPTB. The conduit system of current collection dispensed with the need for overhead wires. In aesthetic terms it was welcomed, as it lessened considerably the visual impact of the street tramway. On the other hand, from an economic perspective it was a distinct liability. Maintenance costs were high and the Board was obliged to retain the services of specialist permanent way teams to ensure that each section of conduit was kept free of obstructions and in sound condition.

Travel from overhead wire equipped tracks to the conduit was effected at transfer points, known as change pits. North of the River Thames these were situated at Highgate Archway, Manor House, Stamford Hill, Lea Bridge Road (Lower Clapton), Well Street (Hackney), Mile End, Limehouse and Iron Bridge (Canning Town). Trunk routes from the northern and eastern suburbs were worked by tramcars adapted to use both methods of current collection.

When trolleybuses arrived on the scene, access to central London termini was gained through the extension of overhead wires in streets, where none had previously existed. As has been mentioned previously, this approach by London Transport ruffled a few feathers, but not enough to delay seriously the bulk of the conversion programme. Such delays as there were occurred when suitable places for trolleybuses to end their journeys were conspicuous by their absence. A lot of haggling took place before the authorities permitted the construction of turning circles. One of the major successes was obtaining permission to link the former tram termini at Holborn and Farringdon Street to form the Holborn loop for trolleybus operation.

As for the other locations where tracks ended, the LPTB managed to arrange suitable turning points at Bloomsbury, Smithfield, Moorgate, Liverpool Street Station, Aldgate and Leman Street (London Docks). However, not even the persuasive powers of Messrs Pick and Ashfield could get the City of London authorities to budge, when it came to the tram terminus in Aldersgate Street opposite Fann Street. This was the end of the line for routes 13, 51, 71 and 77. The southern extremity of Goswell Road was

left Hampstead Depot is depicted in operational days before it became a repository for all the system's waifs and strays. Car 582 awaits its turn on route 15. Nearer the camera is the traverser, which also serves as a temporary storage area for a stack of side destination boards. Note the movable gantries used by tram cleaners to reach the upper deck windows. Alan B. Cross

facing page Many trams working the Hampstead services sported a three line destination box. Seen in Pancras Road, Kings Cross, car 527 is eking out its last days before the inevitable meeting with the scrappers. In the background is the façade of the Great Northern Hotel. Henry Priestley/ National Tramway Museum

fated to retain conduit tracks, until suitable alternative routings had been implemented for the replacement services. The last tram ran here on 10th September 1939.

Aside from the Aldersgate debacle, everything might have appeared to be going to plan, except there were two potential problems on the horizon. The first concerned

the Hampstead group of routes. When faced with the task of clearing trams from this area, Frank Pick had taken soundings from T. E. Thomas as to the merits of converting the whole lot to motor bus operation. Hampstead Heath did attract crowds at Bank Holidays, however, on a daily basis lower passenger numbers on routes serving

Parliament Hill Fields and from Camden Town to South End Green, Hampstead made conversion to trolleybuses a financial risk. An impetus to employ motor buses was given by the abandonment of tram route 19 south of the Archway Tavern. Replacement arrived in the form of a strengthened service on bus route 134.

Another local matter to be sorted out was the fate of Hampstead Depot. Situated in the middle of the one way streets of Agincourt Road and Fleet Road, it was opened in 1914 with a capacity of around 150 vehicles. In practice this figure was never reached; proposed tramway extensions in the area failed to materialise. The place became a convenient halfway house for all the waifs and strays of the system. Cars stored out of service, or otherwise unwanted, lined the stabling roads. Vehicles awaiting the attention of the scrap man also entered the portals of Hampstead Car Sheds. Initial plans for conversion to a trolleybus depot were quietly dropped in favour of maintaining the status quo. The location remained a retirement home for old trams.

These arguments about routes and rolling stock deployment were academic for many locals, who actually cherished their trams and wanted them to stay. Members of the well known Hampstead literary and artistic community were concerned that the famous all night service from Holborn would be axed by the new regime. Trams ran at hourly intervals past midnight. They served Malden Road, Prince of Wales Road, Great College Street, Pancras Road and Grays Inn Road. Party goers, shift workers and night owls were charged fourpence for the privilege of a ride.

One famous resident, who grew up in Lissenden Gardens just off Highgate Road, was John Betjeman, later to achieve national treasure status as Poet Laureate. His poem *Parliament Hill Fields*, which describes a journey home on a route 7 tram, beautifully evokes the atmosphere of the period:

Till the tram went over thirty, sighting
terminus ahead,
Past municipal lawn tennis and the
bobble hanging plane:

This excerpt brings to mind an incident in the poet's childhood. Sir John Betjeman recalled riding on the open top deck of horse trams with the intention of trying to grab the bobble shaped fruits attached to the Plane trees, which are such a feature of the metropolitan landscape.

Alas, not even the remonstrations of literary notables could move London Transport. After due deliberation it was decided to stick to original policy and railless electric traction triumphed with new poles and wires being erected. Tram services 3, 5, 7, 15 and 25 followed the path prescribed by Lord Ashfield and they duly succumbed to trolleybuses on 10th July 1938.

A more intractable problem than that presented at Hampstead was the continued existence of the Kingsway Subway and its associated tram routes. Service 31 ran from Wandsworth to Hackney with a Sunday extension to Leyton (Bakers Arms); service 33 cars travelled from West Norwood to Manor House; service 35 ran from Forest Hill to Highgate (Archway Tavern). All three routes began in south London and traversed the Kingsway Subway to terminate in north

The tram terminus was situated opposite Swains Lane on Highgate Road, Parliament Hill Fields. The conductor of car 559 poses for the photographer, while car 523 waits at the end of the track. The steamroller in the background is employed on construction works for the new trolleybus turning circle.
Henry Priestley/National Tramway Museum

London. Travel patterns established by these services needed to be maintained, until the conversion programme moved south of the Thames.

The Kingsway Subway, which provided a through tramway from Victoria Embankment to Theobalds Road, was opened for single deck tramcars on 10th April 1908. It represented a farsighted attempt to speed up communication between the two halves of the LCC network. Unfortunately it remained unique and the opportunity was

lost to provide the capital with other sub surface lines, which could have alleviated the growing menace of traffic congestion. The last day of single deck operation was Monday, 3rd February 1930, after which date the whole structure was enlarged to accommodate standard double deck tramcars. A ceremonial opening of the new facility occurred on 14th January 1931. It was recorded for posterity on the newsreels, and the film, as viewed by cinema audiences at the time, can still be enjoyed on the British Pathé website.

In its rebuilt state the subway was fine for tramway operation, but the physical constraints of the tunnels did not bode well for any type of steerable vehicle, be it motor bus or trolleybus. A trial trolleybus was constructed to ascertain whether it was worth going ahead with the project, but the engineers at London Transport still

had their work cut out to devise practical solutions for the many problems raised. A range of ingenious ideas was explored. These included metal troughs for use as wheel guides and the implementation of right hand running in the tunnels so that vehicles could load and unload passengers at the central island platforms already existing at Holborn and Aldwych tram stations. A simple alternative to all this experimentation might have involved abandoning the subway entirely. Overhead wires for trolleybuses could then be erected top side along Kingsway, across Aldwych and the Strand to reach the Thames Embankment by several narrow streets near Somerset House. However, it was very unlikely that the elected representatives of the City of Westminster would have sanctioned a surface trolleybus route. Thus the whole enterprise of modernising the Kingsway Subway hit more than a few snags.

An editorial in the September 1938 issue of THE MODERN TRAMWAY noted how the LPTB's latest proposals had sparked controversy:

Close upon the announcement that an experimental trolleybus is to be built for the Kingsway tramway subway comes the news that the London Passenger Transport Board are to make preliminary plans for the running of trolleybuses along Victoria Embankment and over Westminster and Blackfriars Bridges. This latter proposal has brought a storm of protest from all manner of people and is justly attracting comment in the National Press. We learn from the Daily Telegraph that no new trolleybus poles are to be erected and that use will be made of existing lamp standards and buildings. The News Chronicle takes a serious view of the situation and suggests that the Board's plans be made known well in advance so that the public may have the chance to consider them.

Reluctantly, the powers that be at 55 Broadway had to acknowledge a setback to their plans. It was not yet regarded as a total defeat, but the practicalities of the situation dictated that services 31, 33 and 35 would continue in operation for the time being. This meant mixed operation of trams and trolleybuses along important thoroughfares in north London. It also meant that Holloway Depot, now deep in trolleybus territory, would have to retain a limited tramway presence. Some staff at the depot would therefore be expected to work on both forms of electric traction. In short, the management and the workforce had to make the best of an unsatisfactory situation.

Even in its latter days the Kingsway Subway still exercised a fascination over tram enthusiasts, casual travellers, tourists and seasoned commuters, who had occasion to use this link across central London. Car 1931 pauses at Holborn Tram Station. It has just descended the ramp from street level in Southampton Row. Passengers boarded and alighted at the driver's end of the tram.

THIS SIDE FOR TRAMS
VIA
VICTORIA EMBANKMENT
⇒⇒⇒ TO

	DIRECT SERVICE
CHARING CROSS	ALL TRAMS
WESTMINSTER	ALL TRAMS
BRIXTON	33
HERNE HILL	33
WEST NORWOOD	33
ELEPHANT & CASTLE	35
NEW CROSS	35
FOREST HILL	35

LONDON OVER THE BORDER

West Ham Depot in Greengate Street was the favoured spot for staging official photographs of the rolling stock. Former West Ham car 264 was almost thirty years old, when this view was taken in 1934. The tram has yet to receive its LONDON TRANSPORT fleet name. This vehicle appears in good condition, but the longevity of the average tramcar worked against it, when it was compared to the latest buses and trolleybuses.
London Transport Museum

THE EASTERN environs of the capital have been described as 'London over the Border'; the traditional frontier between Middlesex and Essex was the River Lea. The arrival of the London County Council in 1889 and the subsequent division of the metropolitan area into postal districts fixed in the popular mind the concept of an East End to be discovered on leaving the confines of the City at Aldgate. Places such as Hackney, Stepney, Whitechapel, Limehouse and Poplar developed their own distinct identities as predominantly working class neighbourhoods, which could be traversed by a network of tramways with connections to lines owned by municipal operators in metropolitan Essex. Chief amongst these, and crucial to the efficient running of the network, was the County Borough of West Ham.

East of the River Lea was classic tramland. Trams seemed a permanent part of the landscape, offering as they did the means of travel to work or to reach the 'green lungs of London' – the parks, Wanstead Flats and Epping Forest. The ride on the top deck was all part of an affordable day out for a family. Frequent services were provided by vehicles which reflected municipal pride. In fact one local council was so proud of its trams that it resisted fiercely incorporation into the LPTB. The management at Ilford fought a long rearguard action to prevent Ashfield and his 'wicked combine' from getting their hands on their green painted tramcars, which served the district and, it was claimed, returned regular profits into municipal coffers.

Aside from Barking Council Tramways, which was a one generation wonder and ceased operation in 1929, the local tram systems were making a determined attempt to move with the times. West Ham, East Ham, Walthamstow and Leyton had all commissioned new rolling stock. Ilford, whose management affected an aloofness from neighbouring operators, had ordered eight new, single truck trams as late as 1932. As well as new vehicles appearing on the scene, there was a spate of track renewals and road improvements. Walthamstow Council had authorised a complete reconstruction of their system in 1924–27; track doubling had taken place throughout, with the result that only the Higham Hill to Markhouse Road, Leyton route (later renumbered 85) was predominantly single track and loops. The modernisation programme in east London culminated in the extensive rebuilding of the old Iron Bridge at Poplar. A new traffic layout, including provision for trams on services 65 and 67, opened on 15th January 1933.

Appearances suggested that tramway business in the area was thriving and the fares were some of the cheapest in London. In the summer of 1933, at the dawn of London Transport, an observer standing at Stratford Broadway would have been treated to the spectacle of an almost continuous stream of trams. Former West Ham, East Ham, Leyton and Walthamstow cars headed off down local back streets to Chingford Mount, the Docks, Canning Town or East Ham Town Hall. Passengers desirous of a trip round the County Borough of West Ham could avail themselves of a route 10 car, which worked London's only true circular service. It was said that when the sun was shining and the wind was in the right direction, the 33 minute round trip at a fare of only 2½d (1p) could offer a pleasant way of exploring part of the East End with an unrivalled view from the top deck of a tramcar!

Other trams passing through Stratford Broadway included ex-LCC vehicles on trunk routes 61 and 63 from Leyton and Ilford into central London. Impressively, these two services maintained an interval of a car every 90 seconds. Added to this scene was a plethora of motor buses. However, this air of permanence was illusory. Lord Ashfield and the LPTB had no intention of granting the area immunity from the brave new public transport world being prepared for the rest of their domain.

At first the new owners contented themselves with closing East Ham Depot and shuffling the rolling stock about. On the face of it this was a sensible policy to maximise

Stratford Broadway was a major tramway interchange and the hub of the East End network. Car 217 has a short layover before setting out again in the direction of East Ham. Many of the local services were operated by four wheel cars, which made them prime candidates for early replacement by trolleybuses.

resources. Twenty of the Walthamstow bogie cars were despatched westwards to Holloway Depot in September 1933. These particular vehicles were famous for their sprightly performance and, quite frankly, their qualities of speed and acceleration had been wasted on home turf. They were allocated to service 29 from Enfield to Tottenham Court Road. They shared the route with Felthams and other refugees from east London in the shape of ex-Leyton E/3 vehicles. This combination ensured that the route was probably the fastest in the LPTB.

Cars going eastwards in exchange for the former Walthamstow and Leyton vehicles were slower and included the 500 series of ex-LCC rolling stock, which were nicknamed 'tortoises' by the crews. As John Barrie noted on observing the new arrivals on route 29:

I do not believe that the East Enders were very pleased with this deal; they certainly got the worst of the bargain! There were two batches of these cars, 51-62 and 39-46, the letter K having been added to denote Walthamstow. The former cars were built in 1927 and were I think the noisiest, roughest riding, ugliest and most uncomfortable car on which I have ever ridden – but to me they were absolutely wonderful cars; they had one feature that really mattered. Boy, could they shift! In common with the newer type, which were the last cars to be built for London, they were the fastest cars to appear on the London Streets.

When the strategists at 55 Broadway did get to work on serious plans for the East End, it probably seemed a straightforward matter of drafting the requisite legislation, but they came unstuck, because part of the Parliamentary Bill later threatened to turn into a public relations disaster. Paragraphs 32–38 of *The London Passenger Transport Board Act,* 1934 sought powers to convert the conduit tramway from Aldgate along Whitechapel Road and Mile End Road to overhead wire operation. Bearing in mind the bulk of the proposed legislation in the 1934 Act related to the introduction of trolleybuses, this concern about a short

section of tramline in the East End appeared somewhat out of context. At the time it was inferred the logic behind the enterprise may have been to test public opinion by erecting overhead wires along a thoroughfare previously devoid of them. However, an internal report (qv) suggests that the management were trying to abandon the change pit in Mile End Road in an attempt to speed up the service. Whatever the motives of Frank Pick and others, the House of Commons debate on 20th June 1934 flushed out plenty of objections to the scheme.

Several honourable members were worried that the rights of the borough councils were being trampled on by a large and powerful organisation – the LPTB. Historically, the local authorities in the LCC area had a veto on the erection of overhead wires to power the tramways. In addition there was a strong sense of injustice in that wealthy residents of the West End could write influential letters to THE TIMES, whereas in the submission of Barnett Janner, Liberal MP for Whitechapel and St Georges:

I hope that I have said enough to convince the House that the proposal is absurd . . . It is not fair that the East End of London, because it happens to be poor, should be made the scapegoat for the introduction of ideas which are to be tried on them first, and afterwards possibly upon other sections of the community, who will have to accept them because poor Stepney had to suffer in the past . . . as far as Whitechapel High Street, Whitechapel Road and Mile End Road are concerned, the inhabitants are quite entitled to have their magnificent streets without the obstruction of overhead wires . . .

Mr Janner's colleague, Dr O'Donovan, Tory MP for Mile End, after going on at some length about the blighting of the area by the proposal, rather lost the plot by admitting:

I have commented on our great loss of local amenities.

I only wish to say that if we could have an offer of trolley omnibuses all opposition would melt from this side.

Finally, after a number of similarly contradictory statements the worthy doctor resumed his seat. Sir George Hamilton, Conservative MP for Ilford, picked up the baton. He seemed to have a better understanding of what the Board was trying to achieve. He quoted incidences where a tram would lose power on the conduit – in tramway speak the vehicle would be 'stuck on a dead' – an occurrence which would be avoided by the use of the overhead wire system:

If a tram is suddenly pulled up and its electrical connection happens to be at the break of the rails, and the contact is not made, that tram cannot start again. The result is that another tram has to come up behind and push it along. Sometimes one tram is not enough, and I am sure hon Members have seen, as I have, in that very road five trams all pushing one wretched tram in order to enable it to regain contact. That creates a tremendous block of traffic in this great main street.

Although Sir George was certainly guilty of exaggeration in judging the number of vehicles required to animate a stricken sister car, the point was well made. Conduit equipped tracks certainly merited serious study to determine whether they had outlived their usefulness. In the end it was a case of much ado about nothing. The conduit remained from Aldgate to Mile End until the opening months of the Second World War.

This little sideshow of paragraphs 32–38 of the 1934 Act briefly spluttered into life and then died. The whole affair failed to have any significant impact on the trolleybus conversion programme. As part of the bigger picture construction crews crossed the River Lea in the summer of 1936. Walthamstow was finally to gain an electric traction link westwards to the Tottenham High Road. On 18th October 1936, tram route 23 from Woodford, Napier Arms to Walthamstow, Ferry Lane was replaced a greatly extended trolleybus route 623, which continued past the end of the tramlines at Ferry Boat Inn to terminate at Manor House. Thirteen trams were withdrawn to be replaced by 27 new trolleybuses housed at Walthamstow Depot.

Also on their way to the depot were sundry other tramcars deemed fit only for the scrap heap. An extra track had been laid behind the main running sheds at Walthamstow.

Aldgate tram terminus was situated on the boundary of the City of London. The City Fathers were always opposed to any significant tramway encroachment on their territory. Although a policeman is present, potential passengers for car 1312, now reversing to return to Barking on route 67, would have to brave a constant stream of traffic to achieve their goal. Competing buses add to the throng. Note the LCC information sign for trams leaving this terminus. London Transport Museum

Local tram enthusiasts noted down the fleet numbers of the arriving cars as they were shunted towards their fate. Although official London Transport policy was to discourage sightseers, the bush telegraph amongst local children soon started to function. Luckily for posterity, schoolboy observer, David Bayes, was particularly meticulous:

There was a single siding parallel with the fence and cars would be hauled from the shed furthest from Chingford Road to replenish the stocks on the scrap line which accommodated three or four trams. Around four labourers steadily removed brass and other fittings before the car bodies were pulled over on their sides and burned; the trucks were cut up in situ. An old lorry then ran a shuttle service to dispose of the scrap metal.

I had missed the beginning of the contract of George Cohen's to scrap the trams and ex-West Ham 245 and ex-Walthamstow 2005-6, 2007, 2010-1, 2015, 2017, 2021, 2023, 208 and 2040 had gone before I investigated by cycling into Lloyd Park, standing on my crossbar to peer through the strands of barbed wire strung along the top of the boundary fence. After that until 27th May 1938, when the last tram was scrapped there, my visits and observations from that precarious position were almost continuous. An astonishing variety of trams, many unknown to me, ended their days there, prompting me to make copious notes and rough drawings on the spot.

In the period 1936–38 David noted trams formerly owned by Ilford, West Ham, Walthamstow, the LCC and the Metropolitan Electric, which had passed over the threshold of the depot yard. Added to these passenger vehicles were a number of works cars, including trams from the Croydon and London United fleets. The wrecking team managed to cut the LPTB fleet total by some 293 cars.

At the same time that trolleybuses were making their triumphal entry into Walthamstow, East Ham local service 73 breathed its last. The route from Wanstead Park to the Royal Albert Docks was timed at 24 minutes with a through fare of 3½d (1½p). It was originally slated to become a trolleybus route and indeed London Transport surveyors had already planned a turning circle in back streets at the southern terminus by the docks. However, the tram route was paralleled in its entirety by bus route 101 (Wanstead to North Woolwich). Another example of doubling up resources paid off this time, as it was deemed more expedient to junk the trams and let the buses carry the load.

Although trolleybuses were unsuccessful in replacing tram route 73, they had better

luck elsewhere; their invasion of the East End picked up pace during 1937. A factor influencing the speed of the conversion was London Transport's desire to phase out four wheel, single truck tramcars, of which there were many on operational duty in the East End. The bulk of the fleet throughout the metropolitan area consisted of eight wheel bogie cars and these vehicles would be retained until the planned demise of the system.

It can be argued that T. E. Thomas and his team were correct in thinking that single truck cars had no further role to play. Bearing in mind the antiquated state of some of the vehicles they had inherited, it was a reasonable assumption to make. However, the claim that smaller trams were somehow inadequate to cope with passenger flows was untrue. In cities such as Edinburgh and Sheffield modernised fleets of four wheelers lasted well into the 1950s. In fact the West Ham Tramways Committee debated in January 1931 the whole issue of fleet renewal. A skilled workforce had been assembled at the depot in Greengate Street. The craftsmen were well versed in bodywork construction techniques and in the art of producing new vehicles able to withstand bumper loads of dockers, shoppers and football supporters. Enquiries were also made with the English Electric Company of Preston, which had spare manufacturing capacity due to the slump in trade. Plans of semi streamlined, single truck cars ordered for Huddersfield and Edinburgh were studied, but when it

Workers employed in the Royal Victoria and Albert Docks benefited from an intensive tram service originally supplied by West Ham Corporation. Here at the terminus in Connaught Road cars 316 and 1437 await their next passengers. The M class tram at the rear is working route 97 to Chingford Mount. Car 316 at the front still displays its old 9A route number. It will probably finish its journey at Stratford Broadway. Note the Metropolitan Stage Carriage Licence No.6562 on the front bulkhead just behind the driver. Hugh Nicol/National Tramway Museum

came to finance, a combination of Ministry of Transport reluctance to sanction a loan, plus the uncertainty surrounding the formation of the LPTB torpedoed the proposed deal. Thus, again the opportunity was lost to modernise the rolling stock.

Narrow thoroughfares occupied by double track tramways abounded in the area. With an increase in motor traffic, the LPTB deemed it reasonable to instal trolleybuses on these back street routes as soon as possible. After all, trolleybuses could manoeuvre around parked vehicles, so went the argument. The first casualty of 1937 was tram route 85 from Higham Hill to Leyton via Blackhorse Road. Beloved by traditionalist tram enthusiasts, the 85 was a friendly single track and loops affair, run at a leisurely pace by staff well known to the locals. It was replaced on 17th January by an extended trolleybus route 685, which was much more businesslike. Further inroads into tramway mileage occurred on Sunday 6th June, when trolleybuses emerged from the reconstructed

Walthamstow and West Ham depots to take up service previously offered by tram routes 69, 87, 97 and 99. Withdrawal of 94 tramcars followed as a result of this conversion stage.

Almost all trams had now been removed from a swathe of territory stretching from Chingford Mount to the Victoria & Albert Docks, the only exception being route 99A cars, which ran a special service for greyhound racing fans from Plaistow Station to West Ham Stadium, situated just off Prince Regents Lane. Unfortunately for the Board, not enough trolleybuses were available to cover these journeys. Route 99A finally ceased on 3rd August 1938.

The success of these latest east London conversions was dented somewhat by a Ministry of Transport inspection report, written on 1st September 1937. Wiser counsels, who had been urging a less hasty approach to tramway abandonment, appear to have been vindicated. The inspector, A. H. L. Mount writes:

I noted that over long sections of route in, for instance, Ferry Lane, Blackhorse Road, Markhouse Road, etc., which had been converted six months ago, the rails had not been filled in; I understand that this is due to the fact that the serving of the notices of abandonment has been delayed owing to the necessity for retaining rail continuity for negative return, as the result of inability to complete the sub-stations and introduce the all-insulated system. In Leyton High Street also the track will be in use till the 12th September for the purpose of evacuating old tramcars for destruction.

I impressed on the representatives of the Borough Councils the desirability of early removal of the rails and for filling in the rail grooves temporarily, particularly where points and crossings exist and track is badly worn . . .

The inspector goes on to list a number of locations where substations had yet to be completed and placed in operation. In short, a significant part of the electrical infrastruct-

At Whipps Cross, Leyton, car 205 has just entered the reserved track adjacent to Epping Forest. Modern E/3 class vehicles were the mainstay of route 61. There is plenty of activity on this summer's day long ago. Adults and children take advantage of the fine weather. Indeed, it must be warm, because one tramway employee has hung his coat on a nearby traction standard.

ure needed for the new trolleybuses was lacking. As regards redundant rails left in the roadway, this situation was the subject of a debate in the House of Commons on 16th June 1937. Thomas Groves, MP for West Ham Stratford, asked the Minister of Transport whether it was economic to leave disused tram tracks where they were. The Minister replied that a case could be made for maintaining the status quo, until such time as the relevant highway needed reconstruction. Mr Groves then indicated that he did not wish the financial burden of track removal to fall on the local authorities. There the matter rested.

Although Inspector Mount's report did not rate as an official reprimand, his ticking off had little effect on the desire of the bosses at 55 Broadway to get rid of the trams as quickly as possible. Indeed, it seems to have spurred them on to even greater heights. Rumours circulating among some TGWU representatives in the tram workforce pointed the finger at specialist contractors who, they claimed, had been offered incentives by the management to accelerate the infrastructure works necessary for the new trolleybuses. Speaking some decades after the event, George Tapp asserted that many of his east London colleagues were not satisfied that enough care was being taken to ensure a smooth transition between the two forms of electric traction.

The sceptics appeared to be proved correct, when a number of power failures suggested that not everything in the garden was rosy. Even 'The Thunderer' became involved. A piece in THE TIMES for 21st December 1938 highlighted London Transport's latest embarrassment:

Added to the traffic difficulties in the East End of London was a breakdown in the tramway services. No trams were running east of Bow Road, where overhead electric wires operate, and along Mile End Road and Commercial Road dozens of cars were stationary for several hours, while engineers worked to restore the service.

Obeying the message on the stop sign, car 334 lays over at Barking Broadway. Conductor and driver are sitting in the lower saloon, while they take a short break before the return journey to central London. The lack of commercial activity indicates that this view was taken on a traditional British Sunday, when practically all shops were closed.
A. V. Mace

Clearly, all was not well, but undaunted, the conversion programme had pressed ahead to deal with the last ex-municipal system north of the Thames, that of Ilford Corporation Tramways. The local authority had been happily running its trams since 14th March 1903. There were no through services to central London. However, a connecting track did lead to the Ilford Hill terminus of trunk route 63 to Bow Bridge and Aldgate; a similar connection at Barking Broadway to route 67 had been severed in 1931. In some respects those

responsible for running the Ilford trams had not cultivated good neighbourliness. As was shown in the Becontree Estate saga, the idea of letting other operators reach the terminus at Chadwell Heath and possibly beyond was anathema. This isolation policy was reflected in the fact that the Ilford wheel profiles differed from the London norm, thus rendering transfer of rolling stock to and from the area somewhat inconvenient.

New trams to an outmoded design had arrived at Ley Street Depot, Ilford in 1932. One wonders why, in view of Ilford's imminent absorption into the LPTB, they were ever ordered in the first place. As it was, they did not stay long, because the Board sold the whole batch to Sunderland in 1937–38. Their service on Wearside lasted until 1954. As for the remaining single truck cars, the local MP, Sir George Hamilton, found them an embarrassment. In a House of Commons debate he referred to them as 'the ancient trams that come from the borough of Ilford' and one of his Parliamentary colleagues, Dr

O'Donovan, joked that he had no wish to see 'my hon Friend's old bucketing trams' anywhere near his own constituency in Mile End!

The London Transport public relations department did not have to expend much energy in convincing the native population of the modernity of the trolleybus. On 6th February 1938, routes 91 and 93 were withdrawn and the ex-Ilford antiques were quickly hustled away to their doom at Walthamstow Depot scrap yard. There then followed a hiatus of 15 months, before the next conversion. Much of the East End had now been cleared of tramcars; only the rails were left. Trunk services entering the area remained for the time being.

Routes 55, 57, 61, 63, 65 and 67 continued working; they were an accepted part of the landscape and as such did not attract much attention. However, the services terminating at Aldgate did play a part in a dramatic event, which made headlines across the country and abroad. The Battle of Cable Street took

Ilford Broadway was another important interchange point, where trunk route 63 met the Ilford local routes 91 and 93. Former East Ham car 89 is loading passengers for the journey along Romford Road to Stratford Broadway. There appears to be plenty of room on top. One lucky child has bagged a front seat with the best view of the road ahead. Although it belonged to the same organisation, the bus to Victoria Station is competing for passengers to central London.

The face of Herbert Morrison stares out from an election poster on a billboard in Canning Town. Labour had seized control of the London County Council in 1934 and the party was anxious to implement the manifesto for another term in power. Meanwhile, away from the world of politics, car 334 makes the transition from trolley to conduit, while an inspector hops aboard to check all is well. In fact this tramcar seems to be almost devoid of passengers; however, this situation will change before the vehicle reaches its destination at Aldgate.

place on 4th October 1936, when Sir Oswald Mosley and his British Union of Fascists were prevented from marching through the East End. A mass confrontation between police and anti-fascist protestors occurred in the Gardiners Corner area. Newsreel footage depicts trams held up in the melee. There was a rumour that at least one tram crew, sympathetic to the anti-fascist cause, had deliberately stalled their tramcar on a dead section of the conduit, so as to act as a barrier against Mosley and his blackshirts. The reality was that a line of trams built up and remained virtually immobile during the disturbances.

The management at London Transport was well aware that some employees from Poplar, West Ham and Leyton depots, who worked services into Aldgate, supported different sides politically in the left-right divide. Sensibly, no drastic disciplinary action was taken, but staff were later banned from displaying political badges on their uniforms. The story of the tram drivers aiding the protestors entered into local folklore.

In the leafy suburbs, a world away from the strife on the streets round Gardiners Corner, a far more peaceful scene played out in front of the cine camera of Mr Redburn of Leyton. The film, shot in the summer of 1938, is in colour and features a number of ex-Leyton E/3 cars on route 61. Of particular note is the view of reserved tracks on the eastern side of Whipps Cross Road adjacent to Epping Forest.

Moving images of the Battle of Cable Street, the mass of protestors at Gardiners Corner and the altogether more tranquil daily life of the people of Leyton are readily available on the internet. They present an interesting evocation of the life and times of the East End and its tramways.

One of the largest skimishes in the Battle of Cable Street occurred at Gardiners Corner, Aldgate, when mounted police confronted anti-fascist protesters. Stuck in the middle of the mayhem is a standard E/1 class car on route 65.

ELEPHANT TO THE BRIDGES

A FTER A false start by the American, George Francis Train, with his Kennington line in 1861, the tramway presence south of the River Thames was established securely in 1870 and lasted until 1952. In that period the change of traction from equine power to electricity was effected first on Friday 15th May 1903, when the Prince of Wales opened the pioneer LCC conduit line from the bridges at Westminster and Blackfriars to Tooting. In the following months new electric routes were constructed to serve south London; the major interchange at the Elephant and Castle grew in importance. Although the London County Council

did later encounter opposition to some of its proposals in the Dulwich and Blackheath districts, in general terms the completed network hit all its targets as regards traffic objectives. Unlike the situation in the West End and the cities of London and Westminster, the forces opposed to tramways were fragmented and less influential.

When the LCC relinquished control in favour of the LPTB, well established services provided vital transport links and enabled thousands of working people to gain access to their places of employment in the centre of town. Such was the intensity of service that just under 300 tramcars an hour passed

through intersections at the Elephant, the Oval, Vauxhall and Camberwell Green. In peak periods lines of trams would circle the Embankment to convey homeward bound commuters. Trunk routes traversed many of the SW postal districts in the Metropolitan Boroughs of Southwark, Lambeth, Battersea, Wandsworth and they reached Croydon and Wimbledon in the County of Surrey.

So well entrenched was the tramcar in south London, that the planners at 55 Broadway conceded early on the area would be last on the list to lose its railbound transport. Not that this strategy prevented the powers that be from tinkering at the edges. One

Pictured in Balham High Road, car 1727 is one of the rehabs or reconditioned vehicles outshopped in November 1935 from Charlton Works. It lasted until September 1950. Route 8 started at Victoria Station and then made a loop via Clapham, Tooting and Streatham in order to return whence it came, the terminal stub at the end of Vauxhall Bridge Road. Note the rag and bone man's cart parked by the kerbside.

of the most notable examples of piecemeal abandonment occurred on 7th September 1937, when tram route 32 was replaced by a diversion of motor bus route 137. The 32 took 12 minutes to run from Clapham (Plough) to the south side of Chelsea Bridge at a through fare of 2d. It was known to conductors and motormen as 'the chicken run', because they claimed 'you were there and back before you knew it'. It was probably the nearest south London got to a genuine back street route in the East End style. It was worked by four trams with an extra vehicle in rush hours. According to local tramwayman, Stan Collins, the 32 was one of the best earners on the system and conductors would often return to the depot with a sandbag sack full of coppers (penny and halfpenny coins).

Unlike some of the last tram celebrations north of the Thames, it was a muted farewell, which accompanied car 1056, as it left Chelsea Bridge terminus at 11:54pm on Saturday 7th September. It arrived at *The Plough*, Clapham at 12:05am on the Sunday.

As a counter to all this negative activity, a boost to tramway operation was given by the migration of the Felthams at the end of 1936, which gave 'south side' passengers their first real taste of modernity. Cars from the first batch, refugees from the old London United routes, were driven to Putney Bridge Road change pit by 'north side' crews. Staff from Streatham, Telford Avenue Depot then took

above An unknown photographer has parked his car on the Albert Embankment and has asked his wife to pose in front of the Houses of Parliament. Does any reader know who owned the vehicle registered JH 4185? Luckily for us, car 424 has crept into the shot. It is working service 26 to Kew Bridge via Putney.

below The Felthams found a new home in south London. Car 2069 is depicted near Telford Avenue, Streatham in May 1938. At this stage in their career, the front exit of these vehicles was in regular use – hence the warning notice for other road users. The front exit fell into disuse in postwar years. R. Mayes/Terry Russell

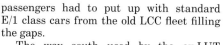

The trolleybus conversion scheme broke the tramway connection from Wandsworth to Hammersmith and beyond. In a few days after this photo was taken route 26 will be truncated at Clapham Junction and trolleybus route 626 will run past this location in Putney Bridge Road. Car 493 of class E dated from 1906 and was scrapped at Mitcham Road Depot, Croydon in September 1937.

Another connection broken by the introduction of trolleybuses was the section of track between Wandsworth and Tooting. Car 626 is working route 12, which will be partly replaced by trolleybus route 612.
Alan B. Cross

over and guided them over the conduit to their new home. In fact the newest arrivals had two homes, because some type UCC cars were allocated to Brixton Hill Depot, which was an operational annex of Telford Avenue. The Felthams were assigned to the 16/18 – Purley to Embankment services; they also appeared on route 10 from Tooting to City (Southwark) and on routes 8/20 from Tooting Broadway to Victoria Station. Unfortunately, due to the frequency demanded by the timetable, it was not possible to run a purely Feltham equipped service. Intending

passengers had to put up with standard E/1 class cars from the old LCC fleet filling the gaps.

The way south used by the ex-LUT Felthams was effectively declared *hors de combat* by the trolleybus conversions of 12th September 1937, when route 30 was abandoned, routes 26 and 28 were curtailed at Clapham Junction and route 12 was cut short to terminate at York Road, Wandsworth. Unnumbered all night tram service from Tooting Broadway to the Embankment via Garratt Lane was cut back to terminate at Wandsworth, Princes Head. The link to Hammersmith and beyond via Putney Bridge was severed and conduit tracks in East Hill, Wandsworth and along much of Garratt Lane were decommissioned. Most of the abandoned rails were removed in 1938 with the exception of the spur serving the Wimbledon Stadium dog track at Summerstown.

This seemingly arbitrary slicing up of established traffic patterns was the cause of inconvenience for many regular passengers. It surely made more sense to retain the Wandsworth to Tooting via Garratt Lane link, but the LPTB's aversion to dual working of trams and trolleybuses over the same route put paid to the idea. For the record, the last tram to traverse Garratt Lane left Tooting Junction at 12:49am on the morning of 12th September and arrived at Jews Row, Wandsworth Depot at 1:11am.

It was not all gloom and doom. At the same time as these abandonments were taking place, a brand new track layout was being constructed at Vauxhall Cross. Five feeder roads supporting no less than 10 tram routes converged on the place. A gyratory system of traffic flow incorporating new conduit tracks aimed to alleviate some of the congestion. The first new section in Parry Street opened on 3rd April 1938, followed by the rest on 15th May. THE MODERN TRAMWAY for April 1938 quoted a cost of £366,000 for one third of a mile of conduit tramway; construction of the whole layout, which included property demolition, took approximately three years. It was projected that the modernised tramway would have to last until trolleybus conversion in the summer of 1942.

Speculation about the wholesale introduction of trolleybuses had been occupying minds in the council chambers of south London and had been causing residents' groups no little upset. The worthy householders adjacent to the Beaufort Street terminus of tram route 34 were up in arms at London Transport's plans to 'festoon' side streets with overhead wires. The elected representatives of the Metropolitan Borough of Southwark had also had enough and Thomas Naylor, MP for Southwark South

above Work is in progress on the reconstructed road layout at Vauxhall Cross. It was a chance for onlookers to observe new conduit tracks being fabricated on site. In those days you could leave your bike by the roadside without undue fear of its being stolen.
London Transport Museum

right Cars 457 and 552 are seen at Vauxhall Cross in 1935. The original street layout at this intersection was deemed inadequate to cope with the increase in motor traffic, therefore a new gyratory system was implemented. As can be seen, the provision of two trolley poles per car was not uniform across the fleet.

East, took up the cudgels on their behalf. In a debate on the LPTB, which took place in the House of Commons on 26th April 1937, he accused London Transport of sharp practice in wanting to place the burden of road reinstatement after tramway abandonment squarely on the shoulders of local ratepayers. As he pointed out, Southwark was one of the poorest boroughs in London and could not afford to pick up the bill.

His speech fairly implies that Lord Ashfield *et al* should leave well alone and not foist their marvellous new transport system on his constituents. His subsequent remarks suggest he may have had his own contacts within 55 Broadway:

I am informed that engineering difficulties will make it next to impossible to introduce the overhead system of trolley omnibuses without impeding traffic and limiting transport facilities. I dare say the Minister is acquainted with the Elephant and Castle, which is known all over the world and particularly in London as a centre of traffic congestion. If the Minister will visit that junction at the peak hours of either morning or evening, he will realise the tremendous problem which faces the Board, if they are going to substitute at the Elephant and Castle or at St George's Circus for the present system, a system which will cause even greater congestion than now exists at those two points.

At present, the trams run in the centre of the highway and the omnibuses alongside the kerb. If trolley omnibuses are substituted for trams, it will not be possible to accommodate at the sides of the highway a sufficient number of omnibuses to deal with passenger traffic, which is now enabled to pass through those congested points with the dual system in operation. I am not an expert engineer, but I am informed that the situation is one to which the engineers of the Board will have to give serious attention and that practical difficulties are such that it will be impossible to remedy them, once the trolley omnibus system has been substituted for the existing system.

Once again, Ashfield's and Morrison's favourite *bête noire*, the junction at the Elephant and Castle, had come back to haunt the planners. And yet again, one can speculate as to the source of Mr Naylor's information. Was it someone high up in the Central Bus Department trying to put a spanner in the trolleybus works?

As it was, the Central Bus Department had no need to try to sabotage others, when it had its own malcontents within the ranks. On 1st May 1937, London's busmen symbolically downed tools and walked out. The strike lasted almost a month until 28th May. Trams and trolleybuses were unaffected

Coronation Day, 12th May 1937, saw the trams being pressed into intensive service transporting school children and their teachers to assembly areas on the Victoria Embankment. A team of officials were on hand to marshal the crowds. London County Council

and electric traction was called upon to transport millions who were now busless. It was a matter of huge embarrassment to London Transport that this withdrawal of labour coincided with preparations for the great national celebration of the Coronation of King George VI on 12th May. The streets of the capital were decked out in flags and bunting.

A special LPTB map was issued to enable visitors to choose the best public transport access to view the Coronation Procession. Unfortunately, half the information contained therein was now irrelevant. Since there were no buses, on the roads the trams did sterling service. All night cars ran from Tooting Broadway, Southcroft Road, New Cross Gate, Downham, Hampstead, Stamford Hill, Highgate and Poplar. These were augmented by normal service cars and by 2 o'clock in the morning potential passengers were queuing at tram stops in the suburbs. On the day of the ceremony vehicles displayed different coloured signs, which corresponded to specific termini in the central area adjacent to the Coronation Procession. Examples of this special arrangement were service 18 (Green-Brown) from Purley to terminate at Waterloo Bridge; service 33 (Brown-Green-Blue) from Manor House to Aldwych Tram Station; service 78 (Maroon-Yellow-Green) from Norwood to Victoria Station. All together some 36 tram routes were included in the day's traffic scheme. The Victoria Embankment, designated a Green area, was reserved for school children. In order to transport them a fleet of 130 tramcars was drafted in. The vehicles were then lined up on the Embankment, where the tracks ran on the river side of the carriageway.

That the big day passed off so well was due in no small measure to the efficiency of the tramways and the loyal, hard working staff. Sadly, the success of the Coronation Day operation was the last time ever that the full potential of the system, albeit after some loss of mileage, could be demonstrated to Londoners. The June 1937 issue of PENNYFARE stated that 45 million passengers had been carried by trams and trolleybuses in the period 8th to 17th May. The trams were further congratulated on transporting some 13,000 school children to their viewing positions on the Embankment. Crews had worked to a very tight schedule and all children had to be disembarked between 9:15 and 10:30 on the morning of the Coronation.

Even Sir Philip Game, Commissioner of the Metropolitan Police, was obliged to modify his fierce anti-tram stance and praise the excellent organisation, when in the space of 45 minutes the masses of young people and their teachers were assembled.

Further new arrivals on the streets of south London appeared in the shape of the main batch of ex-MET Felthams. Streatham Depot had been modified to accept them and this location was a favourite of visiting enthusiasts. A party of LRTL members had been given a conducted tour on 2nd April 1938, to be followed by another on 10th September. They were obviously fascinated by the place. A report in THE MODERN TRAMWAY described the occasion:

New and old members had an interesting time inspecting Feltham and other type cars stationed in the depot, and opportunity was also taken to inspect Car No. 1, our steed of memorable 15th May, and the former MET experimental car No. 2167. Mr. Cook, Southern Area Rolling Stock Superintendent, was our guide on this occasion . . .

The route south for migratory tramcars was now via the Kingsway Subway. The entrance by the Victoria Embankment had been repositioned in connection with preparatory works for the new Waterloo Bridge. Together with the Vauxhall gyratory system it was the last major pre-war construction undertaken by the LPTB on their 'doomed' tramways and, as such, Ashfield and the Board deserve credit for finding the cash to complete the two projects. Praise was heaped on the Permanent Way Department in an article in PENNYFARE for November 1937:

Alterations to the permanent way included re-arranging the double-track conduit junction on the Embankment, running a new double-track curve and the necessary connections at each end to link up with the Subway and Embankment tracks, and removing the old curve and connections.

The work was beset with considerable difficulty, for it had to be done in relays and without interrupting the (tram)cars, which sometimes run at intervals of only a few seconds. Unobstructed space for three lines of road vehicles had to be maintained, and through this dense traffic long lengths of track rail, some weighing a ton, had to be manoeuvred across the road and laid in their correct positions. Several pairs of electric mains had to be altered, for this is a point where the North and South tramway cables are linked up. Another difficulty was provided by the fact that the top of the District Line is only 2ft 6ins below the road surface.

An interesting aside to the rebuilding of Waterloo Bridge was that, in the protracted debate in the 1930s on the form and style of the replacement structure, the LCC were accused of planning to run trams over the new bridge. According to the Earl of Crawford in a House of Lords session on 3rd March 1932, it was the Labour Party to blame for wanting double tram tracks as an extension from the Waterloo Station terminus of route 68. As usual, politicking rather obscured reasoned argument, and of course, the LCC lost control of its transport system in the following year.

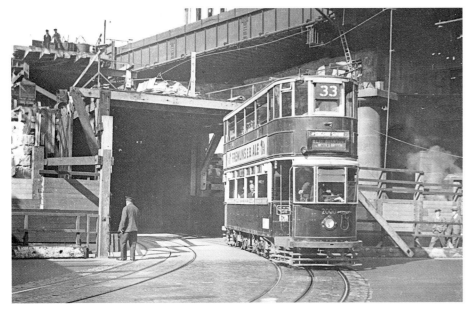

above left New trackwork was needed at the southern entrance to the Kingsway Subway as a consequence of the demolition of the old Waterloo Bridge and the construction of the new version.
C. F. Klapper/The Omnibus Society

left Car 2000 emerges from the Kingsway Subway on to the Embankment. The old Waterloo Bridge is being dismantled. The inspector standing on the left of the picture will have to find some kind of temporary refuge during the reconstruction period. Tram crews received instructions to report bricks or other masonry falling on car roofs. As far as we know, stone blocks detached from the original Rennie bridge did not interrupt the tram service!

above Victoria was an important London tram terminal. An inspector checks with the motorman of car 1627, before departure on route 20. After he has left, car 1093 on route 8 will have the right of way. Note the Little Ben clock tower in the background.
A. V. Mace

left E/1 class car 1667 is depicted at Victoria terminus on 3rd June 1939.
G. N. Southerden

The arrival of modern rolling stock, coupled with new track layouts made it appear that the trunk routes south of the River Thames still had some mileage left in them. Tramway enthusiasts believed that, while there was life there was hope, and they refused to give up on the task of saving the bulk of the south London system. Certainly, by the end of 1938, members of the LRTL and others had drawn up a survival and modernisation plan, based on a comprehensive survey of existing routes. Road widths were measured and an attempt was made to assess passenger flows at various key locations. In this task LRTL volunteers were sometimes assisted by local policemen, who held up the traffic in the belief that the gentlemen with tape measures were on official business for ARP and civil defence!

Indeed, precautions against the possibility of air raids indicated there was enough anxiety about the state of international politics to suggest a reassessment of priorities on behalf of London Transport. However, in spite of the increasing unease, detailed plans for the acquisition of new trolleybus depot sites in Rye Lane and at Stockwell went ahead. It was felt that rebuilding work to replace the tramway infrastructure, such as in the case of Norwood Depot, was not worth the effort.

As was the custom, at 11 o'clock on 11th November tram drivers halted their vehicles for two minutes in celebration of the signing of the Armistice in 1918, which ended the First World War. On a practical note each crew was instructed not to use more than half power for 10 minutes on restarting, lest they caused an overload. After two minutes past 11 as a matter of respect for the fallen, trams passing religious and civic services at war memorials *en route* slowed down. Motormen, conductors and most male passengers removed their hats and no warning gongs were sounded.

In his end of year message to tram and trolleybus staff, dated Friday, 16th December 1938, T. E. Thomas writes with a hint of desperation:

Cheerfulness is infectious . . . When times are good it is easy, but when they are not it becomes more difficult and is, therefore, a greater virtue. Let that be the keynote for 1939 . . .

As Inspector Drury, on duty at Camberwell Green, noted on his copy of the boss's message: 'We're all whistling in the dark now!'

At journey's end outside Wimbledon Town Hall cars 1777 and 1530 await their return to central London. On the right of the picture a trolleybus on route 604 is about to use the turning circle in front of the two tramcars. The 604 route was normally operated by the Diddler type trolleybuses, which were built by the same company that produced the Felthams. Note the scissors crossover in the trackwork. In theory this arrangement permitted quick reversal times. A. V. Mace

SOUTH BY SOUTHEAST

THERE WAS always a romantic notion that the spiritual home of the London tramcar was to be found in the Old Kent Road, at Dog Kennel Hill, along Jamaica Road by the Surrey Docks, in Trafalgar Road, Greenwich in front of the Royal Naval College and in Beresford Square by the Woolwich Arsenal or, indeed, on any of the south eastern approaches to the capital. What was rather less than romantic was the hard headed stance taken by the metropolitan boroughs of Lewisham and Woolwich. Both councils actually valued their local tramways and both had cooperated with the LCC in the last phase of tramway expansion before the dead hand of the LPTB spoilt things.

New housing estates at Downham and at Eltham were supplied with double track lines

giving the residents easy and cheap access to central London and to the main local shopping areas. Most of the network was worked on the conduit, but the 1928–32 extensions were all constructed with overhead wires. The Grove Park to Downham, Bromley Road section was wired by the LCC to accept pantographs and bow collectors as well as the traditional trolley poles. This progressive modernisation was not continued by the new regime, but the LPTB did sanction new works in the Eltham area.

Whereas the investment needed by the Bexley tramways to cope with the 1930s suburban housing boom had not materialised, the well maintained former LCC routes on the other side of the county boundary benefited from modernised

track layouts to cope with the increase in motor traffic. There was already a recently constructed roundabout at the Well Hall end of Westhorne Avenue (also referred to in contemporary documents as Well Hall Circus). In May 1935 work began on a similar gyratory arrangement at Eltham Green by the Yorkshire Grey public house. It should be noted in passing that the junction of the two tramways was the site of a serious accident in March 1934 (see Rolling Stock Appendix).

The project cost £5,960 and was completed in October. It included electrically controlled points, set for service cars on route 46 proceeding towards Eltham Hill and for route 72 trams entering and leaving Westhorne Avenue. The trolley wheel of each approaching tram made contact with

left In advance of the trolleybus conversion programme studies were undertaken to assess traffic conditions on existing tram routes. A service 70 car reverses at the crossover in Bermondsey Street. It is 3:35pm on Thursday, 16th April 1936. Slow moving goods vehicles bound for the Pool of London were often the cause of delays to trams in this area.
Dave Jones Collection

facing page
The construction of Eltham Green roundabout necessitated a realignment of tram tracks. The new layout is already in operation as car 962 slows for the turn from Westhorne Avenue to join route 46 trams on their journeys from Eltham Road to Eltham Hill.
G. N. Southerden

an electrical skate positioned on the trolley wire and this sent a signal to activate both the point mechanism in the roadway and an overhead 'frog' device to switch the trolley wheel to the correct wire. In theory there was now no need for motormen to descend from their driving platforms to spear the rails with their point iron, nor were the services of pointsmen required, as was the usual procedure at nearly all major junctions in the metropolitan area.

In keeping with tradition, where everything was explained down to the last detail, the official TRAFFIC CIRCULAR to employees for September 1935 leaves nothing to doubt: *Notice to Motormen* –

The electrically operated point has been removed from the existing position of Eltham Road and Westhorne Avenue, and is now situated at the Circus at the junction with Westhorne Avenue, and is controlled by a skate on Pole No. 51.

Cars for Westhorne Avenue pass under the skate with power ON. Cars for Eltham Church pass under the skate with power OFF. Cars from Westhorne Avenue to London will automatically operate the points at the junction of the Circus and Eltham Road, when they pass under the

skate at Pole No. 64, whether power is ON or OFF. Cars from London to Eltham Church will automatically operate the points at the junction of the Circus and Eltham Road, when they pass under the skate at Pole No. 64, whether power is ON or OFF.

The signal on Pole No. 50 indicates the position of the electrically operated Frog at Pole No. 51, and shows the motorman whether the Frog has been operated for the route they should take. Motormen must observe the points have been correctly operated. The speed of cars is NOT to exceed four miles per hour when passing under the skates.

As this circular suggests, it was understood by tramwaymen that, unlike their busmen colleagues, they had to possess a detailed technical knowledge of their vehicles and the tracks on which they ran. If anything untoward occurred, one of the first places to look was down at the motors and the running gear. Hatches in the lower saloon floor could be lifted and the services of a tool kit were then employed to sort out the problem.

Someone who would have noticed what was happening on the ground was local

MP, Sir Kingsley Wood, who was a frequent passenger in the Eltham area. As Minister of Health, part of his brief was the eradication of poor housing conditions. His electors remembered him talking to crews, as he made regular trips on vehicles working services 44, 46 and 72. He was concerned that the tramwaymen with whom he conversed had access to decent accommodation in one of the improved public housing schemes adjacent to the tram routes. Ashfield and Pick were well aware of their 'celebrity' clients and in Sir Kingsley Wood's case, maintaining a good relationship was particularly important, as the gentlemen concerned was later appointed Chancellor of the Exchequer, thereby having a large measure of control over the LPTB's purse strings. In fairness to Sir Kingsley, unlike many of his Conservative colleagues, he championed the trams in his constituency.

He was also remembered for his visit to the injured, when some of his constituents had the misfortune to be on board, after a service 72 car ran into the rear platform of a 46 tram on Grand Depot Road, Woolwich on 22nd October 1937. Twelve passengers, the motorman of the 72 and the conductor of the 46 had to receive medical treatment. In

above Reconditioned car 978 proceeds slowly through road works in Bromley Road, Catford. Critics of the conduit system suggested that in areas like this there would be no loss of amenity by erecting trolley wires. The existing use of street lamps supported by overhead cables rather supported this argument.
A. W. V. Mace/R. S. Carpenter

spite of this incident and in contradiction to scurrilous stories peddled by the anti-tram brigade, travel by tram in London was one of the safest forms of getting about the capital. Indeed, it was the transport of choice, when fog blanketed the metropolis. Sydney Harris, editor of the magazine THE MODERN TRAMWAY, noted the effects at street level of what would later be termed smog:

During a real 'pea souper' – a filthy, stinking, sulphurous fog, which made one's eyes smart – south London was blotted out one November night in 1938. Most traffic had stopped except the trams. At Camberwell, depot bound trams signed off as per their normal schedules, but around 11.30pm a small group of hopefuls waited at Camberwell Green tram shelter, knowing full well that some tram would take them towards Dulwich and home, however slowly.

An HR/2 was heard approaching through the gloom. It was No. 120 on service 62 about to enter Camberwell Depot. The anxious regulator tactfully suggested to the crew that they might like to take the huddled passengers part of the way home, say to Goose Green.

There was no argument. The points were reset; HR/2 No. 120 reversed over the crossover. The grateful passengers – almost a full complement – climbed aboard

and the tram vanished into the murk. All the way up Denmark Hill it picked up folk, even between stops, as it crawled along its familiar, reliable steel track, glinting dully in the beam of the tram's headlight.

With fog rolling past outside and windows dripping with condensation inside, No. 120 nosed its way to the crest of Grove Lane, then cautiously descended steep Dog Kennel Hill into Grove Vale, East Dulwich, where the fog gathers thickest. At Goose Green the crew made no mention of reversing, but No. 120 continued its steady way up Lordship Lane, passing three abandoned No. 12 buses at Dulwich Library.

The fog swirled denser at Dulwich Common and an unseen Southern Railway electric train from Crystal Palace (High Level) rumbled over the bridge at Lordship Lane Station. No. 120 crawled up to Horniman's Museum and Down London Road to Forest Hill Station, where more abandoned buses were found littering the roadways.

Once under the railway bridge, the service 62 met a late service 35 tram taking on passengers for Brockley at Perry Vale terminus. It was doing yeoman service amid the wreaths of swirling fog. No. 120 continued its way along Stanstead Road to Catford; the journey from Camberwell took nearly an hour, but nobody complained – the faithful tram got them home. The driver and conductor had to return No. 120 to Camberwell Depot and then make their own way home afterwards, but they kept cheerful. They were proud to serve the public, even though they only received a few shillings overtime pay.

Hardly anyone paid their fares on that tram!

How could they? The tram was crammed tight with passengers and the conductor was out front most of the time, walking, armed with a torch to show the way to his motorman companion. And behind the tram followed a close formation of motor cars using the tram as a guiding star to get them home too!

Yet, in a similar fog, a motor bus on its way from Forest Hill to Dulwich was seen crawling along Crescent Wood Road in the wrong direction, a mile off its route, hopelessly lost! This is sufficient proof of the electric tramcar's superiority in thick fog.

The scenario described by Sydney Harris was an all too common one, in an era when pollution from domestic coal fires and factory chimneys added a disruptive element to wintertime in Britain's largest cities. The journey of car 120 passed through one of the most iconic locations on London's tramways – the four track layout on the steep gradient at Dog Kennel Hill. Aside from the fog shrouded environment, what really is striking from this eyewitness account is the capacity of the average London tramcar to transport above average numbers of people. Aided by their robust construction, vehicles from the tram fleet were often called upon to shift mammoth crowds. This task they were required to do at frequent intervals during the football season.

On 12th February 1938, the crowd at The Valley to watch Charlton Athletic play Aston Villa was given as 75,031. Woolwich Road, a couple of hundred yards from the ground, was the setting for lines of trams catering for local supporters from Greenwich, Woolwich, Plumstead and Eltham. Fans arriving from north Kent changed modes of traction at Woolwich Ferry trolleybus terminus. Observers later confirmed that the actual attendance was well in excess of the official figure. On the day, staff from New Cross and Abbey Wood depots worked extra shifts to cope with the situation.

Spotted amongst the convoy on Woolwich Road were several HR/2 cars, drafted in to work service 58EX, and waiting, after the final whistle had sounded, to return passengers to Lewisham, Catford and to various suburbs in the Dulwich hills. Also present was at least one E/3 vehicle with Kingsway Subway stencils above the indicator boxes. This may have been part of a contribution from Holloway Depot and the tram concerned would have headed back to north London after the match. However, one tram stood out brightly on this winter's day. It was newly painted and anecdotal evidence suggests it was commandeered from the nearby yard at Charlton Repair Works. It is quite feasible that a harassed inspector, probably stationed by the crossover opposite Rainton Road, Charlton, was told to use his initiative to supplement the service. Certainly, London Transport staff out of uniform and therefore, probably fitters from the works, were seen piloting vehicles in the centre of Woolwich. Whatever the arrangement, it worked and thousands of fans, who relied on public transport, got home safely, thanks largely to the efforts of London's tramwaymen.

Of course, the job of the CRD (Central Repair Depot) at Charlton was not just to help out at football matches. The existence of this important facility, which occupied land north of Woolwich Road, was vital for the efficient functioning of the system. Tramway access needed to be maintained until the very end of the conversion programme. This dictated that routes passing outside (36, 38 and 40) would be the last remaining services.

A booklet, titled THE OVERHAUL OF TRAMCARS, was produced at 55 Broadway, and from this we can get an accurate picture of what was going on. It states:
Today all cars are overhauled and renovated in Works at Hendon, West Ham or Charlton . . . Charlton Works are the largest of their kind in the country. Under Regulations of the Ministry of Transport, each car has to be re-licensed annually and certified fit for public use.
The Works adjoin the Angerstein Wharf of the Southern Railway, which facilitates

transport of materials to and from the Works by rail or river. The first portion of the Works was completed in 1908. This was extended in 1911, and the main building was completed in 1926. A stores building was added in 1928.
The buildings, which occupy approximately seven acres, were planned to deal with 1,800 cars annually, but the progressive system of operation has increased output capacity by fifty per cent. In addition, the plant is designed for the manufacture of new parts.
Basically the place supplied just about everything, down to the last nut and bolt, to keep the tram fleet on the road. It also kept 1,200 staff in employment. In tune with the advance of the abandonment programme, structural alterations were effected to

cope with the extra length of the displaced Felthams. When Hendon and West Ham ceased to function for railbound vehicles, the CRD was the sole tramcar repair works on the system, although, as we shall see, some mechanical work was later outshopped to the remaining depots.

In this southeastern corner of the capital the road from the CRD to New Cross Depot was just under three miles; adjacent to this main tram route were the main power station at Greenwich and the Deptford Wharf PW yard. All four locations could be expected to see out the system. At the close of the year 1938, negotiations between the management and the trade unions had progressed to a point that passengers using south London services, based at New Cross and at other 'south side' car sheds, could expect either a fully

Car 1510 waits on Bostall Hill, Plumstead at the loop by Woodhurst Road. The year is 1935 and work has started on equipping this section for dual tram and trolleybus operation. This area suffered badly in the Blitz and rows of houses on both sides of the road were destroyed by enemy bombs. G. N. Southerden

above One of the 'prestige' neighbourhoods served by the trams was Romney Road, Greenwich. To the right of car 95 and the tram stop is the imposing building of the National Maritime Museum, while out of sight on the left are the equally imposing Seamen's Hospital and Royal Naval College. The publicity department of the LPTB promoted the attractions of Greenwich, which could be reached by tram routes 36, 38, 40, 58, 62, 68 and 70. N. Rayfield/LCCT Trust

below McLeod Road, Abbey Wood was the setting for London's longest lived dual operation of trams and trolleybuses. In theory the overhead wires were so configured that a trolleybus could pass a tram on the inside of the carriageway. Roy Hubble/LCCT Trust

enclosed traditional tramcar or a Feltham or a rehabilitated version of the traditional model. Platform staff – motormen and conductors – would then be protected from the worst of the elements by windscreens at both ends of the car.

As local industries picked up orders after the trade depression of the early 1930s, and as a result of the semi-detached suburban housing expansion, passenger numbers remained healthy. This positive situation was also due in part to the fact that several important tram routes were spared the inconvenience of having to compete with buses for road space. The main highway from Eltham to Woolwich fell into this category, as did Downham Way to Grove Park and sections of the Dog Kennel Hill routes from Lordship Lane to Camberwell Green. Even where there was a bus route, the positive fare differential rested with the tramways and, of course, workmen's fares were only generally available on trams and trolleybuses.

After the November fogs caused traffic chaos, nature had another trick up her sleeve. Cold weather brought a traditional white Christmas for Londoners. In fact, the snows over the Christmas of 1938 turned out to be the deepest and most widespread of any festive season in the 20th century. The trams rose to the challenge, as noted by THE MODERN TRAMWAY:

True, there were delays and hold-ups, due to snow and ice freezing in the conduit – sometimes smashing ploughs and causing 'shorts' – but all forms of transport were crippled during that period. Tramways with overhead equipment proved the best of all vehicles under the circumstances. Snow ploughs were much in evidence. These were old LCC type B cars fitted with revolving brooms and the top deck removed. These looked rather attractive, especially in the morning after a fall, and did their work remarkably well.

Fortunately, a number of works cars, former passenger vehicles of LCC classes B and C, were still in existence to carry out the duties of clearing snow from the tracks. In active service for December 1938 were 21 snowbrooms, all on four wheel trucks and equipped for both overhead trolley and conduit operation. The one real drawback for the snow clearing crews was having to stand on open platforms, devoid of any protection against the elements.

Motorists benefited from the work of these vehicles, because the swept path enabled them to proceed along the highway. In this case during inclement winter weather many avid tram haters had cause to repent and thank the London Transport staff. In tram-less areas of the capital no such help was available and motor traffic had to cope with the icy conditions.

As was the custom from previous years, a limited tram service operated over the Christmas period and for the time being thereafter, the local tramway situation was stable. Indeed, trolleybuses had made a very limited impact south of the Thames in the County of London. Unfortunately it transpired that 25th December 1938 was to be the last peacetime Christmas. Events far from the borders of the UK would have a significant impact in the coming New Year.

PEACE AND PHONEY WAR

THE LAST eight months of peace in Europe saw a London tram system down to its bare bones north of the Thames. On a national level this last precious time before the outbreak of war was spent in anxious preparation for the conflict ahead. Although the idea that central government and the local authorities had got everything up to a peak of efficiency is certainly not true, at least the message was beginning to filter through the organisation at 55 Broadway that precautions against air raids should be a priority. As regards protecting the fleet from bombing, railbound vehicles obviously did not lend themselves for easy dispersal, unlike buses, which could be parked away from their home garages in side streets. In the circumstances the wisdom of retaining tramway access to Hampstead Depot became apparent. The 'retirement home for old trams' would later serve a key function in the smooth running of the system.

A sombre note was struck in the January 1939 edition of PENNYFARE. A report indicated the state of readiness of the 84th (LT) Anti-Aircraft Brigade (Royal Artillery, Territorial Army), which had 20 officers and 280 other ranks. All were part time soldiers recruited from London Transport staff. Four times a week there was morning and evening training on the anti-aircraft guns.

Whereas, it might have seemed logical for the LPTB to curtail spending plans in the face of the increasingly martial atmosphere, in reality it was business as usual. Lavish investment envisaged a bright future with cash available for extensions to the Underground, the development of a new fleet of standardised diesel buses (the RT), and, unsurprisingly, a further push on the trolleybus front.

One month after the article on London Transport's riposte to the Luftwaffe, PENNYFARE gave information calculated to depress readers of THE MODERN TRAMWAY and members of the LRTL and TLRS:

Ready for service, car 1120 stands at the entrance to Stamford Hill Depot. Although this tram had received a rebuilt top deck, it perished in Hampstead Depot sometime in June 1939.

All trams will vanish from the streets of London north of the Thames within the next 12 months.

Four hundred new trolleybuses will be required to replace the trams for this part of the Board's conversion scheme. This month (February) the routes from Stamford Hill to Liverpool Street, London Docks and Holborn will be changed over . . . In March and April, two further routes Nos. 11, Highgate Village to Moorgate, and 53, Aldgate to Stamford Hill, will be converted.

At intervals, until January 1940, the remaining routes, which include Bloomsbury to Hackney, Aldersgate to West India Docks, and Aldgate to Barking, Ilford and Leytonstone, will be dealt with according to programme.

There is a finality about the date of January 1940 in this statement. The article implies that, come hell or high water, tramway abandonment was considered sacrosanct, even with the possible accompaniment of the sound of the guns of the 84th Brigade being fired in anger! On the face of it, no thought seems to have been given to the notion that the forthcoming national emergency might just require Spitfires and Hurricanes, plus huge amounts of ammunition, rather than factories and manpower being tied up, producing new trolleybuses, poles, wires, electrical cabling, substations and copious stocks of rubber tyres. In short, it is reasonable to suggest that caution should have been the watchword and that the beginning of 1939 should have been the time to re-evaluate the whole programme.

A counterargument to the wait and see approach was that much of the overhead wiring was already in place for the introduction of further trolleybus services. Also, extensive reconstruction works were in progress to render depots suitable for the trackless vehicles. It would have been uneconomic to leave matters half finished.

On 5th February 1939, tram services 43, 47, 49, 49EX, 71, 75, and 83 were consigned to oblivion. The author's future mother, then resident at Pierhead, St Katharine's Dock, went to watch the arrival of trolleybuses at Dock Street terminus, erstwhile end of the line for trams on service 47. She and a group of school friends asked the duty inspector, whether they could have a ride on one of the trial vehicles as far as Gardiners Corner, Aldgate. The answer was a firm 'No!' Undeterred, the group then got into conversation with a conductor on one of the about to be retired trams. He suggested the kids buy the tram for the sum of 10 shillings (50p) and then have it installed in a playground. Sadly, what seemed like a good idea at the time, later foundered on parental disapproval.

The transaction never took place and the vehicle in question, E/1 class car 757, offered at a discount to the children, was dismantled within the confines of Hampstead Depot.

Car 757 was not alone in suffering this fate. From January to August 1939 a total of 262 trams were scrapped, many of which still had some useful life left in them. A surprise inclusion in the list was car 1001, which had been reconditioned as recently as October 1935. One wonders what sense it made to destroy a vehicle on which money had been spent in the rehab programme. Perhaps a mistake had been made and a fleet number transcribed? This may have been the case, however, there is evidence to suggest that some individuals were less than meticulous in drawing up the condemned lists for rolling stock. All of which chimes in with the prevailing ethos at 55 Broadway, where trams were distinctly *passé*. Basically, when told to clear a depot of its previous inhabitants, employees simply followed orders and redundant tramcars were driven or towed to their last resting places.

If everything had gone to plan, then tram route 11, serving Highgate Village, would have fallen to the trolleybus in the spring of 1939. Because of the gradient on Highgate Hill, powerful four motor cars of class HR/2 were employed; they made the regular journey from the city terminus at Moorgate. The 11 was an all conduit line with quite a tramway pedigree. The section of track on Highgate Hill was originally opened on 30th May 1884, as a narrow gauge (3ft 6ins/1067mm) cable tramway, thus

Car 1001 is depicted at Stamford Hill terminus, where a siding leading from the main highway provided an ideal location for trams to layover before their return journeys. Unfortunately, neither the modern track layout nor the recent reconditioning of car 1001 had the slightest effect on the advance of the trolleybuses. To the surprise of many observers car 1001 was scrapped in July 1939. *Henry Priestley/National Tramway Museum*

giving Londoners a taste of what would later become world famous in San Francisco. The romance of the cable cars was ended, when the line was acquired by the LCC and integrated into the north London network of standard gauge, conduit equipped routes.

Over all this time the denizens of Highgate Village had got used to an open skyline and therefore, it was reasonable to expect that they would not take kindly to the imposition of overhead wires in their select neighbourhood. True to form, when the LPTB commenced negotiations over the location of a suitable turning circle for the replacing trolleybuses, the locals and their elected representatives were not amused. Amidst a welter of correspondence and proposals flying backwards and forwards, it was apparent that there was a lobby for the status quo. Residents were happy with comfortable tramcars and some saw no reason for the changeover. After all, from an operational point of view, service 11 shared tracks with Kingsway Subway service 35 from Archway Tavern to Highbury. It was likely that the 35 would be retained for some time, due to uncertainty over the Kingsway Subway conversion. Finally, both routes were worked from Holloway Depot, which was used by trams and trolleybuses.

John Barrie surveyed the situation and noted:

The only routes left at Holloway were now 11, 33, 35 and 53. The 53 was another peculiar horse-shoe route like the 71, travelling a long way to cover a short distance. It was called the 'Bigals' by the crew. It had two plough-to-trolley changeover points, at Stamford Hill and Manor House. Fortunately the section in the middle, which had not belonged to the LCC, had recently been included in the availability of the 1/- All Day Ticket, so we were able to keep riding this route. Operating the route had become very difficult owing to the varying speeds of the cars employed, and a driver would do half a duty on a vestibuled car and the other half on an open car, a very unsatisfactory state of affairs.

A further difficulty was caused by the fact that many of the motormen on this route were men from other depots, who had not passed out as trolleybus drivers, and in many cases were elderly men, who were unable to adapt themselves to the fast cars that they were handling after a life time on slow-motor cars at such depots as Stamford Hill and Hampstead.

The 53 bowed out on 5th March, and even dyed-in-the-wool tram enthusiast, John Barrie, had to admit that trolleybuses on route 653 gave a better service to the public. At this conversion a purpose built bus, coach and trolleybus station was opened at Aldgate Minories, in anticipation of the closure of the nearby tram terminus on the City boundary at the junction with Middlesex Street.

The new construction work at Aldgate gave a clear sign that the major trunk routes running into metropolitan Essex were not long for this world. Hackney Depot supplied E/1 and E/3 class cars to work routes 31, 55, 81 and 77, while Leyton Depot had the same mix of rolling stock to operate routes 57 and 61. Bow Depot supplied trams for routes 61 and 63; these included cars from the former East Ham and West Ham fleets. Finally, car sheds at Poplar and West Ham serviced routes 65 and 67.

The inevitable happened on 11th June, when the last car on route 55 left Bloomsbury, the final 57 departed from outside Liverpool Street Station, and Woodford terminus saw the back of the 81.

At Gardiners Corner, Aldgate the trams are still putting up a good showing, even though their days are numbered. After abandonment the conduit tracks remained here for most of the war period.
Dave Jones Collection

Here at the Napier Arms, Woodford, the LPTB had to buy a parcel of land just beyond the tram terminus to enable trolleybuses to end their journeys. The provision of turning circles for the trackless vehicles could be problematic. In the meantime, car 880 has just arrived from town and is about to reverse with the minimum of fuss. *Henry Priestley/National Tramway Museum*

Interestingly, on the same day of the conversion fare increases came into force throughout the Board's area. An official communiqué from HQ announced that (quote) 'steps which are being taken have been found necessary as the result of the present revenues being too low to meet statutory obligations' – in other words, London Transport was legally obliged not to make a loss. Pro-tram voices pointed out that the LPTB had already borrowed millions on its hasty tram scrapping programme and had paid top dollar to bus manufacturers and suppliers of electrical equipment, who, quite frankly, had organised their affairs into a cosy cartel in order to extract cash from the coffers at 55 Broadway.

Another attempt to gain revenue came in the form of the discounted sale of three HR/2 tramcars to Leeds. On 22nd May, the Yorkshire city's transport committee had authorised General Manager, Vane Moreland, to offer a price of £750 for each vehicle. The LPTB accepted. Bearing in

mind a single HR/2 had cost £2,921 in 1931, the canny folk in Leeds must have felt they had really secured a bargain! Car 1881 was transported north on 22nd August, and the other two (cars 1883 and 1886) followed in October and November. Further 'exports' at knock down prices were put on hold due to wartime conditions.

The May edition of PENNYFARE carried a major article on London Transport's latest and largest ARP exercise, which involved medical attention for casualties, the use of a converted Green Line coach as an ambulance and the decontaminating of a bus splashed with blister gas. Frank Pick wrote in a letter to staff that everything was being done to 'deal with the protection and safety of the Board's staff and properties' and in short, 'much could be done to minimise the consequences of war'. He ended the letter with the rather blunt statement – 'those who are prepared need not fear war'. As for members of the 84th Anti-Aircraft Brigade, they were informed of their release date from

embodiment or temporary military service – 'on Saturday, September 2, all personnel can count on being back at their drill halls at the latest by 10pm' ran the text in the July number of PENNYFARE. Unfortunately, the 'Ack-Ack Boys' were not to know that the Wehrmacht had other plans for the start of September.

After dark on 11th August 1939, a test of blackout facilities across the metropolitan area featured trams equipped with subdued interior lighting and masks covering headlights. Although not a total blackout in the sense that would soon become well known to citizens – at one stage Westminster

Bridge and the Houses of Parliament remained defiantly illuminated – the whole exercise was deemed a success. Even though the tension was rising, several mundane events played out in the last days of peace. At Brighton on the south coast the Corporation and the local omnibus company had reason to thank Lord Ashfield, as he had been instrumental in advising on transport policy. In 1936 the LPTB had lent trolleybus no. 61 for assessment purposes. The trolleybus bug had then bitten and by the autumn of 1939 the locals were ready to say goodbye to their remaining trams.

As far as we know, Lord Ashfield was not amongst the official invitees from London Transport, who attended the closing celebrations, when the last Brighton tramcar entered Lewes Road Depot at around 2am on the morning of Friday 1st September. At precisely the same time, some 800 miles to the east, German troops were massing on the Polish border in a macabre opening ceremony for World War 2. Back in the metropolis,

above left On Sundays some route 55 trams were extended to the Rising Sun Inn by Epping Forest. In the last spring of their existence trams on routes 81 and 55 are seen in Woodford New Road. Many east London folk took a tramride to gain access to the countryside.
George Kemp/LCCT Trust

The rails at Aldersgate terminus ended on the boundary of the City of London. The busy life of the square mile has ceased on this Sunday, as car 890 waits for the return to West India Dock on route 77. This particular London terminus was never converted to trolleybuses.
W. A. Camwell/National Tramway Museum

frantic preparations were going on for the evacuation of children, hospital patients, the sick and the vulnerable. Over the next three days London Transport was mobilised for the emergency situation. Between 5:30am on Friday morning and midnight on Sunday around 600,000 children and adults were dispersed from the capital. According to PENNYFARE in its wartime austerity edition for November 1939, 154 trams took 12,700 evacuees to Waterloo Station and 111 trams and trolleybuses transported 9,100 to Clapham Junction. All in all, 533 trams were on evacuation duty over the five days until Tuesday 5th September.

After Hitler let slip the dogs of war on Friday, Neville Chamberlain confirmed the worst in his broadcast to the nation on Sunday. As the words of the Prime Minister faded into the aether, air raid sirens began to wail. Trams were halted in their tracks and crews and passengers made their way to the nearest shelters. Fortunately there had been a mass programme of trench digging in the summer months to facilitate shelter construction in parks and open spaces. Sandbags were now to be seen everywhere as a protection against bomb blast damage to public buildings, tram depots and many private dwellings. Luckily, this sounding of the sirens proved to be a false alarm.

As a result of the commencement of hostilities the remaining 1,255 tramcars in the London Transport fleet were earmarked for white painted fenders and entrance steps, as well as the now widespread use of head-lamp masks. Of course, some vehicles never made it to the repainting stage. Scrapping of redundant trams continued until May 1940, when car 1264 was the last to be sacrificed.

The outbreak of war might have seemed a good time to postpone the tramway abandonment programme, but the message had not yet reached Messrs Ashfield and Pick, as tram service 77 from Aldersgate to West India Docks was axed on 10th September. In fairness to London Transport the route had already been fully wired for trolleybuses, except for the short section to Aldersgate terminus, which was abandoned by electric traction. John Barrie, our youthful enthusiast in north London, had ventured out with his camera to take a few last week snaps of the 77. On this occasion his enthusiasm got the better of him and, when challenged by a policeman to explain his activities, there followed in his own words 'a clash of personalities', until things were sorted out. As John later recalled, it was unlikely that Nazi spies and saboteurs would be interested in sending pictures of Hackney Depot E/1s back to Berlin! Members of the LRTL out on tram spotting duties were then instructed to carry their identity cards and gas masks

with them, together with a copy of THE MODERN TRAMWAY to prove they were not enemy sympathisers.

On 17th September, the aircraft carrier HMS Courageous was sunk by German submarine U-29 off the coast of Ireland. Among the 519 crew members who perished was Able Seaman E. I. Dullam, formerly an assistant tester in the tramways electrical engineering section. He had joined London Transport in July 1934 and was the first casualty of the war. Sadly, many more were to follow on the home and overseas fronts.

top George Kemp was also out with his camera in the first week of the war. Car 1909 is depicted in Well Street, Hackney. Blackout precautions are in force – fenders have been painted white and headlamp masks fitted. Note the taped crosses on neighbouring house windows. These served to minimise the blast damage caused by flying glass. Shortly after this photo was taken, George was asked by a policeman to cease photographic activity! George Kemp/LCCT Trust

above Ilford Broadway was the terminus for trams on route 63 to Aldgate. Two ex-Walthamstow cars, famed for their speed and noise, provide an intensive service. Again there is plenty of evidence of competing motor buses in the line of vehicles waiting at the traffic lights. D. A. Thompson/LCCT Trust

The grim reality of the first wartime winter was beginning to take hold, when traditional Guy Fawkes bonfire festivities were banned. Therefore, there were no fireworks on 5th November to accompany the last trams on routes 61 and 63. The colourful scene at Stratford Broadway, so resplendent with tramcars a mere six years ago, was now devoid of railbound vehicles. Bow Depot saw the withdrawal of 70 trams, of which 18 former East Ham and West Ham bogie cars were eventually transferred to Abbey Wood Depot. With the withdrawal of service 61 there perished the unique reserved, double track by the side of Whipps Cross Road. The site of this private right of way is still accessible to walkers and cyclists today (2013).

There remained the anomaly of route 11. Rumours circulated among locals that, because of the national emergency, the trams were being retained indefinitely. One conductor in an HR/2 on the descent of Highgate Hill claimed that the trolleybus infrastructure along the road was going to be uprooted and dropped on the Germans. When asked the reason, he replied, 'Well, it's obvious. Hitler wants the Poles!' No doubt, this example of gallows humour caused a few wry smiles among the passengers on the lower deck. The officials at 55 Broadway were probably less amused by the whole drawn out affair, but they finally managed to crack the problem. John Barrie was on hand to witness the end of trams to Highgate Village:

The 11's were converted on the 10th December, and had the most unspectacular last car I have ever seen. I think I was the only person who turned up to see Car 146 make its final departure from the Village, in the words of the local press 'unwept, unhonoured and unsung'. On the same date Service 31 was diverted from Holborn Hall to Agricultural Hall, the long disused third track at Islington being brought back into use for this purpose. Hackney Depot became entirely trolleybus, its E/3's being transferred to Wandsworth and Thornton Heath depots. The operation of Route 31 was transferred to Holloway Depot, the HR/2's being used for this purpose.

Two days after the powerful HR/2 trams were banished from the hill, the first snows arrived, heralding almost two months of harsh winter weather. The situation was aggravated by the blackout and the total lack of street lighting. Bus and trolleybus drivers had a difficult task as it was, without the added danger of icy roads. The spectacle of trolleybuses on replacement route 611 having problems getting a grip on Highgate Hill just served to emphasise the usefulness of the trams and their fixed track.

The loss of the 31 from Rosebery Avenue to Hackney and the subsequent closure to trams of Hackney Depot resulted in a reshuffle of vehicles across some south London services, operated by depots at New Cross, Camberwell, Clapham and Wandsworth. Also south of the Thames early in the New Year, on 15th January 1940, the section of track between Tooting and Wimbledon Stadium at Summerstown was decommissioned, leaving trolleybuses the task of carrying the punters.

As the New Year started, nearly 8,000 London Transport staff had been called to the colours and fuel rationing had forced the management to withdraw 1,266 buses. Curtailment of a number of bus services had been taking place over several months; in March London Transport admitted that it had to reorganise more than 500 bus and coach routes. Passengers were urged to use trams or trolleybuses, where possible, thus saving precious raw materials. However, in spite of the depressing effect of the blackout, the civilian population had yet to experience any of the horrors of aerial bombardment.

Also at the turn of the year THE MODERN TRAMWAY surveyed the scene:

Latest news of the present rolling stock reshuffle appears to be as follows:

Most HR2 type are still retained at Holloway depot for service on the 35 route. Route 31 now operating from this depot. E3 type cars now to be found on routes 26 (principally), 16 and 18, 2 and 4, 40, 72. Rebuilt E1 class cars on 26 route. Walthamstow type cars on routes 26, 12, 28, 16 and 18. West Ham and East Ham type cars now attached to Abbey Wood depot and working 36, 38, 40 and 46 routes. HR2 type cars working on 34 and 66 routes.

Luxury tram No. 1 is reported to be covered with sandbags and in use as an air raid shelter at Streatham depot. Several Felthams are said to be sharing the same fate. Shortage of spares for Felthams is reported to be the reason for this surprising action.

No further surplus trams are to be broken up. London Transport announce they are to be stored for future use. The only trams without windscreens are to be found on routes 65 and 67.

There is no reason to doubt the authenticity of most of this report, although it did take a few weeks for the anti-scrapping order to be fulfilled. Abbey Wood would later receive the bulk of the former east London vehicles. The fate of car 1 was of particular interest to enthusiasts. It was very much a one off tramcar and, as such, many drivers considered it was too complicated to master, hence it was seconded to ARP duties. It was believed that only six drivers had been trained to handle the vehicle. However, as we shall see, Bluebird did reappear in due course.

Winter held the capital in an icy grip and the first few weeks of 1940 saw the country blanketed in snow. On 5th February the bitter weather conditions contributed to a serious accident at Downham change pit, when the motorman of a car on route 54 lost control of his vehicle and it skidded into a stationary tram waiting to pick up power from the conduit. According to news reports, a tramwayman and 17 passengers needed medical attention and the accident caused a three hour delay in the service. Luckily such incidents were rare. The climate had become more clement, when Easter 1940 brought out the bank holiday crowds and extra trams to cater for them. The so called Phoney War was at its height and people seized the opportunity to return to some form of normality. Routes 65 and 67 still ran from Bloomsbury and Aldgate to Barking Broadway. They were the last East End services, but preparations were already well advanced to terminate their existence.

The edition of PENNYFARE for July 1940 gave the following information:

Now only three tram services are left anywhere north of the Monument. Commercial Road lost its two tram routes over-night on Saturday 8th June: 130 trams of routes 65 and 67 were put into store, 147 new trolleybuses stole over their road – creatures of startling quiet in the clamour of Poplar. It meant the swapping of horses, this silent revolution – Training 250 tram crews, average age 40, for nine days; putting up 660 steel poles, 28 miles of wire; enlarging Poplar Depot half as much again and rebuilding the old part, adapting West Ham Depot as well; clearing one part of Poplar Depot at a time to take up rails, lay a new, smooth floor, and put down temporary rails; on the first day, pulling up temporary rails and laying timber over inspection pits, while trolleybuses kept coming in – 100 of them belong to Poplar alone.

For those who collect statistics. To-day 256 miles of trolleybus route, 102 miles of tram route; north of the Thames the only trams are those on the Embankment and Kingsway routes. Trolleybuses number 1,671; trams 1,127.

Poplar Depot was built by the LCC in 1906 and contained space for 96 trams on conduit tracks. During the conversion process a temporary change pit was installed at the depot entrance and cars then navigated their way inside, courtesy of recently erected overhead wires. Thus, in one final flourish of expensive rebuilding the trolleybus conversion scheme came to an end. In the nine years from 1931 to 1940 just over 200 route miles (322km) of tramways had been closed.

above Downham change pit in wartime – it was here the collision took place, that caused a number of casualties. Car 936 is probably on its way back to New Cross Depot. G. N. Southerden

below Time is almost up for car 1066 on route 65 at East Ham Town Hall. It is 8th June 1940 and trolleybuses will be taking over tomorrow. The conductor is watching out for the safety of passengers boarding and alighting. Car 1066 will be despatched to Hampstead Depot to see out the war. J. C. Gillham

STORM AND STRESS

THE WAR was coming closer to the British Isles. After the Dunkirk evacuation and the fall of France in May and June of 1940, the enemy was in a position to inflict considerable damage to London and to other provincial cities. The aerial assault on the capital began on 6th July, when a daylight raid brought down trolleybus wires in New Malden. Overhead wire crews managed to fix the damage in four and a half hours, but this was just a small taste of what was to come. Night bombing started on 24th August.

On a practical level during the first air raids crews stopped their vehicles and took shelter with the passengers. This practice was modified in the light of experience and in the Blitz most trams just kept going, unless the situation became too dangerous. Aside from a direct hit, the real menace was delayed action bombs at the roadside. As regards 'sticks' of incendiaries, the crews attempted to knock them off the roof of the tram with any long handled object. Sometimes trolley poles were swung to get rid of the offending explosives. All of which implies great bravery on the part of motormen and conductors.

Bomb craters presented the greatest obstruction to the tramways. A list of wartime service disruptions in the Blitz can be found in an appendix after the main text of this book. In some circumstances a relief bus service was organised. The LPTB in their wisdom had trained over a thousand tram drivers for motor bus work in emergencies. Often, buses were not called upon and it was a case of running shuttle trams either side of the crater, until the permanent way repair teams could splice in new rails or restore power to the conduit.

Unfortunately the repair gangs were going to have plenty of practice in devising ways of keeping the trams running. Official instructions, given during the height of the Blitz, were practical and concise:
Damage to Tracks, Enemy Action . . . In order that tram services may be restored as soon as possible after damage by enemy action it may be necessary in some cases for trams to run over skeleton (unpaved) track; during the black-out a red lamp will be placed at each end of such open track and, before a tram can proceed, the Conductor must remove the red lamps and, after the passage of the tram, replace the lamps in position on the track.

In many respects it was easier to deal with overhead wire equipped routes, because temporary (skeleton) track and wiring were in theory a more straightforward job, than rebuilding the conduit. Theory became practice in the first serious incident of the Blitz, when a high explosive bomb blast on Thursday, 5th September 1940, destroyed wiring on part of Westhorne Avenue, Eltham. Cars on route 72 reversed as near as they could to the obstruction, until repairs could be made. The task took five hours and was completed in time for the rush hour the next morning.

Monthly editions of PENNYFARE carried details of the tragic loss of life of staff and their families. By the end of October the magazine reported that 62 members of staff had been killed, together with 14 wives and 16 children. In one incident a Clapham Depot tram conductor, his wife and two children were fatally injured in an air raid. As a response to wartime depletions in the workforce, caused by male employees joining the military, women were employed from late autumn 1940 as tram conductors. By June 1941, the number of women in service with London Transport was stated to be 6,250; however, as far is known, no females were ever employed as tram or bus drivers.

Another move to ease transport problems was the use of tram staff on a regular Thames steamboat service from Westminster Pier to Woolwich. The 10 mile trip, costing 9d return (7d for workmen), began on 13th September, but unfortunately the 80 minute journey failed to appeal to the masses and this novel idea of trams taking to the water ceased on 2nd November. Alarming reports of marine tram crews spotting the odd rogue mine floating in the Thames probably did nothing for passenger serenity!

In order to minimise the dangers of flying glass after bomb blast, anti-splinter cotton netting was affixed under a coat of varnish to tramcar windows. It has to be said that London Transport was particularly ill

Officials from the LPTB dragged their feet when it came to protecting the tram fleet from blast damage. As can be seen here, diamond shaped 'peep holes' were later cut in the window netting. Car 1143 is pictured in McLeod Road, Abbey Wood. W. J. Haynes

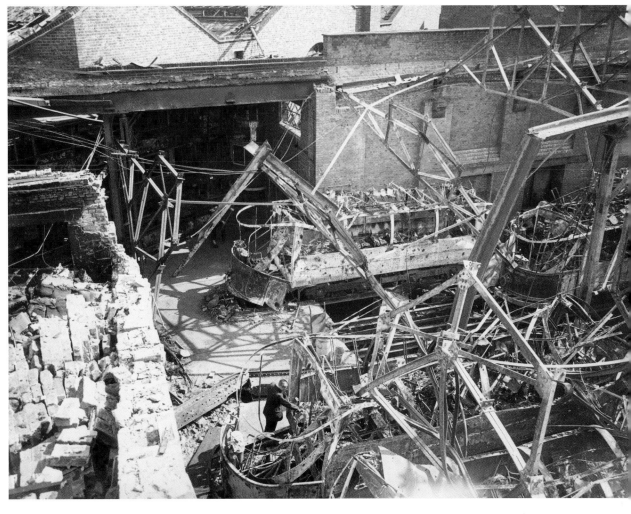

The bombing of Camberwell Depot caused the destruction of many vehicles, among them was one of the HR/2 prototypes, the remains of which can be seen in the centre of the picture. The official LPTB photographer has risked life and limb in climbing on to the damaged roof of the depot. The date is 11th September 1940. All photos of bomb damage had to be passed by the government censor.
London Transport Museum

prepared in this respect. The work took about 12 months to complete, by which time most of the damage had been done to passengers and vehicles. Diamond shaped peep holes were later excised from the netting, so that people seated on the lower and upper decks could have a restricted view of their whereabouts.

Vehicles were now a precious commodity and, after tram scrapping ceased in May 1940, somewhat later than THE MODERN TRAMWAY had predicted, full use was made of Hampstead Depot as a convenient holding area for spare tramcars. It had received some trams displaced from Poplar and Bow depots by the trolleybus conversions. A single conduit track, all that remained from the original routes, served to maintain the connection from the depot in Cressy Road to the main car shed at Monnery Road, Holloway. The journey was known to some staff as the 'tramcar waltz' and at least one wit suggested a Tram & Trolleybus Department brass band should supply accompanying music to the six reversals

needed to complete successfully the obstacle course. Fortunately, wrong road working was less of a problem due to the wartime lack of motor traffic.

The reserve fleet was called into action after the night of 8th September, when Camberwell Depot received direct hits from a high explosive bomb and sundry incendiaries. The attack effectively wrote off 30 tramcars. Nine days later Clapham Depot found itself in the firing line. Here another 16 vehicles were reduced to matchwood. Structural damage caused access to both depots to be severely restricted. Among the cars drafted in from Hampstead were a number of vehicles without vestibules, therefore, obliging the crew to return to working on open platforms. Observant passengers, having to put up with this make do and mend arrangement, probably noticed in the lower saloon that many of the trams still had fare charts relating to north London services, which no longer existed.

Kingsway Subway route 35 was severely

disrupted by air raid damage in the autumn of 1940. Vernon Burrows was on hand to witness the upheaval:

The service was frequently run in two or three sections. south London rolling stock damaged by the bombing was partly replaced by removing all HR/2 cars from Holloway Depot. This had a negative effect on the 35s, but the service between Archway Tavern and Bloomsbury was augmented by unvestibuled E/1 cars transferred from Hampstead Depot. Of course, fire regulations decreed that wooden bodied trams weren't allowed through the Subway. However, 'in extremis' several standard E/1 cars did slip through, when enemy action affected the availability of rolling stock. Also going south from Holloway were a number of ex-Leyton E/3 cars.

Further trouble erupted on 8th November, when Abbey Wood Depot was blitzed, losing eight trams in the process. The misery was completed on 27th December, after an attack on New Cross Depot reduced the fleet by

Clapham Depot lost a number of trams in the Blitz. The vehicle in the centre of the picture was damaged beyond repair. Elsewhere workmen are endeavouring to tidy up the mess. Part of a tramcar roof has lodged itself in one of the inspection pits. There is obviously less damage to the rack of spare conduit ploughs on the right of the picture. The building was eventually reconstructed and it was to have a colourful existence. In the 1960s it housed the Museum of British Transport. London Transport Museum

another six vehicles. According to PENNYFARE, staff responded well in the hour of need:

Courage of a 40-year-old labourer on the permanent way of our trams has been brought to the notice of the King, who has awarded a Commendation.

On the night of 27th December 1940, two H. E. and 15 incendiary bombs fell on a tram depot. In the words of the official account Labourer Ernest Fox displayed exceptional courage and zeal and took the lead with seven other men in dealing with the bombs.

The account goes on to relate that Mr Fox scaled the roof of the depot and traversed its whole length (300 feet) in his search to extinguish incendiary devices. All the while the raid was continuing and yet more bombs were falling. Bravery of a similar order was been shown on a daily basis by conductors, motormen, fitters and other members of the PW department, who were often out on the road, exposed to the elements and to enemy fire.

Most of the trams lost in the four depot bombings were ex-LCC E/1 class cars. At Abbey Wood one former West Ham (class WH) tram also succumbed, and at Camberwell seven E/3 class cars and 15 HR/2 vehicles perished. The two most famous casualties of the Camberwell raid were cars 1852 and 1853, the only prototypes of class HR.

Although news was strictly censored, contemporary reports suggest that London Transport and its staff rose admirably

to the challenge of maintaining services throughout the Blitz. Across the nation there had been an almost complete moratorium on tramway abandonment. The much maligned trams came into their own, supplying vital urban transport in very difficult circumstances. Other cities in the UK outside London suffered bomb damage, and two, Coventry and Bristol, were put out of the tram business altogether by damage to tracks, wires and underground electrical feeder cables. However, tramways in the metropolitan area survived anything the Luftwaffe could throw at them; the battered and bruised system made it past the last major raid of the Blitz on the night of 10th and 11th May 1941.

The so called 'great fire raid' of Saturday/Sunday 10th and 11th May, did much damage to conduit tracks in the central area. A large conflagration at the Elephant and Castle caused widespread destruction. For a

Two London Transport tower wagons guard the entrance to Farringdon Road. Tracks formerly used by route 17 have been severed by a large bomb crater. Squads of civil engineers, workmen and employees from the utility companies were mobilised to deal with these situations. Since trolleybuses had already replaced trams on this section, it is safe to assume that the services of the conduit PW team will not be needed.
London Transport Museum

few days no trams could reach the Victoria Embankment or the southern portal of the Kingsway Subway. On 18th May the Subway was reopened, but no attempt was made to renew the permanent way spanning a large hole at the northern end of Southwark Bridge. The City terminus of routes 6, 10, 46, 48, 52 and 60 at Queen Street Place was then abandoned. Trams had to reverse at a newly inserted crossover on Southwark Bridge and this arrangement was later made permanent.

On the subject of bridges, several temporary structures were erected over bomb craters, so that trams could coast across and pick up power from undamaged sections of conduit. Other traffic was forbidden to use these rudimentary bridges and signs proclaiming

DIVERSION – TRAMS ONLY

were posted either side of the obstructions. Generally speaking, the damage was made

good in a couple of days. Often a serviceable single track would open first, before normal double line working was resumed. As usual, the LPTB repair crews showed great ingenuity in all they did, and in truth, by the summer of 1941 they had had plenty of practice in devising alternative solutions, which provided quick service restitution after air raids.

Throughout the first years of the war many miles of tram track lay disused in London streets. It has often be said that this situation represented a wasted resource at a time of national emergency. Conduit tracks were less susceptible to blast damage than trolleybus overhead wires. In theory former tram routes in north London could have been reanimated, if only on a temporary basis. Certainly, there was the possibility of removing the rust from the rails on tracks leading to Moorgate and those linking the East End with Bloomsbury. However, as far

as we know, no such arrangement was ever made.

If the tracks were of no further use, then the metals could be employed in the war effort. Here the picture was very mixed. At the start of the conflict scrap metal prices ranged between 45 shillings and 50 shillings (£2.25 – £2.50) a ton; this did not encourage some local authorities to take the plunge. In a House of Commons debate on 18th March 1940, the topic was aired by William Thorne, MP for West Ham, Plaistow, who

Several tram routes used the Old Kent Road in south London. The date is 16th January 1941. As was the case on many occasions through tram services were restored before the highway was fit for motor traffic. Tramcar speed over these sections was limited to a maximum of five miles per hour. For those with a technical interest in conduit trackwork, this view is a mine of information.
London Transport Museum

was obviously well aware of the situation on his home patch. As usual, there was still doubt over who would foot the bill for the roadworks involved. THE MODERN TRAMWAY quoted from the reply of Mr Leslie Burgin, Minister of Supply:

Each mile of idle track represents between 300 and 350 tons of top grade steel. Mr. Burgin hopes to get 100,000 tons of rails, about half the amount from London. The work will have to be done in daylight as Defence of the Realm regulations say that

no road shall be blocked by repair work during black-out time. Several miles of tramlines are to be taken up at Leyton, it is announced, at a cost of £73,000.

In order to encourage the scheme, the government had increased the scrap metal price for tram rails to £6 a ton. On the face of it this action seemed a handsome gesture, but the problem of finding the cash for track removal remained. Late in 1941 Finsbury Borough Council took umbrage over a Ministry of Supply directive that the Council would not be indemnified in respect of accidents caused by lines being taken up and the road surfaces being reinstated. THE MODERN TRAMWAY added fuel to the fire by pointing out rather facetiously that the 'free highway maintenance' by the tramway authority had now ceased and that local ratepayers were in for some nasty shocks, if the Council had to pay out compensation

for mishaps caused by the 'more flexible transport system'!

As regards the rolling stock situation, it is true to say that after the last trolleybus conversions in 1940, London Transport was over endowed with tramcars, although, as has been mentioned, not all of them were in a roadworthy, or indeed, a very presentable state. After routes 65 and 67 ceased, the service required a fleet of just over 800 trams to fulfil traffic commitments. A survey conducted by members of the LRTL was published in THE MODERN TRAMWAY for June 1941. It noted that on 31st August 1940, the LPTB tram fleet consisted of 1,081 cars, of which 167 still lacked windscreens. One presumes the delay in publishing this information was due to the censor having to assess whether it would be useful for the enemy to know the transport situation in London.

The capital's embarrassment of riches as regards tramcars attracted attention from the provinces. In August 1941 a party from Sheffield called to inspect the ex-East Ham and West Ham cars sharing duties on routes 36/38, 44 and 46 out of Abbey Wood Depot. An initial offer of ten vehicles was made to the Yorkshire city, but no enthusiasm was shown to pursue the matter. Plausible reasons for this rejection were that the former Eastenders lacked air brakes and would have been the only bogie cars in an otherwise single trucked fleet. Another concern centred on the BTH 509 motors of the London vehicles, which did not find favour with the Sheffield rolling stock engineers. Therefore, what could have been an interesting wartime transfer failed to come to pass; most of the members of classes EH and WH later survived until the end of the system in July 1952.

Respite from the bombing came in June 1941. The Third Reich had directed its attention to the attack on the Soviet Union.

Air raid alarms in the capital were then sporadic in nature, until the flying bomb threat materialised in June 1944. During the Blitz the trams had become indispensable to London. Many Londoners acknowledged a level of fatalism in the idea that the noise of tram travel drowned out the dreaded whine of falling bombs. Every passenger then prayed the descending explosive did not have his or her name on it.

Tramway workers – motormen, conductors, permanent way gangs, fitters, engineers, depot staff, cleaners and overhead linesmen – had ensured that the service continued under the most testing of circumstances. It was a shame the publicity department of London Transport did not give enough credit, where it was due. On 11th December 1940, the Duke of Kent paid the first of several royal visits to LPTB services. Two bus garages and a trolleybus depot occupied his schedule. A month later he was treated to a conducted tour of Neasden Depot of the Underground. Although various

celebrity appearances at London Transport installations were arranged in a morale boosting exercise, the trams and their gallant, hard working staff were left out.

Insult was added to injury, when a film purporting to illustrate the vital role of wartime transport in the capital, ignored the tramways completely. *City Bound* (1941) focused entirely on buses and tube trains, thereby implying these two forms of transport had overcome the Blitz by themselves. A more general overview of life, entitled *London 1942*, also managed to present a tramless scene to the watching world. It appeared that, even when performing heroically, the stigma attached to tramways remained.

The date is 1st May 1941 and an enemy landmine has effectively suspended the tram service in Effra Road, Brixton. The air compressor for the pneumatic drills is taking power from one of the trolley wires. In theory it was an easier job to repair non-conduit tracks, however, as is apparent, it was still a major task to put everything back together again. London Transport Museum

DOODLEBUG ALLEY

In the early 1940s factory workers were vital to the nation's wartime economy. Here at Hardens Manorway on the boundary between Charlton and Woolwich queuing pens were installed to ensure an orderly return home for the employees of the nearby Siemens Works. Several inspectors were on hard to marshal crowds on to the waiting tramcars. And, of course, nobody would have dared to jump the queue! London Transport Museum

A T THE start of 1942 it was announced that, of the 146 former members of staff now incarcerated as prisoners of war, a total of 13 individuals belonged to the Tram & Trolleybus Department. In a sense they were the lucky ones. Less fortunate colleagues featured in the lengthening Roll of Honour lists of those killed in action or who were missing, presumed dead. Also departed from the scene, although not as a direct result of the violence of war, was Frank Pick, who died on 7th November 1941.

As a counter to all the grim news civilian morale was boosted by the knowledge that Great Britain had two potentially very powerful allies against the forces of Nazism. New Cross Depot staff celebrated that fact. They were in the forefront of the 'Dig for Victory' campaign and had helped cultivate a field at Brockley Hill. Forty acres of grassland yielded a harvest of 170 tons of potatoes. One of the plots was named 'Ashfield' in honour of the Chairman, while a nearby allotment was christened 'Uncle Joe', after another rather different Chairman. In due course a further extension of the tramway workers' farm was

known as 'Uncle Sam'. Boxes of produce were taken by cart to the nearest tram route and then transferred to the front platforms of passing vehicles. This ad hoc distribution system was used throughout the war.

The increasing number of individuals engaged on vital war work not only required home grown food, but also reliable transport to get from home to their places of employment. The aptly named 'Battle of the Queues' occupied minds at 55 Broadway. Unfortunately, policy decisions on dealing with overcrowding, which emanated from London Transport, appeared to be contradictory. Those patient souls waiting in line for a tram home were not helped by a series of service cuts in the latter half of 1941. Sixty-four trams were withdrawn from the schedules. The biggest loss came on routes 68/70, which suffered a 20 per cent reduction. The official word was that the axe would fall primarily on evening and Sunday workings; therefore, peak hour passengers should not suffer unduly.

One of the routes targeted was the 46 from Southwark Bridge to Woolwich, Beres-

ford Square. Cars on this service passed through Eltham and it was in this area that an interesting example of transport coordination occurred. The road from Woolwich to Eltham was served exclusively by trams. The route had opened in 1910 and during the First World War trailer cars were employed to move large numbers of workers travelling to Woolwich Arsenal. By the time of the Second World War the original service 44 had been joined by the 46 and 72. Passenger numbers had been augmented by the growth of suburban housing estates. An increasingly difficult situation with moving large numbers of workers vital to the war effort was alleviated somewhat by the extension of express buses on routes 21A and 161, which ran non stop from Eltham to Woolwich. Of course, workmen's fares were not available on the buses, which charged a premium rate of 4d per journey. In spite of criticism from Arsenal employees, London Transport stuck to its guns on the unavailability of workmen's fares for bus users. They were only ever introduced on a strictly limited basis, when buses replaced trams on certain sections of route, such as the old East Ham service 73.

Local housewives in Eltham, who were accustomed to use the trams to visit the department stores in Lewisham and Woolwich, were asked to restrict their shopping times to a period from 9:30am to 3pm, so as not to interfere with peak hour traffic. Rudimentary passenger shelters, officially described as 'portable', were erected at main stops. They were flimsy looking affairs, which at least did keep the rain off those at the head of the queue. More substantial queuing pens appeared in the Woolwich and Charlton areas to cater for long lines of homeward bound workers. On 12th April 1942, a statute came in force that required orderly queues to be formed at tram and bus stops.

In pre war days LCC posters had extolled the virtues of visiting Castlewood, Shooters Hill, Bostall Woods and Avery Hill Park by tramcar. Also lying near or a short walk from the main tram routes were other popular green spaces such as Woolwich Common, Eltham Park and Charlton Park. Not all children had been evacuated in 1939. Some had remained at home and others had returned, so that many families were reunited in the intervening months. Parents and their offspring did their bit for the war effort by endorsing the 'Holiday at Home' campaign. Conductors on services 44, 46 and 72 were well aware that two tram stops on Well Hall Road by the Welcome Inn and the junction with Shooters Hill Road were favourite jumping off points for families wanting some fresh air and exercise.

In fine weather and during the school holidays grandparents, mothers and children would join cars on routes 36/38 in central London and then ride to the end of the line at Abbey Wood. There they would lose themselves in the local greenery surrounding Bostall Heath and Lesnes Abbey. Although leisure riding on public transport was officially frowned upon, it was accepted that citizens under stress needed places to

unwind and, since the trams offered cheap fares and did not use precious imported fuel or rubber, they were the vehicle of choice for many picnickers, ramblers and working people on their time off.

This south-east corner of the metropolis was representative of the situation throughout south London, where places like Wimbledon Common, Tooting Bec, Greenwich Park, Blackheath, Peckham Rye and Brockwell Park were all within easy reach of a tram stop. An idea of the atmosphere of the time can be appreciated in the iconic British colour film of 1944, *THIS HAPPY BREED*, which shows crowds relaxing on Clapham Common. Trams running along South Side *en route* to Tooting complete the scene.

Since the upheaval of the last trolleybus conversions of 1940, there had been no loss of track mileage and only a number of relatively minor adjustments to tramway routeings. The first major shake up on the service front occurred on 1st April 1942, when routes 2A/4A and 22/24, formerly operated by Clapham and Streatham depots, were organised into rejigged services 22/24. According to the official TRAFFIC CIRCULAR Clapham Depot was to assume sole ownership of the new 22/24. Cars bearing

either route number shared common tracks from Savoy Street, Strand on the Victoria Embankment as far as Stockwell. There the two diverged; the 22 went anti-clockwise via Clapham, Tooting, Streatham and Brixton, until it reached Stockwell again. The 24 did the south London circuit from Stockwell in a clockwise direction. These trams provided extra capacity for office workers in the Vauxhall and Albert Embankment areas.

In compliance with instructions from the Ministry of War Transport, enhanced tram services on existing tracks were the preferred option. New bus routes paralleling tramways were definitely unwanted and the Board then decided there were still further economies to be made. A campaign began in the summer of 1942 with the aim of eradicating so called redundant or little used stops. As might

With arrival of American forces on these shores there were at least some soldier enthusiasts with cameras and a supply of film. They were more fortunate and better paid than their UK brothers in arms. On 21st July 1943, a picture taken for the folks back home depicts a standard E/1 tramcar 1170 on the Embankment in the shadow of Hungerford Bridge, which leads to Charing Cross Station.
Anthony F. Tieuli/Terry Russell

have been guessed beforehand, a number of passengers disputed the findings of the Board's 'experts' and resented losing their favourite stopping place. A suggestion that they would all be healthier by being made to walk further to the next stop predictably drew further criticism! The main targets for this campaign were buses and trolleybuses, as it was felt that savings on the use of rubber tyres could result.

The trams were not immune from the LPTB diktat on stopping places, but they got off very lightly in comparison to their trackless contemporaries. Whereas London's buses had traditionally stopped on demand, electric trams in London and elsewhere in the UK had always had fixed stops. Indeed, various pre-1933 metal signs indicating
ALL CARS STOP HERE
survived into the corporate image era of the LPTB, and many ex-LCC style signs soldiered on until the end of the system in 1952! A photographic appraisal of the various styles of tram stops is included in the companion volume LONDON TRAMWAY TWILIGHT.

The fleet was augmented in a small but significant way by the return of car 1 to active service in mid-June 1942. It was taken out of mothballs, or at least divested of its sandbag coverings, and declared fit for duty. Based at Telford Avenue Depot, Streatham, car 1 was still dependent on sufficient staff being willing to drive it. A number of motormen

admitted to being scared, when asked to take the former LCC flagship luxury tramcar out on the road. Stan Collins of Streatham Depot begged to differ and he writes with affection about the pleasure of driving Bluebird in THE WHEELS USED TO TALK TO US. As he says, 'I always called it my baby'. However, motorman Collins was in the minority and car 1's appearances were often confined to peak hour only journeys on routes 16/18.

Unfortunately, a shock awaited those London tram enthusiasts still unattached to His Majesty's forces, who wished to have multiple rides on car 1. In the autumn of 1942, on 11th October, the much cherished Shilling All Day ticket was suddenly abolished. The Shilling All Day was an institution, which had never been available on motor buses and tubes. Valued as a great benefit for working people and for Londoners on low incomes, it was introduced first by the LCC on Saturday, 3rd January 1925. A link to the past had now been broken. Also axed were the sixpenny child's day ticket and the sixpenny evening tourist ticket, which was valid for unlimited travel after 6pm. However, the Shilling Red, White and Blue ticket issued to HM and Allied Forces on leave in uniform was unaffected. Members of the Home Guard were excluded from this concession and this caused some mutterings about the unfairness of the LPTB's actions.

A further indication that the chill winds of

austerity were blowing through the corridors of 55 Broadway came with the revelation that the famous London Transport red and cream paint scheme was going to be modified for some buses and trams. Wartime shortages were blamed for the change. The new ersatz colour was known variously as indian red or red oxide. In fact it was a shade of brown. Existing stocks of traditional colours were kept for Underground and tube carriages, as it was felt that piebald trains would be unacceptable and 'look ridiculous'! Car 1867 had the dubious privilege of being the first to adopt the new livery. In due course some 21 members of the fleet were so treated, before everything returned to normal at the next repaint.

The year of 1942 drew to a close with no end in sight to the war. Official TRAFFIC CIRCULARS kept up the pressure by reminding staff that 'as loyal citizens it is their duty to refrain from spreading rumours or engaging in defeatist conversation, particularly whilst they are on duty'. On the lighter side, crews were also informed that no less than 102,000 cups and 66,000 knives had gone missing from staff canteens and that it was costing London Transport £8,000 a year to cover the losses! An attempt to lift the gloom, quite literally, was stymied by police reports of tram drivers trying to interfere with head-lamp masks. The depressing combination of winter darkness and the perils of being a motorman in the blackout had obviously taken their toll.

If there were any doubts about the nastiness of war, these were dispelled on Wednesday 20th January 1943, when, just after noon, enemy raiders swept in low over the capital. Reports of German pilots waving as they machine gunned the population of south London added to the distress caused by the disruption to daily life. Among the civilian casualties was G. A. Parker, a retired tram conductor with over 48 years service. Several trams suffered damage in the raid and were towed to Charlton Works. Holes in the roof in one car, caused by cannon shells from a Focke-Wulf FW190, prompted comments from CRD workers that a complete transformation of the upper deck was needed. It appears somebody had unearthed a trolley standard from a scrapped open topper. Predictably, nobody took the idea seriously that a traditional tramcar style of the 1900s should be resurrected.

Car 118 is photographed near Peckham Rye, right in the middle of Doodlebug Alley. The locals embody the spirit of Keep Calm and Carry On. In spite of wartime shortages of materials causing arrears in maintenance, the tram on route 56 still looks in fine shape.

In the February 1943 edition of PENNYFARE there was evidence that the workforce at the CRD had stopped grumbling about the lack of celebrity visits and had used its collective initiative by establishing contact with the Soviet Embassy. This time, as far as we know, T. E. Thomas refrained from criticism of the workers' state! Over a thousand pounds had been raised by the tramcar repairers for medical supplies to Russia. The donation was accepted in person by the Ambassador, Comrade Ivan Maisky. Arthur Turner, Hon Secretary of the Works Committee takes up the story:

Charlton Works have been thanked repeatedly. In September 1942 the shop stewards were invited to the Soviet Embassy and spent 2½ hours in the company of the Ambassador and Mrs Maisky . . .

This gesture in supporting the Allied cause was backed up by numerous donations to WARCO, the LPTB's own fund to support prisoners of war and families of staff killed in the air raids. Staff at Charlton also aided the war effort by producing munitions, military equipment and parts for aircraft.

On Saturday, 6th February, cars from Holloway Depot on route 31 began operating a restricted service on Saturday afternoons and on Sundays. The modified arrangement was in force between Victoria Embankment and Battersea, Princes Head. In itself this curtailment was nothing new. London Transport had been tinkering with tram timetables on many occasions during the war. However, in this case, the loss of the traditional service to north London annoyed regular passengers, even though vehicles returning to the depot still had to traverse the Kingsway Subway. Also the planners had ensured that extra reversals on the Embankment caused delays. All in all, this tampering with route 31 was not a popular move. However, the situation was exacerbated on 20th October at the commencement of the winter schedules, when journeys outside peak periods were terminated at Westminster Station. Regulars on the 31 must have thought they were being unfairly targeted.

Whilst certain services were diminishing, the Ministry of War Transport gave permission in November 1943 for an extension to the system, albeit a very small one. About 75 yards (69 metres) of track were to be installed in Beresford Square, Woolwich. This new construction was in the form of a connecting curve linking the 46, 44 and 72 terminal loop with the 'up' London bound line in Beresford Street. It was designated for specials carrying workers from Eltham to the Thames side factories in Charlton and Greenwich. In spite of its strategic significance for

transporting persons vital to the war effort, the straightforward task of inserting the requisite connection took almost 10 months, before operation commenced in late August 1944.

One thing was certain, enhanced services at Woolwich or anywhere else in the capital would never be short of tramcars to run on them. On 22nd September 1943, a trio of youthful tram enthusiasts, Messrs Price, Meredith and Tatford, managed to convince the foreman at Hampstead Depot that they meant no harm. The sight which greeted them was an assembly of vehicles, 101 in total, which were quietly waiting their turn to be brought out of retirement. Three works cars 08, 029 and 035 formed part of the collection. There were only nine trams with drivers' windscreens – cars 797, 867, 913, 1259, 1284, 1302, 1535, 1584 and 1607. All the rest were unvestibuled refugees from the 1940 trolleybus conversions of Poplar and West Ham depots.

In his Christmas message to staff Lord Ashfield acknowledged that 1943 had been a difficult year, but he suggested the tide had turned for the Allies. His warning that the long suffering citizens of London were 'not out of the wood yet' would ring tragically true in the coming months of the new year during the aerial onslaught on the capital.

On 20th February 1944, one of the last conventional attacks by manned German aircraft caused damage in the Clapham Junction area. Route 34 was cut by a large crater in Falcon Road. A shuttle service either side of the obstruction was instituted, until single line working could be restored. Normal operation on double track was resumed on 14th May. However, the false sense of security engendered by the cessation of enemy activity in the skies was about to be brutally shattered. The summer of 1944 marked the start of the final offensive against the civilian population of London.

The first pilotless flying V1 bomb hit the capital in June. These weapons were known in the vernacular as 'buzzbombs' or 'doodlebugs' and they presented a real threat. In June and July the depots at Thornton Heath, Camberwell and New Cross suffered some structural damage to their respective roofs. In the case of New Cross, 112 trams were variously affected by a V1 explosion, although all were soon back in service. In the next month tracks at the Newington Causeway, Borough Road and Borough High Street junction succumbed to a flying bomb and cars on services 6, 10 and 48 were diverted to run along Southwark Bridge Road. On Thursday, 24th August, three trams at Kennington Gate received a direct hit. There was a heavy death toll and the vehicles concerned – Feltham car 2109, ex-Walthamstow cars

2044 and 2051 – were written off completely. What was left of the cars was then taken discreetly at night to Purley Depot.

Among tram crews the southern approaches to the Elephant and Castle were known as Doodlebug Alley, and motormen responded to the sound of a falling V1 by putting as much power through the motors as they could and then hoping and praying that 'their number wasn't up'. Several near misses were recorded and in one incident on 5th August 1944, an HR/2 at full speed southbound in Lordship Lane, managed to outrun a doodlebug, which fell on the Co-op in Lordship Lane, killing 23 people.

Whilst there was a sporting chance of avoiding a descending V1, there was no protection at all against the next Nazi terror weapon. On Friday, 8th September 1944, a suburban street in Chiswick was wrecked by an enormous explosion. The first V2 rocket had struck the capital. On 11th November, trams were rerouted from the one way section in Shardeloes Road, Brockley, because of debris from a rocket attack. Single line working was adopted in the adjacent Malpas Road. Cars were passed through by travelling inspectors being used as human tokens.

At 12:26pm on Saturday, 25th November, the crowded Woolworths store in New Cross Road was totally destroyed. Many women and children were among the 168 persons killed by the V2. Crews and passengers from passing trams, together with workers from the nearby depot, ran to the scene and attempted to pull out casualties from the rubble. Contemporary reports indicate that debris from the blast covered the roadway from the Town Hall as far as New Cross Gate Station. Although tram crews were by this time fairly battle hardened after their experiences of the Blitz, the horror of that day stayed in the memory. The author well remembers talking to an eyewitness in the early 1960s. He was a former tram conductor, who was now taking the fares on the 89 bus route. He recalled that many of his fellow colleagues were traumatised by the event and that for days after the carnage trams would pause briefly outside the tragic site for crew and passengers to pay silent respect to the dead.

One of the last incidents of the war to affect the tramways was on 8th January 1945, in Green Lanes near Manor House, when extensive damage was caused to both tracks. Cars on route 33 had to wait until 10th April, before full repairs had been completed. The final chapter of this tragic saga played out at Parkers Row, Bermondsey on 2nd March 1945, when a V2 crater interrupted cars on services 68 and 70. The nightmare of death and destruction was over.

HUMAN RESOURCES

O N 30TH JUNE 1934, after one year of existence the London Passenger Transport Board employed 19,558 tramways staff; the Central Bus section had 34,148 employees. In a total workforce of some 75,468 individuals, women made up a tiny minority. Whilst it may seem fairly bizarre to modern eyes, there was a huge gender imbalance. Before dealing with the male majority, it is worth considering what contribution was made by women. In the 1930s traditional male attitudes to female staff conditioned the employment policy of the LPTB. Although wartime needs in the 1914–1918 conflict dictated that conductresses were to be seen on buses and trams, they disappeared from view after the armistice. It was felt that men returning from the trenches deserved their jobs back.

Certain clerical jobs were retained by unmarried women and a number of war widows. When one of the female clerks, typists, telephonists or canteen assistants got married, she would normally leave paid employment with the Board. Her new husband was then expected to support her financially. Because of the appalling casualty rate among men fighting in the First World War, many women were unable to find partners. PENNYFARE carried details of staff social and sporting activities. In the News Section for TRAMWAYS (February 1934) a retirement was reported:

We regret to record the retirement on medical grounds of Miss G. D. McIllroy, traffic clerk at Effra Road offices . . . Miss McIllroy joined the service of the London Tramways Company in June 1893, and was transferred to the LCC undertaking in January 1899. During the war, Miss McIllroy, like so many others, took over duties normally performed by male

above Changing the points was just one of the tram conductor's tasks. When the job fell to the clippies they were the equal of any of their male colleagues. London's tramway workers always regarded themselves as different to the 'bus people'. They had their own traditions and practices. Women employees shared this feeling of comradeship and exclusivity.
Dave Jones Collection

right On 17th May 1941, the Effra Road Ticket Works was severely damaged by bombing. The women employed here, including several wearing tin hats, soon set to work in clearing up the rubble. Stacks of uncut tram tickets have survived the raid. Luckily, no incendiary devices fell on the building. What we see here is the result of blast damage from an enemy landmine.
London Transport Museum

staff, and, for some time, acted as assistant night inspector at one of the depots.

The ticket works at 51–53 Effra Road, Brixton, turned out between six and seven million tickets annually. The task of checking the stock was allocated to female staff. The same situation applied to certain skilled operations in the electric motor assembly shop of Charlton Works; this delicate work required nimble fingers.

One of the many important changes occasioned by the Second World War was the re-employment of women platform staff right across the transport spectrum of the LPTB. Conductresses or 'clippies', as they were called, became a common sight on the trams. They did not graduate to become drivers. On this point London Transport caved in rather cowardly to the demands of the TGWU, whose hierarchy preferred not to grant the status of motorwoman to any of the eager lady applicants. However, not all union members were so reactionary. On occasions during the latter half of the war female depot staff were called upon to shunt rolling stock within the confines of the buildings. After the worst of the Blitz was over, it was not unknown for clippies to receive strictly unofficial driving lessons under the guidance of the motorman.

Some crews 'in the know' christened the countrified section of track across Woolwich Common 'the Ladies Mile'. In fact this term was erroneous because the route from Nightingale Place to the junction of Academy Road and Shooters Hill Road was only about half that length. With few houses and widely spaced stops it was an ideal location to learn the skills of tram driving without drawing undue attention to oneself. As it was, taking charge of a 44, a 46 or a 72 tramcar, ambling sedately up the gentle slope towards the Welcome Inn and Eltham Common, would not have been a particularly overtaxing exercise for any novice, man or woman, provided an experienced motorman was on hand to deal with emergencies.

The man at the front of the tram – the fellow who worked 'the handles' – otherwise known as the driver or motorman, was at the controls of a large, well constructed, solid vehicle on the public highway. Although not concerned with the task of steering said vehicle, he nevertheless had to judge speeds and braking distances. He had to remain alert to the antics of other road users and to potential passengers, who had to step out into the road in order to board the tram. He was expected to possess a good working knowledge of the mechanics of his tramcar. When things malfunctioned, causing a breakdown, he was the first person with the requisite skills to attempt repairs.

At the start of the London Transport reign in 1933, the motorman, more often than not, had to stand for an eight and a half hour shift on an open platform with no windscreen or vestibule to protect him from the elements. No wonder they were a hardy lot and they earned every penny of their 73 shillings (£3.65) weekly wage. The chap on the back platform, the conductor who collected the fares and punched the tickets, was paid the same. Bus drivers were paid 86 shillings and 6 pence (£4.32); bus conductors received 79 shillings and 6 pence (£3.97) per week. Wage differentials between bus and tram workers endured almost to the end of the tramways in 1952.

The figures represent an average pay packet without any additions for overtime. Tramway crews could expect around £200 per annum. In the context of the standard of living for 1933, the average annual earnings were £142–14s–0d (£142.70). The magazine GOOD HOUSEKEEPING declared that the weekly cost of food for a middle class family of four amounted to £1–4s–0d (£1.20). In London and the Home Counties the unemployment total was 13.5 per cent of the workforce; there was generally no shortage of applicants for jobs with London Transport.

Throughout the 1930s wage rises were very moderate. At the outbreak of war in September 1939, tram drivers and conductors were on a basic weekly wage some nine shillings (45p) above that of July 1933! There was a guaranteed 48 hour week of six days. Paid holidays amounted to 12 days a year. Rest day working was voluntary, but attracted a 25 per cent increase over basic pay rates. Overtime was sometimes available; however, there was a pool of 'spare men', usually up to 10 per cent of the staff, who would be available to take up any slack. Until 1936 there were no meal breaks and staff had to fit in a bite to eat and a hot drink around their duties. Hours of work could encompass 'spreadovers', whereby a crew member would be asked to be on duty from 6am to cover morning peak travel until 9am, and then return for a stint from 4pm to 7:30pm. A perk of the job was the receipt of a 'sticky', which was a pass that allowed free travel on just about all LPTB services with the exception of Green Line coaches.

Crews were provided with caps and clothing. Tramway platform staff wore a navy blue serge uniform with red piping on trouser seams, jacket lapels and on the cap top. Central Bus staff had white piping; the Underground workers had orange piping on their uniforms. In May 1937 Norwood Depot drivers and conductors were issued with an 'experimental' brown uniform. Women conductors were dressed in grey worsted. They received a tailored jacket and had the choice of a skirt or grey trousers.

In this 1937 view the inspector at West Norwood smiles benignly at the camera. Whether he was such a jolly chap, when called upon to reprimand a tram conductor or driver, we shall never know. Some officials were respected by the crews, others were just tolerated. The motorman, who is wearing his summer issue white cap top, obviously just wanted to get on with the job.
W. J. Haynes

Cap badges were of the familiar London Transport circle and bar (bull's eye) design. Motormen and conductors had to wear a licence badge with the letter T followed by the official number of that individual. Busmen wore a badge with the letter N. Staff were expected to be smartly dressed, making sure that their shoes were regularly polished! In the summer months from 1st May to 30th September white cap covers were worn.

Duties reserved for the conductor of each tramcar centred on the issuing of tickets and collecting of fares (qv). He or she was also expected to deal fairly but firmly with any recalcitrant passengers, who appeared likely to infringe the rules and engage in drunken or anti-social behaviour. At peak times when gathering passenger fares became arduous, a 'snatcher' would come aboard to assist the conductor. Snatchers were usually experienced members of staff who went from tram to tram.

It was also part of the conductor's remit to deal with the trolley rope at change pits and at termini. Some conductresses had trouble keeping both feet on the ground, when faced with a highly sprung trolley pole. Usually the tram driver would then help out his female colleague in distress. Another task allotted to the conductor was to fetch a tea can from one of the cafés en route. The motorman would normally sound his gong three times to indicate to his fellow crew member that they were approaching the designated café. There was a strong *esprit de corps* among tram crews.

In July 1934 PENNYFARE devoted a whole article, entitled *My First Day*, to the experiences of three tramwaymen – a driver, an inspector and a conductor. These firsthand accounts have a genuine ring to them:

A MOTORMAN: My first day as a motorman was hardly one continual round of pleasure. I started off all right, but soon got a nasty sensation. I struck a patch of tarry rail just before a compulsory stopping place. At first I though the magnets were not going to act, but when I dropped some sand we stopped all right, but a bit too suddenly. No one complained, however, except my conductor, an old hand, who said to me at the end of the journey: 'If you drove a mule like you drive that tram, he'd kick your brains out. Don't jerk on the reins, boy.'

The next thing was a youth driving a Ford van cutting in front of me from the offside and just clearing the buffer by about an inch. After my heart had made up its mind to re-start beating, I drove on, but my right eye still seemed to have a bit of a cast to the offside for several days. At the end of the day I was tired out, and when parting my mate said: 'Good Night, the first ten years are the worst!' . . . H. L. S.

A REGULATOR: As a tramway regulator, I found my duties very different from what I expected, the viewpoint was different, my former chums were chums no longer, at least when on duty, but just motormen under my charge, and for whose time-keeping and behaviour I was responsible.

Formerly, I had been chiefly concerned with the running of my own car: now I was held responsible for the headways and timekeeping of about a hundred cars and crews of various services. Then there were the worry and confusion arising out of breakdowns and delays. 'Keep a cool head,' I was told, and I soon had my abilities tested in this respect. I was on duty at Shoreditch Junction and shortly after commencing work a 'No. 43' became derailed on the curve from Kingsland Road into Old Street. The car left the rails and finished its course on the kerb outside the Kings Head, with a bump, and the first thing the top-deck passengers knew was that someone in the saloon bar was holding up a tankard. Fortunately no one was hurt, and there was but little confusion to traffic, as the car had cleared the tracks and other cars could get by. The trouble came when the breakdown gang had to get the car back on its track again, and I had plenty of work to get things squared up. I can assure you that at the end of my first day I was all in . . . F. P.

A CONDUCTOR: I had passed a stiff examination at the Training School for conductors, with high marks, and felt confident as I reported for work. When the C. D. I. told me off at short notice on my first day for a job on a subway car, I was not, however, quite so sure of myself. But, I could only do my best – so away we went.

I had a full car to Wandsworth and back, and satisfied everybody except an elderly gentleman who couldn't understand why West India Docks was sometimes a suburban point and sometimes a Central London terminus. One doesn't get much time for lengthy explanations on subway cars, especially when going through the 'chute' with a full load from Southampton Row. I enjoyed the excitement and the hustle. I was boarded by three ticket inspectors, but they couldn't find even a small mistake. They looked so disappointed, I felt sorry for them.

We also had a collision case, a lorry running into our stationary car, and one or two cases of attempted excess riding . . . H. H.

These personal memoirs from the summer of 1934 bring the tramways to life. One wonders if the motorman's tale of the youth driving aggressively constitutes the first historical mention of 'white van man'! As for the newly promoted inspector, we can sympathise with his having to give orders to former pals from the depot. The conductor, known only as H. H., had his work cut out dealing with the customers on the Kingsway Subway route 31 car. Explaining the intricacies of ticket prices in a stage fare system was a common occurrence, as was handling inspectors or 'jumpers', people employed to go from tram to tram, checking up on the conductors.

Just to conclude this round of personal experiences, a conductor (W. P. from Wood Green Depot) wrote to PENNYFARE in February 1935:

A Busy Year – A tram conductor, from January 15th 1934, to January 2nd 1935, I punched 227,439 tickets, and took £1,548-8s-6d. in cash, in 302 working days. This, of course, does not take into account the incidentals of ringing the bell, turning the indicators and trolley, cancelling prepaid and other tickets.

The provision of sports and leisure facilities was very important for the LPTB. In this the new Board built on the traditions inherited from the former Combine companies and from the LCC and some of the larger municipal operators. Both Ashfield and Pick took part in fostering interest in major sporting competitions between different sections of the London Transport organisation. Activities of members of the T&T Division (Trams and Trolleybuses) featured regularly in PENNYFARE and its sporting supplement. There were some hard fought contests, such as the football final of 10th May 1934, which attracted a large crowd to the Clapton Orient ground. After going 1–0 down to a team from Hackney Depot, conductor Callard of New Cross proved an inspiration to his side. He netted twice and the South Londoners won the day. The Mayor of Hackney presented the trophy and very generously added one guinea (£1.05) to a collection for the LPTB benevolent fund.

Leisure activities ranged from indoor favourites, such as snooker, billiards and darts, to outside pursuits including tennis, swimming and the traditional field sports, football, rugby and cricket. Every year depots organised Christmas parties for children from poor families. On at least one occasion, the boss himself, Lord Ashfield, adopted the traditional garb of Santa Claus to distribute presents to the kids. This gesture says a lot about the Chairman. He genuinely saw himself as a man of the people.

Lord Ashfield was guest of honour at a dinner for the Southern Officials of the T&T Division, held on 2nd April 1938, at the Empire Restaurant, Victoria. According to the report in PENNYFARE the Chairman was greeted by 'a spontaneous and warm hearted cheer', after which everyone sat down to an excellent meal. The reporter from the staff magazine then takes up the story:

The toasts – Proposing that of the L. P. T. B., Inspector C. R. Short, who pointed out that, in a manner of speaking, the trolleybus was the child of the tram, and made humorous reference to the net profits on tramway working which were handed over to the Board by his previous employers, gave Lord Ashfield many openings for witty repartee and the delightful reminiscences of which he is past master.

Lord Ashfield then regaled the assembled dinner guests with several anecdotes from his days as an office boy in America. He found a very receptive audience. There was obviously no denying he was a popular Chairman and that he had the natural ability to communicate easily with all ranks of his organisation.

No doubt, the view from the top seat at 55 Broadway was a progressive, optimistic one; moreover, the Chairman often stated that he was head of a harmonious family, where hard work and diligence brought their own rewards. However, there were cracks in the LPTB edifice. One of the most obvious grey areas was the relationship between the Central Bus and the T&T staffs. Although trolleybuses were in the process of supplanting trams, the customs and working practices of the tramways were transferred to the newer form of electric traction. This schism between the bus and tram traditions was to last until the final trolleybuses were withdrawn in 1962.

Tramwaymen could point to a number of occasions, when they and their busmen colleagues had not seen eye to eye. The unrestricted competition and reckless driving of Pirate buses in the 1920s had resulted in loss of trade for the trams. In the 1926 General Strike bitterness was felt towards those individuals, working for the omnibus companies, who had ignored the strike call or had caved in too easily to management demands. Tramway staff employed by municipal operators, and this included the London County Council, regarded themselves as public servants with a mission to supply reliable cheap transport to the working classes. Busmen, on the other hand, were characterised as an effete lot, only interested in making money for themselves and their capitalist bosses. Proof of this attitude was the fact that buses offered no workmen's fares and had been allowed into the fashionable and wealthier parts of the capital, excluded to the trams. And finally, the bus people were paid more!

Prejudice there certainly was, but the notion that the trams versus buses issue in some way mirrored the left/right split in contemporary politics is an oversimplification. There were communists, socialists, liberals, conservatives and fascists in both camps. The inauguration of the LPTB in 1933 brought about an uneasy peace between the bus and tram organisations; this lasted until the Coronation Strike of 1937. Deadlock was reached between the LPTB and the TGWU over a proposed reduction in busmen's working hours. A faction from the bus crews, branded militant communists by their opponents, had been accused of stirring up unrest. The upshot was a withdrawal of labour beginning on 1st May 1937.

Although T&T staff were members of the TGWU, they had a different set of working agreements with the Board, consequently trams and trolleybuses continued to serve the citizens of London. A busless transport system led inevitably to overcrowding on the tubes and railways as well as on vehicles belonging to the T&T Division. A tense situation was not helped by articles in the BUSMAN'S PUNCH which claimed to represent the rank and file movement. One of the leaders of the movement, Bert Papworth, spoke to a mass rally on 16th May at Hyde Park:

Any means we can adopt to call out other sections of London Transport to support us, with the will to win and victory, we shall adopt. If it means picketing every tram and trolleybus depot, every country service bus depot, and every tube station, in addition to the Main Line railways, the London busmen will undertake that task. If it means that we have to throw

The French press picked up on a lightning strike at Clapham Depot in March 1936. The matter was soon sorted out and the crews returned to work after downing tools for forty-eight hours. Only the depots at Clapham and Telford Avenue, Streatham were affected. As can be noted in this group scene, driving goggles for motormen on open fronted trams were worn round the cap band of the headgear.
Dave Jones Collection

LONDRES:- La grève des tramways à Londres. Les Wattmen rassemblés dans la cour du dépôt de Clapham après avoir décidé la grève. (Col. Hall Dépêche 13.4.36 ST.

our bodies across the lines of the London tramway system, we shall throw our bodies across, in hundreds and hundreds!

Rhetoric such as this had the opposite effect to that which was intended. Only one tram depot, Wood Green, voted to come out in sympathy with the busmen; the majority of tramwaymen had no such sympathies. In fact there was a joke doing the rounds of the depots concerning how a crew member should word an official accident report after his tram had mowed down 'a handful of barmy busmen sunbathing on the tracks'. Note the complete lack of working class solidarity, whereby tram crews believed that busmen had so much money that they could afford to relax, take the family to the seaside and sunbathe during the strike.

The strike ended on 28th May, but for months afterwards there was a real feeling of 'them and us' among the crews. An incident illustrating this situation was described by John Barrie:

A tale told by a colleague who was formerly a tram conductor on the 81 at Hackney is well worth relating. His car had broken down outside Leyton Depot, so he had been lent a Leyton car of the E/3 type. This incident happened just after the bus strike, during the period when bad feeling still existed between the crews of both types of vehicle.

On the return journey to Woodford the tram conductor got into an argument with a bus driver who passed some uncomplimentary remarks about trams getting in the way and holding everything up, to which the tram man replied 'We could leave you behind any time.' The bus driver, who was of course unaware that this was a different type of tram, scoffed at this remark, and said 'I would like to see you try!'

The tram conductor then informed his driver of the occurrence, the tram driver saying 'Wait until we get into Lea Bridge Road; we'll show him.' As the bus concerned was an old open staircase LT type, the tram driver did not have the slightest difficulty in showing the bus a completely clean pair of heels, and left it far behind.

Away from the open road and out of sight of members of the general public, the workshop and depot employees played a vital role in keeping the system functioning. Bus maintenance staff at Chiswick Works were paid more than their tramway colleagues employed at the CRD in Charlton. The wage scales reflected whether a man was skilled, semi-skilled or unskilled. In 1935 a skilled member (craftsman) of the Charlton Works could earn 80 shillings (£4) a week, whereas someone on the lowest unskilled grade took home 60 shillings (£3). In many respects the animosity between bus and tram men did not translate on to the works floor. Communications between Chiswick and Charlton were cordial and technical information was freely exchanged. Indeed, when the CRD took on the role of servicing trolleybuses, a number of bus maintenance procedures were common to both establishments. At the CRD specialist work, enacted by trained craftsmen with their own sets of tools, coexisted with mass production of mechanical components,

above The conductor of car 2236 is stowing the trolley rope in preparation for the switch on to conduit tracks for the journey to Moorgate. At the same time the change pit attendant guides the plough with his fork under the tramcar. This scene is at Manor House, north London, but the routine at change pits was repeated day in day out all over the capital. W. J. Haynes

right The motorman of car 393 has taken on the duty of offloading a temporary stop sign. For him it was all part of a day's work, even though the 'dolly' sign was a dead weight to carry. John H. Meredith

bodywork fitments and interior furnishings for each tramcar. Trucks and running gear were dismantled, repaired, cleaned and reassembled; large lathes ensured that flanged wheels were turned to the correct profile.

In this hive of activity the needs of the workforce were catered for by a modern canteen. An official press release from Headquarters stated that LPTB canteens offered '67 varieties of meat dishes and 32 different desserts'. Added to this cornucopia was the rather cryptically named delight of '24 various forms of vegetables'. Canteen workers' wages varied according to seniority. A male supervisor was paid £4 a week. In June 1937, across the whole London Transport organisation daily meals were provided for 30,000 staff.

Maintenance of the conduit system and the permanent way was carried out by teams of men, many of whom had specialist skills in locating electrical faults and dealing with track problems. Their contribution was vital, but it was not a popular job. The bulk of the work had to be carried out at night after regular services had finished. PW gangs then had to work to tight deadlines, especially when replacing rails and pointwork. Up above them on non-conduit sections the overhead linesmen laboured; they maintained span wires and ensured that trolley wheels passed smoothly through frogs and section feed breaks in the running wires.

Although there was no recognised category of skilled worker, the difference between semi-skilled and unskilled was reflected in the pay structure of permanent way employees. In 1936 a semi-skilled man could earn 70 shillings and 6 pence (£3.52) a week, whilst an unskilled colleague was paid 68 shillings (£3.40).

Also vital to the smooth operation of the tramways were the plough shifters at change pits and the pointsmen stationed at important junctions. Both categories of workmen were obliged to stand out in all weathers to perform their jobs. Their conditions of service reflected poorly on the claims of London Transport to care for the welfare of employees. Only in post war years did pointsmen and plough shifters receive some protection from the elements by the provision of small canvas shelters furnished with a single seat. When pointsmen had finished their work shifts, conductors would normally alight from passing trams and operate the points with a four feet long metal rod. This point iron was part of the standard equipment of each tramcar.

If Ashfield was the pinnacle of the organisation, then pointsmen and plough shifters formed the base of the employment pyramid. The following account was written by Charles Dunbar. His father was once an LCC motorman; however, the onset of deafness prevented him from continuing and he had to accept other jobs on the tramways.

He and another elderly man were offered the job of sharing between them the duties of change pit attendant when the LCC and LUT lines were linked at Summerstown. Summerstown, however, was not too bad. The headway was only 14 minutes and the cars in each direction came along fairly close together, so that for most of his time my father had nothing to do. In those days there was a coffee stall on the pavement with an adequate awning and side curtains and here my father used to sit on a mineral water box lent by the proprietor of the stall.

The closure in May 1934 was a bitter blow to him as the only job that was available to him was that of a pointsmen at Amen Corner, Tooting. This was a terribly exposed place in winter for a man in his late 60s, as there was nowhere at all to shelter. My father and his relief fixed up some newspaper bill boards on railings at the back of the pavement, but the frequent services gave them little chance of taking advantage even of this meagre protection. Two and a quarter years of this finally undermined my father's health and he had to retire a few months before his 69th birthday. He died a little over a year later.

In a society that predated the modern welfare state and the NHS, life could be very tough for those on the lowest incomes. The plight of Pointsman Dunbar and his fellow workers should have stirred the management

When the snows arrived in winter, mechanical assistance was available in the form of a dedicated fleet of snowbrooms such as car 024. Even then these two brave souls have had to engage in some hard manual work in an effort to clear the right of way. In those days the ethos was 'The Service Must Go On' – certainly, nobody had heard of the wrong kind of snow causing service cancellations! London Transport Museum

After the war canvas huts were supplied for pointsmen. There is a conveniently placed peep hole, so that the chap holding the point lever can check which trams need switching to the Brockley bound track. Car 180 is turning from Lewisham High Road into Malpas Road. Automatic points were rare in London and the services of pointsmen lasted until the end of the system in July 1952. John H. Meredith

into positive action. In spite of fine words and noble sentiments coming from the mouths of such notables as Ashfield, Pick, Bevin and Morrison, very little was done to alleviate their situation. Technology could have helped out at major junctions, where the installation of automatic points on the power or coast principle would have spared individuals having to stand, pulling a lever on the pavement. As it was, the issue of a pair of stout boots, a mackintosh and a sou'wester made outdoor tramway staff look more like members of the RNLI than the LPTB!

Although in theory recently retired staff and those with medical problems caused by their work could apply to the London Transport Benevolent Fund for assistance, in practice the help available was limited. Many working men, who had survived service in the military in the First World War, felt that it was beneath their dignity to apply for 'charity', even though they may have paid in small sums regularly to the fund. Only, when the second world conflict came around, was there a concerted effort to improve the situation. The London Transport War Comforts Fund (WARCO) was headed by John Cliff and at the end of 1939 had 42,997 subscribers giving 1d (0.4p) a week. The fund was constituted to assist any staff members and their immediate families, who had suffered illness, injury or bereavement as a result of wartime disruptions or enemy actions.

One of the 'named' sponsors of WARCO was A. E. Jago, a tram driver based at Abbey Wood Depot. On 9th November 1939, he was elected Mayor of Woolwich. As well as fulfilling his civic duties, he continued to be a familiar face on the front platform of a 44 or 46 tramcar. Another way of 'doing one's bit' was to join the Local Defence Volunteer Force, commonly known as the Home Guard. The LPTB Tram & Trolleybus Division contributed just over 3,000 men, who formed two of London Transport's six Home Guard battalions.

Lord Ashfield received an approach from the War Office in May 1940; he was asked to form an LPTB unit of the Home Guard. Its stated purpose was to protect depots and vehicles against sabotage, attack by fifth columnists, or against any form of enemy attack, especially by parachutists. In practice many individuals took turns on fire watching duties and assisted ARP wardens in checking for infringements of the blackout. There was also a lighter side to the tramway Dads' Army, as reported in the HOME GUARD (SUPPLEMENT TO PENNYFARE) June 1941 edition:

45th Battalion. The Home Guards of Clapham Tram Depot held a dance at the Balham Labour Hall and spent an enjoyable evening. During the evening a

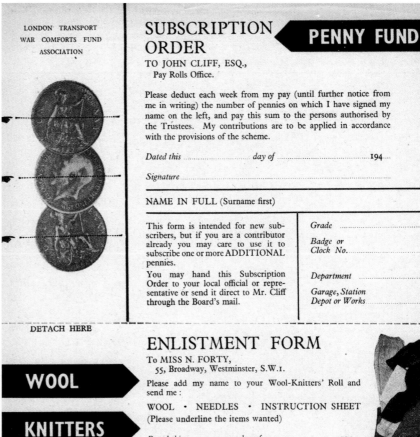

presentation of Sam Brown belts was made to both Platoon Commander C. Ward and Second-in-Command H. Taylor, by Sergt. Sinclaire, the band leader, on behalf of the boys of the Platoon in appreciation of duties performed by them.
The band of six men was formed entirely of Home Guards from Clapham Depot.

Even in the midst of the mayhem of the Blitz, the fact that tram drivers, conductors and depot staff could form their own dance band says much about the morale of the period. As for WARCO, it continued for some

months after the end of the war; it had dealt with over 14,000 cases of LPTB personnel suffering personal hardship or bereavement in air raids. The London Transport Roll of Honour bore the names of 810 serviceman and 453 civilians, who had lost their lives. This total includes 48 tram staff, who had died on duty and 800, who had been injured.

A story of heroism in the Blitz was printed in the January 1949 issue of the LONDON TRANSPORT MAGAZINE. It focused on the retirement of Inspector Jim Carter at the ripe old age of 73. His wartime experiences were not untypical of the everyday dangers faced by staff:

Inspector Carter reached retiring age – 65 – at the beginning of the war, but volunteered to stay on. Throughout the worst bombing he never missed a night's duty and was always at the scene of trouble to keep the night tram services in operation. Then back to Clapham Depot at 5:30 to see the early trams into service.

'Cars were smashed, tracks were torn up, and we had plenty of near misses,' said Inspector Carter, 'but none of my lads (as he calls his team of night crews) was seriously injured or killed.

'I had my share of luck in the raids,' he said. 'A stick of bombs came whistling down. There were two great explosions in the air directly above my head and others in the

jobs on the trams were regarded as being unattractive. The term 'dead end' was often used. Demobbed servicemen, including some with previous experience in the fields London Transport required, believed they could find better paid work with more career prospects. The situation was particularly acute amongst track workers. In spite of some mechanical help, there was still much physical 'pick and shovel' labour, taking place in the outdoors in all weathers. After the lifting of the blackout major permanent way maintenance tasks were carried out at night and in the early hours. This work pattern was yet another disincentive to potential job applicants.

Gone were the stalwarts of the 1930s, men like David Arthur Whitenstall, who was employed as a permanent way ganger at Rye Lane Depot. In 1935 he was elected Mayor of

hoist by their petard, because the tramway PW department had been run down in view of the dismantling of the system, forecast for 1942/43. This unsatisfactory state of affairs remained for the rest of the life of the tramways. It is worth noting that in March 1948 a pay increase was granted. A semi-skilled track hand could earn 111 shillings (£5.55), while an unskilled colleague took home the equivalent of £5.35.

Throughout the early post war period there was a general tendency to level up the tramway pay structure towards that of the Central Bus Division. This was a wise move in view of the unfairness felt by tram staff. A 44 hour week was introduced in 1947, together with a Sunday rate of time and a half. Pay rises in the spring of 1948 meant that motormen and conductors were on a

If the tram on which you were conducting had only a single trolley pole, then the ritual of swinging the pole had to be observed at termini. This task could be hazardous, but on this occasion outside the Napier Arms, Woodford there is little motor traffic to disturb the crew member of car 1187.
D. A. Thompson/LCCT Trust

buildings around. The pair with my name on had collided in mid-air.'

For 'outstanding devotion to duty and good conduct throughout the war period' he was awarded the British Empire Medal in the 1948 New Year honours list.

Inspector Carter was not the only one to extend his service with the Board. Many clippies stayed on after peace returned in August 1945. They were needed, as were many skilled and semi-skilled workers in depots, at the CRD and out on the permanent way gangs. It soon became apparent that

Greenwich and on 9th November of the same year he was invited as a guest by the Lord Mayor of London. Mr Whitenstall had started as a labourer with the LCC Tramways in 1906, and had served on Greenwich Council for 10 years.

In spite of the best efforts of management, at the beginning of 1947 there were still vacancies for 127 men, who were needed to repair and replace worn rails and points, as well as look after the unique demands of the conduit system. In this particular case the planners at 55 Broadway had been

basic wage of 125 shillings (£6.25) per week, which was an increase of 71 per cent since the 1933 formation of London Transport.

It is fair to say that, despite manpower shortages, loyal tram staff made some effort to maintain standards in the early post war period. Some regarded themselves as the forgotten few of the transport system, but others were keen to see the job out to its inevitable end. In the abandonment scheme of September 1950 to July 1952, many former tramway staff made the successful transition to working on the buses.

The plant had successfully colonised many vacant lots and had softened their impact on the observer. Added to the human woes was the natural disaster of the 1946/47 winter, where the weather was so severe that coal stocks for power stations froze on the ground.

The trams carried on and great credit is due to all those who battled the elements and the critics in order to maintain and, on many occasions, to enhance the service. Contrary to accounts written after the event, the tramways were not in their death throes, nor were they a constant embarrassment to London Transport. The south London services and the three routes traversing the Kingsway Subway had survived almost intact. They were a fact of life and, furthermore, they were an important factor in the economic life of the capital. Only in the years 1949–52 did the combined influence of politicians (both local and national), newspaper reporters, town planners, transport professionals, motoring organisations and commercial vehicle manufacturers serve to intensify the campaign of vilification which, with the benefit of hindsight, reflected little credit on any of the anti-tram protagonists.

THE IMMEDIATE post war period was a time of austerity and continued sacrifice for the population of London. The epithet most often used to describe this era is 'drab'. The capital showed signs everywhere of the recent conflict. In the summer of 1947 a contemporary commentator remarked that the view from many a tramcar top deck was characterised by bomb sites and Buddleia.

above The date is 7th July 1947 and the location is the famous Elephant and Castle road junction. The spirit of the age is captured by the poster on the bomb site billboard. A very simple message: WE WORK OR WANT, fairly sums up the mood of postwar austerity. Buses and trams, including one Feltham, mingle with a fabulous array of private cars, vans, goods vehicles and cyclists. Passengers waiting to board trams had to brave streams of traffic. No loading islands had been constructed for their benefit. London Transport Museum

right After the gloom of the blackout the lights go on again. Through some of the most dismal streets of South London this route 68 tram stands out as a welcoming sight. The two dockland services 68 and 70 played a supporting role in the 1951 feature film 'The Pool of London'. D. A. Thompson/LCCT Trust

The Second World War in Europe came to an end officially on 8th May 1945. VE Day was marked by popular celebrations throughout the country. In London crowds of people spilled out on to the main thoroughfares. Trams were called upon to convey revellers to the Embankment and from there large groups made their way to Trafalgar Square, Westminster, Piccadilly and the usual fun spots of the West End. Although bus services were disrupted in the heart of the capital, the trams got off quite lightly and delays were minimal.

Tramcars working that day were part of a fleet of 1,046 cars, of which only 734 were required in peak periods. Thus, there was definitely no shortage of rolling stock, although lack of maintenance due to wartime neglect and scarcity of raw materials had left many vehicles looking distinctly battered and bruised. The official line should have been that the stay of execution granted to the tramways was now up and that measures would be put in place shortly to resume the pre war abandonment programme. However, press reports in August and September indicated that the phasing out of tram routes would certainly not occur for some time. The EVENING STANDARD for 18th August put the priorities of the Board succinctly as 'more buses, more trains'. Shortages of materials and manpower were quoted as being uppermost in the minds of the LPTB, whose senior members pleaded for more time to restart modernisation programmes.

In the September 1945 issue of THE MODERN TRAMWAY some real progress was noted:

It is with pleasure that we record the provision of a new loading island on the L. P. T. B. tramway system, in Streatham High Road . . . on the 8–20, 10, 16–18 routes. It is a well built structure, elaborately lighted, and fulfils a useful purpose as the road is here very wide and the tracks a long way from the kerb on the down side. It is also noted that an unusually large number of freshly painted cars, looking very smart, have recently come into traffic.

Although very welcome as an attempt to improve road safety, the establishment of the Streatham passenger refuge was really an example of 'too little too late'. Another small concession to changing road conditions occurred on 17th April 1946, when the Croydon terminus of route 42, previously outside the Greyhound in the High Street, was transferred to the next crossover south of the town centre, opposite Coombe Road. It was stated that this move would improve traffic flows, away from the narrower roadway at the Greyhound.

One vehicle not using the new terminal arrangements was ex-Croydon car 376. It caught fire on 13th February 1945 and the burnt out remains were then towed to Purley Depot, where it was dismantled in the November of that year. It heralded a resumption of tramcar disposals, which were also taking place at Hampstead Depot. In March 1947, Hampstead finally said farewell to its tramway connections, as cars were moved to Purley. This arrangement was short lived, because trams stored at Purley were shifted again on to Wandsworth by 7th September 1948. Purley was used as a repair depot and finally, after 1st January 1950, as a regular running depot.

Another more spectacular way of achieving a reduction in the tram fleet was through accident damage. Fostered by newspaper reports, there was a widespread belief among locals that trams on route 34 in Cedars Road were being driven at excessive speeds. Although officially denied, there is evidence to suggest that a group of recently demobbed servicemen, some ex-RAF types among them, enjoyed the excitement of descending the slope at full pelt. On the evening of 3rd July, the inevitable happened and car 1780 derailed at the bottom of Cedars Road hill. It had achieved sufficient momentum to traverse Lavender Hill and it then overturned in Queens Road. Thirty-three people were injured and the car was a complete write off.

As an antidote to all the news of tramcar destruction, the folk at Charlton Works had obviously been busy and had begun to make inroads into the maintenance backlog. Unfortunately, in the general tidy up of the fleet the opportunity was not taken to remove the blackout masks on tramcar headlights. These remained until the end of tramway operation. Blast damaged trams, where windows had been covered by wooden sheeting, were restored to full fenestration. Some vehicles needed body strengthening and tie bars were fitted to the lower deck in order to counteract possible structural failures. In fact, there was a concerted effort to shore up the older members of the rolling stock in view of the decision to retain the railbound vehicles for the foreseeable future.

The reintroduction of full lighting

above Lambeth Palace is the London residence of the Archbishop of Canterbury. At least one wartime prelate made regular tram journeys from here to the House of Lords! As a patriotic gesture the chauffeur was left at home. In more peaceful times car 1834 kicks up the dust on Lambeth Palace Road. D. A. Thompson/LCCT Trust

left London trams retained their headlamp masks after the war. The tram stop was a relic from pre-LPTB days. The growth of motor traffic made boarding a tram all the more dangerous, thus bolstering the arguments of the tramcar's critics. J. Wills/LCCT Trust

made the winter streets of 1945/46 much less gloomy. Passengers benefited from better interior illumination of tramcars, and the removal of anti-blast netting from car windows also improved the outlook. Londoners of a literary bent, who were sympathetic to the trams, could rejoice in the reappearance of 'the Galleons of Light', as celebrated some decades earlier by H. G. Wells. Arnold Bennett in LIFE IN LONDON summed up the experience of many in a sentence: 'They roll along day and night without a pause; in the middle of the night you can see them glittering away to the ends of the county'. The glittering spectacle of all night trams had first been witnessed by Londoners on the evening of New Year's Day 1899. The tradition, begun in horsecar days, had continued into the electric era. As from 18th June 1946, several previously unnumbered services received an official route designation. It was said that route stencils for abandoned north London services 1, 3, 5 and 7 were salvaged from scrapped vehicles and had been retained at Hampstead Depot for this very eventuality. The figure 1 had to be added to Feltham number blinds for cars working night services.

The 12 months after the cessation of hostilities had witnessed a valiant effort to restore tramway rolling stock and infrastructure. At the same time politicians and planners were mulling over road and housing schemes, which had been suggested in the comprehensive COUNTY OF LONDON PLAN 1943. It was stated quite categorically that there would be no place for trams in the rebuilt London of the future. Then came the official announcement from 55 Broadway, on 15th November 1946, that motor buses would replace the remaining trams. Residents of Sherard Road and Lassa Road, Eltham, proposed holding a street party to celebrate the news. The trolleybus turning circle pencilled in for their streets would now never leave the drawing board. Similar sentiments were felt across south London. Inevitably, speculation started about the existing trolleybus system as to whether it would be a one generation wonder.

Deliveries of sufficient numbers of the RT type motorbus, on which so many official hopes had been pinned, were uncertain, and a provisional date of 1950 for the resumption of tramway abandonment was published. Priority was also given to the replacement of the aging bus fleet, of which there were in January 1947, 5,925 double deck and 1,116 single deck vehicles. The trams would have to wait their turn for extinction. In the meantime the Board made tentative overtures to the few remaining city tramway operators in Britain. These soundings were in regard of the sale of the more modern members of the LT fleet. A precedent had been set by HR/2 cars 1881, 1883 and 1886, which had been purchased by Leeds in the autumn of 1939. As matters turned out, the Felthams and Luxury car 1 would eventually join the three HR/2s in the Yorkshire city.

While management took their time in coming to a decision on tramcar sales, other folk employed on the tramways were very quick off the mark. In spite of the staff shortages among permanent way workers, THE MODERN TRAMWAY for July 1947 had some good news:

On 12th May, a repair gang repaired a broken rail in four minutes, trams only being slightly delayed. Such action in London is commendable; would that all tramway activities were accompanied by as much seeming enthusiasm. Possibly because a number of new rails are available in the P. W. Depot near Charlton, track repairs are being done at many places on the 36–38–40 routes, rails being renewed and joints tightened, and the surrounding setts regrouted. Complete renewal of one of the tracks at the Blackwall Lane junction in Greenwich is at hand, and the whole of the conduit and live rail construction could be seen by those in that neighbourhood when repair was done.

London's emergency track repair gangs often worked in daylight and during the school holidays they might attract a number of youthful observers, to whom the replacement of conduit yokes and T rails (qv) must have seemed quite fascinating. Granite setts adjacent to the rails were a common form of street paving and were considered almost indestructible. Unfortunately, they were also slippery when wet, and cyclists in particular had to be aware of the dangers in inclement weather.

With new tracks came new schedules. Passenger numbers had picked up sufficiently after the war for an improvement in services. Commencing 12th November 1947, there was a general revision of timetables. The main beneficiary was route 31, which was extended from Battersea, Princes Head to Wandsworth High Street. At its northern end cars terminated on the three track layout at Islington Green. On 12th December, trams working service 44 were extended past their traditional terminus opposite St John's Church to a crossover just west of the Eltham Green roundabout. True to the old LCC temperance tradition, the reversal point appeared on indicator blinds as Middle Park Avenue and not The Yorkshire Grey, which was the public house adjacent to the terminus.

The decision on the final destination of the 44, provoked amusement among staff. After all, the bus people had never flinched in their policy of naming terminals after pubs. In defiance of the LCC teetotal tradition, the two docklands routes 68/70 were well known to be a drinker's paradise, passing as they did a multitude of inns and public houses. A correspondent of the new LONDON TRANSPORT MAGAZINE, which had replaced PENNYFARE, noted in the December 1947 edition, that he counted 50 public houses on the journey from Greenwich to the Elephant and Castle. The 68 was a 10 pubs a mile route!

The ghost of the old LCC Tramways appeared for the last time with the extension

In the early postwar years the capital was still served by a network of electrically powered public transport. As a reminder of days gone by, this scene in Plumstead Road, Woolwich serves to recall the environmentally friendly legacy that was abandoned in favour of diesel buses. Two trolleybuses follow car 1840 on service 38 to the Victoria Embankment. The road surface here was paved with granite setts. These were very durable, but had the disadvantage of being slippery when wet. A. D. Packer

of the 44. Any lingering influence of the old ways of municipal operation was finally extinguished by the passing of the 1947 Transport Act. On 1st January 1948, the London Transport Executive (LTE), under the auspices of the British Transport Commission (BTC), supplanted the LPTB. Chairman of the new LTE was Lord Latham. The talents of the previous incumbent, Lord Ashfield, were now needed by the BTC. Aside from Lord Latham, there were seven members of the Executive: Sir Edward Hardy, A. H. Grainger, John Cliff, Sir Richard Burbidge, L. C. Hawkins, A. B. B. Valentine

The northern ramp leading to the Kingsway Subway remains to this day as a historical relic. Car 1908 awaits the green light to emerge into the traffic. After the failed pre-war trolleybus experiment it became increasingly obvious that tramway replacement services would not be able to use the subway. E. R. Oakley/TLRS

and T. E. Williams. None of these gentlemen, save for John Cliff, had had any meaningful connection with tramways, nor did they possess specialist knowledge pertaining to tramcar development in the capital.

Ironically, one of the last public statements from the old Board concerned the impossibility of obtaining enough new buses to replace the trams. The whole abandonment programme was in abeyance for some years, until the supply situation improved. Finally, in order to stifle any false hopes, it was announced that no new trams would be acquired. Another public statement, this time over the airwaves of BBC Radio on Friday, 28th November 1947, aimed to balance up the argument. A young Croydonian, Barry Cross, gave an assured and informative talk, entitled 'My Hobby – Trams'. Although unlikely to move the mandarins at 55 Broadway, the narrative focused on a number of advantages of tramway operation – cheap fares, frequent services, enhanced passenger carrying abilities – all of which were threatened by the LPTB scrapping scheme.

As regards the policies of the recently established London Transport Executive it was a case of 'plus ça change, plus c'est la même chose'! In short, no reprieve was granted to the tramways. A Government White Paper confirmed that the proposed Elephant and Castle roundabout was being shelved, the inference being that nothing could be achieved until the trams were out of the way. The only project in south London to get the green light was the rebuilding of Creek Bridge, which would affect routes 68/70.

In the spring of 1948 work began on renewing tracks in Kennington Road, Clapham Road, Clapham High Street and at Victoria terminus. The paving adjacent to the rails on the Embankment also came under scrutiny by the PW department. An LTE official announcement confirmed that 15 miles (24km) of track would be repaired in 1948. In June, gangs were noted attending to the permanent way in Upper Tooting Road, Basildon Road, Camberwell New Road, London Road (Croydon) and Brixton Road.

Clapham was also the centre of activity for a report in the May issue of THE MODERN TRAMWAY:

On 13th March, a London tram became a film studio for a day. Richard Attenborough, as the hero of 'London Belongs to Me' rode to and fro for two hours or more between Clapham and Balham . . . he is shown seated in a transverse seat in the lower saloon, an elbow on the window sill which forms a convenient arm rest – a piece of furniture entirely lacking even in the newest buses.

Sadly for devotees of the silver screen, who were also tram fans, the scenes on the lower deck of an E/1 car disappeared on the cutting room floor and the tram presence in the completed film was restricted to a few general shots of London streets.

Another celebrity occasion occurred at the opening of the Hackney Borough Council Road Safety Exhibition on 22nd May. What

was billed as a routine display of safety ideas and posters, was graced by the presence of James Callaghan MP, Parliamentary Secretary to the Minister of Transport. Mr Callaghan talked to members of the LRTL at their stand and engaged in a full and frank discussion on tramway abandonment in London and its impact on road safety. The future Prime Minister (1976–1979) was then reported by THE MODERN TRAMWAY to have operated 'a working scale model layout of a typical modern tramway system, with reserved track, loading islands and tramway subways. A tramcar controller, supplied by London Transport, operated another and larger tramcar model in the balcony'.

Sadly, this was about as far as the LRTL got in persuading the Labour Government to get involved in modern tramways. Of course,

it was nice of London Transport to lend a full size controller, but then they had a stack of them from scrapped tramcars.

In the late summer of 1948 a one way traffic arrangement for New Cross, implemented on an experimental basis, foreshadowed many gyratory systems being planned for the capital. The existence of tramways was blamed for the tardiness in establishing such 'modern' traffic schemes. To some extent this was unfair, because single one way tram tracks were in use at several locations in south London, notably on the approach to Loughborough Junction via Milkwood Road and Lowden Road, and on the outskirts of Woolwich town centre along Grand Depot Road, Greens End and Woolwich New Road. It would have been a straightforward job to lay short sections of new track, but it was

The dockland route 70 was part of London folklore. It began here on Tooley Street near the warehouses of the Pool of London in the shadow of London Bridge Station. Trams then conveyed passengers in a leisurely fashion as far as Greenwich, Church Street. The sun is out and for a moment the hectic pace of metropolitan life is stilled. Time to settle down into a lower deck seat and read your newspaper. A. V. Mace

obvious at this late stage of the game that no significant improvements to the track layout would be sanctioned. Only when the Festival of Britain opened in 1951, was the LTE forced to provide new conduit tracks for a revised road layout.

This chapter ends with the demise of Albert Stanley, Lord Ashfield. The acclaimed 'Father of London Transport' passed away on Thursday, 4th November 1948. Obituary notices were full of praise for his qualities of leadership, compassion and devotion to duty, which, combined with a clear sense of purpose, had guided the fortunes of the LPTB and thus influenced the lives of millions of Londoners. Members of the pro-tram lobby, such as it was in 1948, had mixed

feelings. Although he was instrumental in the commissioning of the modern Feltham type tramcars, Lord Ashfield had then set his cap against tramways and was one of the chief architects in their destruction. Like almost all transport professionals of his era, he failed to appreciate the huge impact that motor traffic would have on the streets of London. The bus and underground railway networks now mark his metropolitan legacy, which endures into the 21st century. However, the tramways were not so fortunate. On Ashfield's watch a major mass public transport system was starved of investment and consequently it perished. A valuable asset was thrown away with little thought for the future.

facing page A winter's evening with the threat of fog in the air is the setting for a brightly illuminated tramcar, which was a welcome sight for homeward bound passengers. Here at Catford a tram on route 54 makes its way to Grove Park. The photographer has used a longer exposure time for this picture, hence the 'ghostly' figures of pedestrians. A. V. Mace

below Track repairs are taking place in Islington on 4th November 1948. Red flags and TRACK UP warning signs alert other traffic to the situation. Removing granite setts individually in order to uncover tramlines was in theory an easier task than drilling holes in a modern asphalt or concrete road surface. Car 1922 passes by under a cat's cradle of trolleybus wires. Author's Collection

REQUIEM

IN THE SPACE of 15 years from the inauguration of the LPTB until the death of Lord Ashfield the foundations had been laid for the events of 1949–1952 – the last years of the trams – which have been recorded in companion volume LONDON TRAMWAY TWILIGHT. It will have been noted in the present work, how forces ranged against the tramcar had been gaining in influence, even before the Government imposed unification of the capital's transport systems. The advent of the LPTB only served to accelerate the dismantling of the network. The main losers in this process were people on moderate or low incomes, for whom cheap fares and a very reliable all weather service were vital in their daily journey to factories, shops, offices and places of employment. Courtesy of the Shilling All Day tram fare, even the poorest student could gain knowledge of the metropolitan area; the ticket was the key to discover London's patchwork heritage, its varied neighbourhoods and its historic buildings.

Millions of passenger journeys went unrecorded. They were considered a routine part of London life, unworthy of the written word. However, we can now attempt to recreate this vanished world. Dr Gerald Druce gives a previously unpublished, detailed account of his daily ride to work:

During the years 1945–50 your correspondent lived at Norbury, just on the Croydon side of the municipal boundary with the County of London and, for part of that time, worked near Croydon Parish Church.

The associated travel involved a direct tram journey from Norbury Station (the northernmost extremity of the former Croydon Corporation Tramways) to West Croydon on service 16/18. Good timekeeping was essential, if he was more than 2 minutes late for the 8am start, he lost a quarter of an hour's pay.

Also 'Workman' fares applied on cars leaving Norbury or Purley up to 7:30am, this fare was only 4d (1.67p) return from Norbury Station to the 'Greyhound' pub, which was then in Croydon High Street (a shade over 3 miles or 4.8km), instead of 4d Ordinary single or 3d (1.25p) single 'Cheap Midday Fare'. The last applied on Mondays to Fridays on cars leaving Norbury or Purley between 10am and 4pm. It was advertised by reversing the route boards on the side of the tram beneath the windows to display 'CHEAP MIDDAY FARES' prominently in white letters on a red background. Up to 30th September 1950, the fare structure within Croydon was completely separate from that inherited from the LCC, which applied to the remainder of the extant London tramways.

Despite the alleged poor reputation of the trams for reliability, he used to catch route No. 26 [see note] of service 16/18 without fail. A Telford Avenue working, it was almost always a Feltham. The route number was displayed on blue enamel plates with white numbers fitted into a socket on the near side window of both cabs. Instead of a destination the rear indicator blind was turned to 'WORKMAN', only used up to 7:30am.

The stop for Norbury Station was just on the Croydon side of the line of granite setts marking the borough boundary, here on the south bank of the River Graveney. Watching for the reflection in the shop windows opposite the bend of the road, the unmistakable shape of a Feltham could be seen approaching. Clanks from the spring-loaded tongues of the trailing crossover, a hiss from the air cylinder accompanied a shudder from the brake rigging as the tram came to rest. Few people alighted, the queue for the tram crossed the nearside carriageway to the annoyance of the bus driver pulling away from his stop sited, as usual, just before the tram stop. Boarding involved two easy steps to climb on to the level platform, then across to the stairs opposite. These had a right angle at the bottom, then a straight flight to the upper deck. At this time in the morning there would be few empty seats.

This section of the route was ideal from the operator's viewpoint, it had a busy rush hour in both directions of travel. Southbound, the tram ran through densely built residential areas and then traversed the commercial and retail region of central Croydon. From Norbury there was no competition from a parallel bus route into Croydon. Also, the route gave good connections to some large factories; in those days a substantial proportion of the local population was employed in precision engineering. During slack hours, especially on Saturday afternoons, shoppers going to and from central Croydon kept the trams busy. South of Croydon there were few passengers, several 'red' and 'green' bus routes competed, these going beyond the tram terminus.

The tram route did not follow the railways closely, but had good interchanges for London-bound commuters at both Norbury (nine trains per hour to Victoria in 1950) and Streatham(six and three trains per hour to London Bridge and Holborn Viaduct respectively). Hence, the conductors were kept busy as some northbound passengers rode the relatively short distance to one of these stations, others went all the way to the Embankment, where the stops between Westminster and Blackfriars were only a short walk from the Ministries and commercial offices or by purchasing a transfer ticket continued through the Subway to Holborn or Bloomsbury.

At this time (1945 to 30th September 1950) the fare structure was a legacy from the days when this service was provided jointly by Croydon Corporation and the LCC. Northbound, for this historical reason the 11d (4.6p) ordinary return and the corresponding 4d single 'Cheap Midday Fare' were available only from the LCC boundary to 'London Terminus'. Both these fares permitted a wide range of transfers to London termini, other than that of service 16/18, and were also valid through the Subway to Holborn and Bloomsbury. However, the 7d (2.9p) ordinary single to London termini extended by two fare stages into Croydon as far as Warwick Road. A separate set of 'Cheap Midday Fares' applied south of Norbury as well as low-value transfers on to service 42 to Thornton Heath High Street by changing at the 'Pond'.

The track with overhead wires from Norbury to Purley had been relaid in concrete with tar macadam surface by Croydon Corporation in the 1920s in anticipation of through running with the LCC to London. Consequently it was in good condition compared with much of the track elsewhere in south London. Connected to a further mile on the LCC side of the boundary, service 16/18 had the benefit of the longest continuous stretch of overhead wiring on the post-1941 tramway system.

There were no steep inclines on the Croydon part of the route. So the drivers could take full advantage of the good turn of speed possessed by the Felthams on level ground. They rode with a gentle side-to-side swaying action. The ex-Walthamstow bogie cars, which kept them company at Telford

Avenue, were even faster. Sadly they rode abominably and could be heard a mile off! A legacy of the municipal boundary, the overhead wires were insulated at the boundary between the two operators. The section on the LCC side must have been close to the limit for current supply. At night, if more than two cars were climbing the relatively gentle incline from the Graveney Bridge to Streatham Common simultaneously the lights dimmed.

From your correspondent's stop the tram continued its southbound journey towards Purley by squeezing under Norbury railway bridge, where the roadway had to be lowered before through running with top covered cars could begin. Then it climbed the gentle gradient between the rows of shops contemporary with the opening of the tramway and past England's first pedestrian-operated traffic lights, installed in 1932. Although less than half a mile away, the next stop at Tylecroft Road was also a fare stage. The LCC datum for fare stages was the 'London Terminus'; Croydon worked from North End in the town centre. Thus, in the 'collision' of the two systems, the inevitable happened and this fare stage was shorter than its fellows.

Past the shops, the residences had long front gardens, provoking the thought that road widening for reserved track would have been possible at the expense of removing the drastically pollarded plane trees flanking the road, their roots corrugating the asphalt pavement. The pavements through the shopping areas between Norbury and the Pond were wider than usual, so loading islands would have been feasible at stops to eliminate the nuisance and potential danger of crossing the inner carriageway to board a tram. Along this stretch the stops were well spaced. There was a crossover at the next request stop and yet a third at Warwick Road; the first of these, south of Norbury railway bridge, was replaced with plain track around 1947. Badly sited on the gradient, your correspondent never saw it used. Croydon had been as addicted to crossovers as the LCC.

In tramway days the Pond at Thornton Heath did exist, not as a grassed roundabout, the quiet surrounding road providing sanctuary for the northern terminus of the local bus routes. These duplicated the tram route southwards all the way to Purley and continued beyond the Croydon boundary. During the rush hours it also served as the terminus of the frequent short-workings of bus route 115 to the factories along Purley Way. For the rest of the day a quarter hourly service on the 115 was more than adequate.

Before it was demolished for rebuilding as a bus garage at the start of 1950, one had to be quick to look through the narrow entrance into the depot as the tram passed. The adjacent Brigstock Villas, the former HQ of Croydon Corporation Tramways, disappeared at the same time. Most of the cars, the ex-Croydon bogie trams 375, 377–395 & 397–399, together with the ex-LCC E/3s 1904–1912, were transferred to Purley Depot for the remaining life of services 16–18 and 42. One consequence of this change was the need to provide new fare timetables to include the extra stages for cars coming from Purley to work service 42. These E/3s were the only ex-LCC cars to run regularly on service 16/18. When the Felthams began their migration to Leeds, they were replaced with ex-Leyton E/3s following the abandonment of the services operated by Wandsworth Depot.

Southbound, the single trailing point leading to the narrow entrance of Thornton Heath Depot was followed immediately by the junction with the single track and loop branch to Thornton Heath High Street, exclusive to service 42. It was notable as the last London Transport tram service, which did not use any ex-LCC track. Consequently it used the overhead entirely. Connecting densely populated residential areas with the retail and commercial centre of Croydon, service 42 cars ran every 3 minutes, making it one of the most frequent services on the system. Moreover, it was reputed to be profitable. So the next stage of the journey from the Pond to central Croydon saw up to 35 trams per hour in each direction.

At West Croydon trolleybus overhead for the 630 and 654 services crossed the tramway at right angles and green LT country buses on services 405, 409, 411 and 414 turned left from their terminus beside the railway station to parallel the tramway for the remainder of the route to Purley. Here the main shopping area through North End and the High Street began. Fewer poles of the overhead obstructed the pavements, as some span wires were secured to rosettes on building frontages instead.

One department store was on the site of the original shop owned by Joshua Allder, who was also a director of the Croydon Tramways Company, when it began horse tram services in late Victorian times. One of Allder's staff was also authorised to act as an occasional ticket inspector on the tramway.

The road narrowed beside the Elizabethan Whitgift almshouses, enforcing the only length of single track on the 16/18 route. Unfortunately, this section also included the road junction with George Street, which was controlled by traffic lights. By 2010, the buildings opposite the almshouses had been demolished to widen North End, which is now pedestrianised. Here the second generation trams of Croydon Tramlink on their way from George Street to Crown Hill cross the route your correspondent is describing. The Victorian Town Hall, built on the site of Croydon Central railway terminus, is now the Central Library. In front is a memorial to the 1914–18 war, notable in depicting unpleasant aspects of that conflict.

In the morning your correspondent alighted at West Croydon to walk along Waddon New Road, the shortest way to his workplace. Returning home, he went to Crown Hill for the stop outside the (now defunct) Grants Department Store. Besides lengthening the ride, this diversion enabled him to board before the crowd waiting at West Croydon. This time he expected a car from Thornton Heath Depot, either route number 11 or 13 (every tram on a specific service had a route number within a single sequence, regardless of depot allocations).

In the evening rush the conductor had an easier time as cancelling workman return tickets did not involve a cash transaction. The car was busier than in the morning, because many factory and office workers left at about the same time, but the shops were already closed. The journey time was about the same each way, as every request stop was likely to be called.

Included in this account are references to running numbers, described in LCC days as 'route' numbers (pronounced 'rowt' by tramway staff). Each tram depot sent out cars in a numerical order in compliance with the timetable. These numbers were displayed on the small blue plaques referred to in the account. Most members of the travelling public were unaware of the practice. In the London Transport era, contrary to LCC tradition, the words route (pronounced in the conventional manner) and service were practically interchangeable; they were used in the sense we understand today.

The comment about the variation in power supply either side of the former Croydon/LCC border brings to mind the fact that Croydon continued to generate power for trams in its area, while electricity supplies on the main system usually came from the former LCC power station at Greenwich. LPTB trams in

Car 1909 is depicted in North End, Croydon just before the junction with George Street on the right. Single track leads into the High Street. The Whitgift Hospital on the right of the picture was built in 1596 and still exists today; much of the area is now a pedestrian precinct. The modern Tramlink line crosses where the photographer is positioned. D.A.Thompson/LCCT Trust

west London were powered by the generating plant at Lots Road, Chelsea.

Alternating current was fed to substations, where AC was converted to DC at 550 volts to be distributed via section feeder pillars, placed every half mile along tram routes. The metal feeder boxes had switches which could isolate any section from the main supply. Although the system normally worked well, there were several incidences in the early years of the LPTB, when power supplies were just about adequate. At times of peak use, it was not unusual to witness a line of trams proceeding slowly with lights dimmed.

One feature of London life was the regular occurrence of winter fogs. Although romanticised by poets and song writers, the appearance of a dense blanket of fog played havoc with the transport system. Steerable vehicles, such as buses and trolleybuses, were frequently restricted to walking pace, as familiar landmarks and whole streets disappeared in the murk. Tube trains were normally the least affected, but on the surface the Southern Electric was handicapped by long stretches of manual semaphore signalling.

Tram conductors would assist their drivers by lighting a torch or flambeau, when the fog was particularly impenetrable. Progress was then limited to walking pace, as the conductor with torch aloft set out along the tramlines, trusting always that his tram was following behind. There are plenty of accounts of London tramcars being followed by a string of motorists all endeavouring to get home in one piece. On occasions like this they had cause to thank the trams and their alleged railbound limitations.

As was apparent, the trams with their fixed track gave a good account of themselves. This is revealed in the following extract from Gerald Druce's memories of a 'Foggy Day in London Town'.

Your correspondent assumes that the fog developed during the time he was indoors somewhere in the capital. Returning, he took the tube to the station then known as Charing Cross (now Embankment) and was fortunate to find tram No. 380, a rehabilitated Croydon bogie car, on service 18 optimistically showing the destination THORNTON HEATH POND, advertising the intention to return to the depot, a mile or more beyond his destination.

Outside the rush hours it was unusual to find many passengers travelling along the Embankment, that night the tram was almost empty, so his favourite place, the front bench seat upstairs, was vacant. The clear view from there was one of the best features of a 'rehab'. The shiny rails for a few metres ahead could be distinguished

in the light from the street lamps and the headlight struggling to penetrate the gloom, as the car gradually eased its way across Westminster Bridge. The journey was made before the special track layout for the Festival of Britain was constructed.

The difficult turn from the semi-reserved track over the bridge was safely negotiated, straight on at the right hand turnout for the Albert Embankment and Vauxhall, then to the next junction by Lambeth North tube station, where we needed to turn right. We cautiously progressed to 'The Horns' at Kennington, turning right there on the trailing junction to join the track from the Elephant and soon after, at the Oval, encountered two sets of facing points, going first to the left, then right into Brixton Road. Further on, the light from the shops in Brixton Road improved some illumination, but it was a different matter on the long climb up Brixton Hill. The long front gardens meant no illumination from the houses, the gas street lamps contributed little.

The difficult conditions experienced by bus drivers became apparent. Parked, nose to tail, were twenty-one buses abandoned in the inner lane. They had carefully kept clear of the tram tracks. For the tram driver a different problem arose. Up to now the road had been reasonably level, so the driver could coast as much as possible to minimise the danger of over-heating the resistances, but, even climbing the hill, the speed on the top series notch of the controller (the slower speed, about 8 to 10 mph, at which all the resistances were cut out) was too fast for these conditions. Fortuitously, the line of buses provided a visible background to prove that forward progress was maintained.

Eventually, the car arrived at Streatham change-pit, where the conductor could just see enough to locate the trolley on the overhead wire. Strangely, your correspondent does not recollect passing a tram in the opposite direction; nor can he vouch for any of the apocryphal stories claiming that a motorist following a tram in thick fog ended up in the depot!

The customary Christmas Message from the Chairman was printed in the December 1948 issue of the LONDON TRANSPORT MAGAZINE. Lord Latham praised his organisation's high tradition of service to the public. In the photo montage surrounding the text were 12 images of the Executive's activities over the past year. Attention was paid to the successful staging of the Olympic Games and the role the tubes in particular had played in transporting 98,000 people a day to the main events at Wembley. A picture appeared of the victorious LTE Tram & Trolleybus football

team, who had managed to win a national trophy for the first time in 44 years. Aside from this sporting achievement there was no mention of the tramways, which at the end of the year had 748 trams scheduled during the Monday to Friday peak periods. The system would live on for another three and a half years.

It can be argued that the ultimate fate of the London tramway system was sealed some years before the advent of the LPTB in 1933. The new organisation, under the direction of Lord Ashfield and Frank Pick, ensured the network then suffered a lingering demise. Although popular with the travelling public, the trolleybus turned out to be a stop gap measure, until it was later discarded in favour of the diesel bus, thereby ensuring that large sums of money were spent on not one but two abandonment programmes, which cleared electric traction from the streets of the capital and added to the vehicle exhaust emissions problem.

George Gundry, sometime resident of Kingston-upon-Thames, keen observer of the local tramway scene and regular visitor to the Continent in the 1920s and 1930s, enquired of an official in Paris what were the reasons for that city's tramways being abandoned. The answer he received was short and sharp: 'La politique, la finance!' On this side of the Channel many politicians at both local and national levels, irrespective of party affiliation, had enthusiastically promoted anti-tram propaganda. Herbert Morrison, once a fervent supporter of London's municipal tramways, effectively abandoned them to their fate. He decided on a strictly business model for the new LPTB, which in many respects gave the blueprint for the nationalised industries created by the postwar Labour government.

Lord Ashfield, Frank Pick and the rest of the Board members endorsed the findings of the 1931 Royal Commission. They allowed wasteful competition between buses and trams on trunk routes into the capital. Most damning of all, they decided that major investment in rolling stock, improved passenger facilities and modernised track layouts, to include segregated rights of way, would never happen. The results of these ill considered decisions remain with us today.

A wonderfully atmospheric image captures a typical London fog, as it swirls round car 1363 at Blackfriars on the night of 7th December 1935. This vehicle will shortly reverse at Somerset House on the Embankment and will then probably head back on route 66 to Forest Hill. The tram behind on route 36 will continue to Abbey Wood.
Getty Images

END OF THE LINE

THE EXTINCTION of London's tramways was postponed by the advent of the Second World War. It was originally planned that the tram network would survive until 1942/3. After hostilities had ceased, a period of austerity, characterised by shortages of manufactured goods, meant that the supply of new buses was delayed. The events of the years 1949–52, which encompass the rundown of the tramways until the closure of final routes in South London, are described in detail in companion volume LONDON TRAMWAY TWILIGHT.

There was no love lost for the trams at 55 Broadway, SW1, headquarters of the London Transport Executive. In fact, their continued presence on the streets of the capital was viewed as something of an embarrassment. Rebuilding the metropolitan infrastructure after the destruction of wartime bombing included the 'modernisation' of the transport system; this process found no place for the railbound vehicles. All of which was in stark contrast to what was happening in the rest of war torn Europe.

The author's father, who was a civil engineer attached to the Allied Control Commission, found it strange that he was now actively engaged in approving the repair and reinstatement of tramways as part of the postwar planning of German towns, rather than ripping them up, as was the case in his native land.

Since the change in policy from trolleybuses to diesel buses in 1946, preparations for the conversion programme had continued apace. Depots had to be reconstructed as bus garages and routes altered to suit new traffic arrangements, although problems arose again in finding suitable terminal arrangements for the replacement vehicles. The intention to integrate new bus services within the existing network was only partly fulfilled. The traditional tram route structure was retained to a large extent. Critics were quick to point out that opportunities had been missed in the staged replacement programme, which was to commence in 1950.

The LTE publicity machine fed local news media with variations of the core anti-tram propaganda of the 1930s. They were successful in creating a posture where few people had a good word to say about the maligned trams; the vehicles that had served their communities for decades now firmly belonged to the past. Londoners were in a hurry to get to the future and, in doing so, they conveniently forgot about cheap fares and the fact that there always seemed to be a tram in sight, even in the worst of weathers, especially in adverse conditions such as fog and snow. Environmental concerns, including the pollution from exhaust fumes emitted by hundreds of new buses, appear to have merited a low priority. Certainly, the imminent wholesale abandonment of electric traction on South London's streets stirred no dissenting voices in official circles.

The postwar conversion programme began on 1st October 1950 with the withdrawal of tram routes 12, 26, 28, 31 and 34, plus trolleybus route 612. In the process Wandsworth Depot lost its electrically powered inmates. The brave new transport world also hit passengers in their pockets with the simultaneous withdrawal of workmen's fares, return and transfer tickets, which had been a feature of tram travel. The die was cast and stage one was followed at intervals of around three months by further tram service withdrawals. Stage eight saw the end of the system on 5th July 1952.

Each conversion stage prompted farewell celebrations. Tram enthusiasts, who were by now pretty familiar with last nights, recorded on film the passing of their favourite vehicles. The size of the crowds of onlookers varied according to the locality and many folk turned out, in the words of one newspaper reporter, 'to give the battle scarred warriors of the streets a right royal send off'. By now the public mood had mellowed somewhat and the respect given to the departing tramcars was akin to that

Victoria Embankment bound car 1954 stops for passengers in Loampit Vale, Lewisham just round the corner from the High Street. At this compulsory tram stop, traffic halts to allow a mother and child to reach the pavement. In the intervening years this location has been completely redeveloped in connection with the construction of a new transport interchange, featuring a bus station, Lewisham Rail Station and the Docklands Light Railway terminus. A. V. Mace

above An E/3 class car on route 46 meets a new RT bus at Lewisham Clock Tower at the former junction of tram routes to Catford and Greenwich. After the demise of the trams a one way scheme with traffic lights was instituted here. A. V. Mace

right Dusk at Southwark Bridge terminus. Trams crossing this bridge played a minor role in the 1947 Ealing Studios comedy '*Hue and Cry*'. London Transport Museum

accorded a terminally ill relative. The press and the cinema newsreels exploited the nostalgia theme. Column inches were given over to personal reminiscences dating back to horse tram days. Accounts of romantic encounters on Edwardian top decks shaded the valedictory tone of the stories. However, from reading the reports it appeared nobody seriously doubted the wisdom of the whole tramway abandonment process. Right at the death a fitting tribute did emerge in the form of a film entitled THE ELEPHANT WILL NEVER FORGET, which is now widely regarded as one of the finest documentaries of the era and has subsequently garnered many awards. Finally, London's trams had their place in the sun.

A fiery end awaited most members of the fleet at what was nicknamed 'the tramatorium' just off Penhall Road, Charlton. Here a yard had been laid out with storage

above County Hall forms the backdrop to this scene on Westminster Bridge. Both cars are E/3 class vehicles, engaged on Kingsway Subway duties. A. V. Mace

right A car working Kingsway Subway route 35 pulls up behind a sister vehicle at the Elephant and Castle. Many buildings hereabouts were lost in the Blitz. Note the attire of the pedestrians – everyone appears to be in their Sunday best. London Transport Museum

tracks to receive the doomed vehicles. The scrappers went to work with a will on each new intake of cars evicted from their depots by the conversion programme. The 737 trams scheduled in active service at the end of 1949 had dwindled to 323 by New Year's Day 1952. In contrast the motor bus strength at the end of 1952 was quoted at 7325 vehicles.

After the rails fell silent, conditions in the scrap metal market made it financially favourable to pull up miles of tramlines. The *laissez faire* attitude of pre-war days, where long stretches of redundant track were simply covered over by asphalt, was not repeated. This time a thorough job was done to eradicate all traces of the trams. A lone relic was spared. The northern portal of the Kingsway Subway still stands today. It acts as a fitting reminder of a transport system, which at the peak of its efficiency, served London so well.

above Romney Road, Greenwich displays a surfeit of public transport. Car 1856, working from New Cross Depot on route 38 to Abbey Wood, accelerates past an RT type bus on route 53. Apart from the loss of the tramway, this scene remains unchanged today. A. V. Mace

left A Walthamstow 'rocket' – fast, furious and very noisy – car 2050 heads through New Cross on its way to Woolwich. London Transport Museum

right A standard E/1 class tram is depicted on route 6 at Southwark Bridge. In peak periods fifty-three trams an hour departed from here on services 6, 10, 46, 48, 52 and 60.
London Transport Museum

below A wet day in south London is enlivened by the appearance of a Feltham and an E/1 rehab, both working peak hour extras. The length of the Feltham permits the display of two separate advertisements.
London Transport Museum

APPENDIX

MAPS

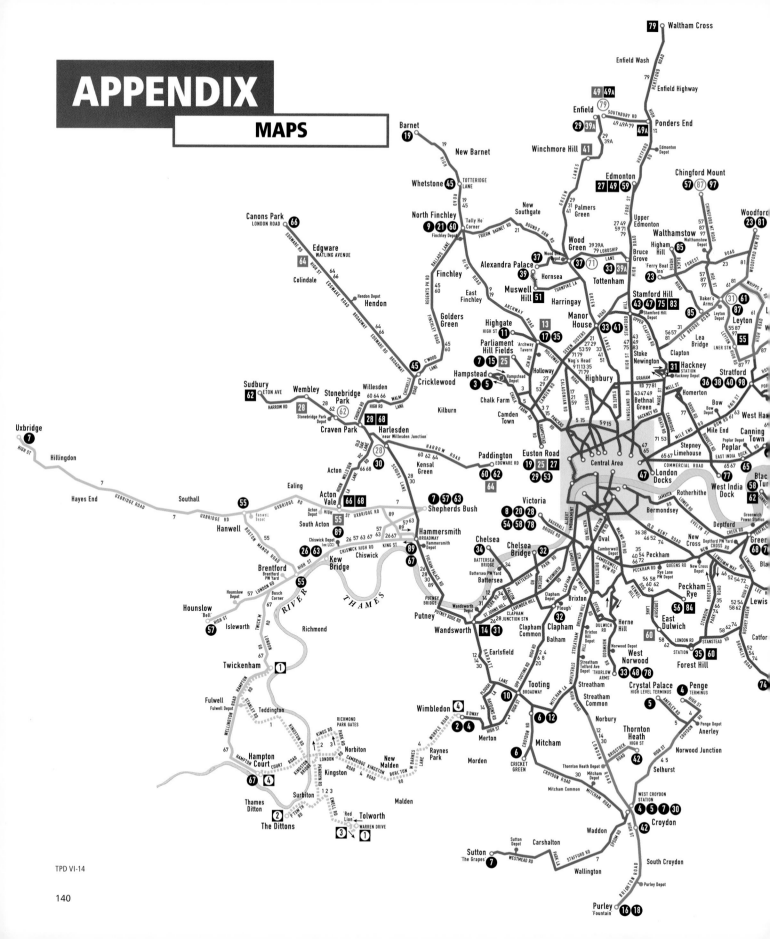

LONDON PASSENGER TRANSPORT BOARD TRAMWAYS

at their maximum extent
July 1933

updated with October 1934
revised route numbers

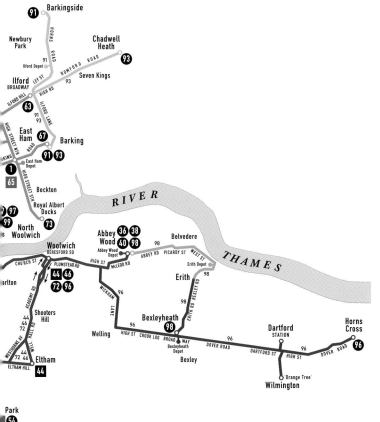

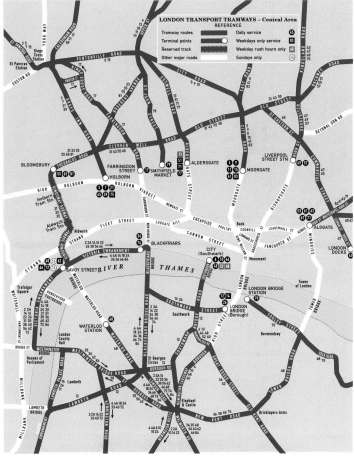

APPENDIX

MUNICIPAL AND COMPANY TRAMWAYS ABSORBED BY THE LPTB

As MINISTER OF Transport, Herbert Morrison, was obliged to use official sources when formulating plans for a unified system of public transport for London. He obtained his tramway information from the Annual Returns for 1928–29, which would have reached his desk at the end of January 1930. This official Ministry of Transport document covered all UK tramway and trolleybus undertakings. As regards the metropolitan area, the facts and figures contained therein fairly represent the apogee of the network, before operations were run down.

In historical terms London's tramways had virtually ceased expanding by the outbreak of the First World War. However, the LCC built several extensions in the period 1920–32; the last being Westhorne Avenue, Eltham, which for obvious reasons does not figure in the 1928–29 Return. It should be noted that Barking Council abandoned tramway operation in 1929, as it was hopelessly uneconomic to continue. The council did lease two sections of track to East Ham and Ilford respectively, in order to maintain service connections with the outside world.

All tramways on this list were built to standard gauge (4ft 8½ins/1435mm), and were electrically powered. The total route mileage does not include depot or service tracks.

An ordinary adult average fare is quoted; the equivalent workman fare was usually about half that of the ordinary average. Expenditure figures were based on the Tramways Revenue and Capital Accounts, which were submitted annually to the Ministry.

MUNICIPAL

Barking Urban District Council Tramways:

1.58 route miles; 5 trams;
485,303 passengers carried;
0.95d average fare per mile;
14.21d traffic income per car mile;
26.42d working expenditure per car mile.
(0.49 route miles leased to East Ham; 0.76 route miles leased to Ilford).

Bexley U. D. C. Tramways & Dartford Light Railways Joint Committee:

10.29 route miles; 33 trams;
8,053,795 passengers carried;
1.03d average fare per mile;
18.22d traffic income per car mile;
15.01d working expenditure per car mile.

Croydon Corporation Tramways:

9.28 route miles; 55 trams;
17,172,578 passengers carried;
0.85d average fare per mile;
12.75d traffic income per car mile;
12.24d working expenditure per car mile.

East Ham Corporation Tramways:

8.34 route miles; 55 trams;
21,804,654 passengers carried;
0.93d average fare per mile;
13.34d traffic income per car mile;
10.89d working expenditure per car mile.

Erith Urban District Council Tramways:

5.42 route miles; 19 trams;
5,371,644 passengers carried;
0.78d average fare per mile;
15.27d traffic income per car mile;
18.45d working expenditure per car mile.

Ilford Corporation Tramways:

7.15 route miles; 38 trams;
15,880,953 passengers carried;
0.91d average fare per mile;
16.59d traffic income per car mile;
12.74d working expenditure per car mile.

Leyton Corporation Tramways
(leased to the LCC):

8.82 route miles.

London County Council Tramways:

166.28 route miles; 1,817 trams;
713,035,141 passengers carried;
0.56d average fare per mile;
14.62d traffic income per car mile;
12.38d working expenditure per car mile.

Walthamstow Urban District Council Tramways:

8.93 route miles; 64 trams;
23,687,260 passengers carried;
0.83d average fare per mile;
13.00d traffic income per car mile;
11.25d working expenditure per car mile.

West Ham Corporation Tramways:

16.35 route miles; 127 trams;
55,066,664 passengers carried;
1.00d average fare per mile;
15.21d traffic income per car mile;
12.55d working expenditure per car mile.

COMBINE

London United Tramways Company:

45.87 route miles;
190 trams;
68,193,967 passengers carried;
0.90d average fare per mile;
16.32d traffic income per car mile;
14.13d working expenditure per car mile.

Metropolitan Electric Tramways Company:

53.46 route miles;
313 trams;
107,605,629 passengers carried;
0.91d average fare per mile;
13.56d traffic income per car mile;
13.20d working expenditure per car mile.

South Metropolitan Electric Tramways & Lighting Company:

13.08 route miles;
52 trams;
12,979,981 passengers carried;
0.97d average fare per mile;
15.73d traffic income per car mile;
13.99d working expenditure per car mile.

APPENDIX
ROLLING STOCK

TRAMCARS WERE built to last. In the first decade of the 20th century the new electric vehicles represented the state of the art in craftsmanship. Their appearance and livery styles reflected municipal or company pride. Bodywork was constructed mainly of wood; this was supported by metal running gear, which conformed to an accepted pattern of either a four wheel (single truck) or an eight wheel (bogie) model. Both types usually sported two electric motors fed from an overhead wire. Connection to the overhead was by means of a trolley pole. Many covered top trams had two trolley poles, one for each direction of travel. LCC experiments with bow collectors and pantographs on the Downham to Grove Park section were not pursued by the LPTB.

The LCC made a determined effort to eliminate open top cars from the fleet. For many operators clearances beneath overbridges were one good reason for retaining open tops. Throughout the capital many roadways were lowered under railway bridges to accommodate covered top tramcars.

In London there was the added complication of the conduit system (qv) of current collection. Many ex-municipal tramcars never possessed equipment for conduit operation. All trams, company or municipal, engaged in through services with the LCC were dual equipped for trolley and conduit.

Much of the fleet inherited by the LPTB in 1933 looked distinctly old fashioned, when compared to the latest buses and trolleybuses. Hard wooden seats, coupled with open platforms, open balconies on the top deck and sometimes no top deck cover at all, were hardly calculated to attract passengers desirous of upholstered comfort. The very longevity of the tramcar worked against it. The stark truth was that lack of investment in the renewal and replacement of rolling stock eventually proved fatal. Double deck vehicles were the norm; the layout of each car was configured for a crew of two people – the motorman and the conductor. A positive aspect was that trams in London could be driven from either end, thus obviating the need for turning loops

or intricate reversal procedures. Trams were never equipped with horns; a foot operated gong sufficed to warn other road users.

Since all traffic in the UK keeps to the left, the entrances and staircases were positioned accordingly to accept passengers boarding or alighting at the rear of the vehicle. The only exception to this rule occurred at Holborn and Aldwych tram stations, where passengers using the Kingsway Subway entered and disembarked at the driver's end of the car. Just after the First World War there were proposals to alter the rule of the road to conform with continental Europe; however, London and the rest of the country remained very firmly insular in its outlook. It has also to be said, in the context of modern tramcar construction across the globe, this insularity dictated that the traditional British double deck tramcar represented an evolutionary dead end as regards vehicle design.

Some half hearted experiments involving single deck trams, with a front entrance and a single crew member, acting as driver/conduc-

Car 290 was inherited from the former West Ham fleet. It was posed outside Charlton Works for an official photo. It has been beautifully restored and will eventually take its place among the collection of historic vehicles, which now resides at the London Transport Museum in Covent Garden. It has since been repainted in full West Ham Corporation Tramways colours.
London Transport Museum

tor, had been conducted by the old London United Company. The concept of one man operation on lightly trafficked routes did not prove viable in the 1920s. In many respects the idea was years ahead of its time, but unfortunately, the LUT did not possess the resources to develop the project further. The Combine's one long term success was the introduction of the Felthams. These all enclosed vehicles had separate entrances and exits, which were positioned to speed up passenger flow through the vehicle at tram stops.

Details of the post war fleet are given in LONDON TRAMWAY TWILIGHT. For the final 14 years of operation the London system relied solely on bogie cars to transport passengers. Of the last single truck cars, scrapped in the spring of 1938, car **290** (ex-West Ham car 102) was preserved and is now part of the London Transport Museum collection. The only other four wheel London tram in captivity is LCC Class B car 106, which entered the LPTB fleet as snowbroom **022**. This open top tram is now preserved at Crich.

Before the demise of the smaller single truck vehicles, the bulk of the eight wheel fleet had already adopted a body style very much based on the standard LCC bogie car. Throughout the 1930s efforts were made to provide windscreens for previously unvestibuled trams, but this upgrade by the LPTB took time and it is noticeable that even on the last tram to trolleybus conversion in the summer of 1940, there were still appreciable numbers of unvestibuled cars in service. Driver's windscreens are variously referred to as vestibules or platform screens. After overcoming opposition from the Metropolitan Police, the effect of their installation was to make life more comfortable for crews and passengers, especially in cold or inclement weather. Unfortunately, windscreen wipers on London trams were conspicuous by their absence, although some drivers perfected ingenious arrangements, whereby hand operated wipers cleared rain from the swivelling panes of the windscreen.

Each tramcar had to carry a Metropolitan Stage Carriage (MSC) licence plate. All trams, buses and taxis were required to submit to an annual police inspection to verify the vehicle's roadworthiness.

The reconditioning or 'rehab' scheme of 1932–37, as discussed in PENNYFARE of August 1934, was intended to give at least some semblance of modernity to the fleet. A group of trams numbered **936, 692, 1001, 1038** and **1144** formed part of the first experimental batch of vehicles, before the main scheme was implemented. The plan was to recondition 250 cars of Class E/1, that had been constructed between 1907 and 1912. In practice the accelerated pace of the trolleybus conversion programme meant that only 150 trams passed through Charlton Works. Each reconstruction cost around £400; however, the original trucks and motors were retained. Although the maximum traction type bogies were efficient and well engineered, they ensured that the 'rehabs' retained their 1907 riding qualities. The opportunity was lost to instal more modern equipment. The fleet numbers of rehab or reconditioned vehicles are given at the end of the rolling stock section.

The arrangement of driving controls on London's trams was very conventional, harking back to the early days of electric traction. Trams relied upon magnetic track brakes for service stops. Although reliable in all types of weather, this system had the serious disadvantage of being very noisy and hard wearing on the rails. Around 1925, Croydon Corporation equipped their 1902 bogie cars with air brakes, in the vain hope that the LCC would accept them on through route 16/18. They continued with air brakes for the rest of their existence, running local route 42.

The Felthams, LCC Luxury car **1**, standard E/1 cars **1103** and **1104** and 'Bluebell' car **2255** also had air brakes. Car **1103** was wrecked on 25th March 1934 in an accident at Eltham Green. The manner of its demise highlighted the inexperience of London's tramway workers with air operated brakes. Having dewired and lost its trolley head at Well Hall Circus, car **1103** was coupled to car **988**, with the latter pushing. The duty inspector ignored the rule, whereby stricken trams should be pushed to the nearest crossover, in order to be shunted and then towed in the correct fashion. He instructed both crews to head for Lee Green change pit, where the disabled vehicle could pick up power again on the conduit.

Unfortunately, the 'pusher' braked sharply at the junction of Westhorne Avenue and Eltham Road and the steel-stranded tow rope (allegedly tested by the LCC to withstand a 10 ton breaking strain) failed. With no electric power to operate magnetic or air brakes, car **1103** broke free of its moorings, sailed across the junction, derailed and capsized, when it struck the kerb on the other side of Eltham Road. Four stubborn passengers had defied the inspector and had remained on board. They sustained injuries, but, luckily, there were no fatalities.

Personal observation by Dr Gerald Druce suggested that the Maley & Taunton air brakes on the ex-LCC vehicle (Bluebird) operated more smoothly than those on the Felthams. Car 1's air brake could not be applied whilst the controller handle was on a power notch. The air brake on the Felthams operated in the converse manner to the automatic compressed air brakes provided on railway trains. As the Felthams ran as single units, there was no need to allow for failed couplings, so air under pressure was admitted into the cylinder to press the brake shoes against the wheels. Hence the system did not fail to safety, if air pressure was lost. Leakage was not a danger during the brief time at service stops, even on gradients, but questionable for longer periods such as the layover at termini. Having roller bearings on all axles, the cars were free running, so a loss of air pressure in the brake cylinder, when stationary on even a slight gradient could be serious. This happened at Leeds, when car 507 (ex-LPTB **2070**, ex-MET 324) ran away at Roundhay, on 4th September 1952, while the driver was absent. Ironically, about 1948 this car was one of the first trams to be fitted by London Transport with quick release to exhaust the brake cylinder more rapidly in order to release the brake shoes upon starting.

The Felthams were equipped with two 70hp motors. In the years following the First World War the LCC had begun to fit

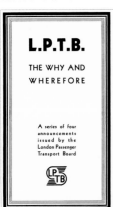

more powerful traction motors. These were intended to speed up the service in response to bus competition. Two English Electric 525 volt, 63hp motors were fitted to many standard E/1 cars. Other vehicles of the same class received Metropolitan Vickers MV 124 motors rated at 61hp. The two HR cars **1852** and **1853**, plus the whole of the ensuing HR/2 class had four motors. In response to their 'hilly route' designation, each bogie contained two 35hp motors, connected electrically in series. The HR class had equal wheel bogies instead of the standard maximum traction truck of two driving wheels and two smaller pony wheels.

Some of the slowest cars in the fleet were from the **552–601** series. Although their bodies were constructed new in 1929–30, they inherited the trucks and electrical equipment from scrapped single deck, Kingsway Subway trams of classes F and G. They possessed two 42hp motors.

The original intention was to repaint all trams in the standard LPTB red and cream livery, but for various practical reasons this did not happen. It was obvious from the initial rolling stock reports that the unsatisfactory condition of some vehicles merited a quick withdrawal; therefore they were spirited away, still wearing their old paint schemes. From mid-1934 onwards the well known LONDON TRANSPORT fleet name in gold lettering was applied to the waist panel of each vehicle. Fleet numbers, also in gold edged in black, were applied in the range **1** to **2529**; vehicles acquired from the LCC retained their original numbers.

Advertising material displayed on tramcars provided a useful way of generating extra revenue. The LPTB encouraged this commercial activity by exhorting potential advertisers to use tram sides and dash boards to promote their wares. The result was that vehicles certainly looked more colourful. Rates in 1936 for a 20 feet by 20 inches (6.096 metres by 508mm) full length side were fixed at 5 shillings (25p) per week. A smaller advert on the dash, measuring 20 inches by 30 inches (508mm by 762mm), was priced at 1 shilling and 6 pence (7½p) per week.

Vehicles listed are sometimes referred to as London's 'First Generation Trams'. The second and current generation are now in operation in the Croydon area; their fleet numbers 2530–2559 follow on from those of the LPTB. Modern London Tramlink tramcars seat 72 and can carry 174 standing passengers, whereas the traditional variety had seats for 50–60 on single truck cars, and for 73 on a standard E/1 bogie car. Type UCC/Feltham vehicles seated 64. Accommodation for standees varied according to the vehicle type, however, London's trams had a legendary capacity for absorbing crowds. In rush hours and, especially after sports meetings, trams were sometimes packed to the gunnels.

According to official figures the fleet carried 1,013,433,000 passengers in the financial year 1934–5. The number of service car miles run in the same year was 101,576,000. The average period between overhauls at Charlton, Hendon or West Ham was two years; each tram spent an average time of 13 days in the repair works.

The first section of the following rolling stock summary lists single truck cars and their provenance. Construction dates are quoted in brackets. Vehicles designated 'unvestibuled' retained open platforms and lacked driver's windscreens. The second section features larger bogie trams, which made up the bulk of the rolling stock. LPTB fleet numbers are quoted first in bold typeface, then reference is made to the previous numbers issued by former owners of each vehicle.

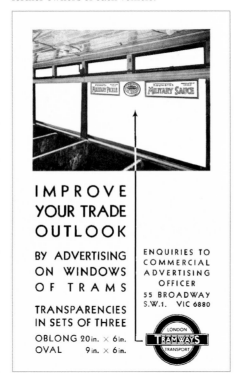

IMPROVE YOUR TRADE OUTLOOK

BY ADVERTISING ON WINDOWS OF TRAMS

ENQUIRIES TO COMMERCIAL ADVERTISING OFFICER 55 BROADWAY S.W.1. VIC 6880

TRANSPARENCIES IN SETS OF THREE

OBLONG 20 in. × 6 in.
OVAL 9 in. × 6 in.

Although care has been taken to verify numbers and dates, official records dating to the 1930s can and do contain mistakes. LPTB policy was to dispose of surplus vehicles by having them scrapped, however, there were some escapees, which were sold and then survived in fields and gardens to begin a second career as temporary accommodation or storage facilities.

London tramcars often inspired feelings akin to affection from their crews. In company with steam engines and ocean liners, they were always referred to as 'she'. As the rolling stock matured with age, the motorman would sometimes remark 'the old girl is in fine fettle this morning' when everything was going to plan. In contrast, the replacing buses and trolleybuses were deemed quite soulless!

4-Wheel, Single Truck Tramcars

5–27. *Ilford Corporation Tramways 1–23*. Top covered, open balcony, unvestibuled. Cars 1–6 (1920), 7–16 (1921), 17–20 (1922), 21–23 (1930). Scrapped in 1938.

28–30, 32. *Ilford Corporation Tramways 24–26, 28 (1909)*. Top covered, open balcony, unvestibuled. 30 scrapped in 1937, rest in 1938.

31. *Ilford Corporation Tramways 27 (1912)*, acquired from Barking Council Tramways in 1914. Top covered, open balcony, unvestibuled. Scrapped in 1938.

33–40. *Ilford Corporation Tramways 33–40 (1932)*. Enclosed top deck, unvestibuled. Sold 1938 to Sunderland Corporation Tramways. Scrapped in 1954.

41–44. *Ilford Corporation Tramways 29–32 (1903)*. Top covered, open balcony, unvestibuled. Scrapped in 1937.

Because of differences in wheel profiles from the London norms, all the ex-Ilford trams remained on their home patch, working services 91 and 93.

48, 49, 53, 56–60. *East Ham Corporation Tramways 13, 15, 21, 24, 25, 27, 28, 30 (1901–03)*. Top covered, open balcony, unvestibuled. Cars **53** and **58** went to Abbey Wood Depot in 1934 to work service 98. Scrapped in 1935–6.

68, 69. *East Ham Corporation Tramways 44, 45 (1919)*. Top covered, open balcony, unvestibuled. Scrapped in 1936.

70. *East Ham Corporation Tramways 35 (1911)*, acquired from Barking Council Tramways in 1915. Top covered, open balcony, unvestibuled. Scrapped in 1936.

71–80. *East Ham Corporation Tramways 36–40, 46–50 (1921–22)*. Top covered, open balcony, unvestibuled. Scrapped in 1935–36.

With exception of the two trams sent to north Kent, these vehicles worked routes in the East End, especially local East Ham service 73.

211–258. *West Ham Corporation Tramways 1–26, 28–43, 45–50 (1904)*. Top covered, open balcony, unvestibuled. Car **234** scrapped in 1934, the rest in 1935–37.

259–267. *West Ham Corporation Tramways 51–59 (1905)*. Top covered, open balcony, unvestibuled. Car **259** had an enclosed top deck. Scrapped in 1937–38.

268–273. *West Ham Corporation Tramways 60–65 (1923–24)*. Enclosed top deck, unvestibuled. Scrapped in 1937–38.

274–281. *West Ham Corporation Tramways 86–93 (1906)*. Top covered, open balcony, unvestibuled. Scrapped in 1937–38.

282–288. *West Ham Corporation Tramways 94–100 (1906)*. Top covered, open balcony, unvestibuled. Scrapped in 1937–38.

289–294. *West Ham Corporation Tramways* 101–106 (1910). Top covered, open balcony, unvestibuled. Car **290** was preserved by London Transport. The rest scrapped in 1937–38.

These vehicles spent their lives in the East End. At least one ex-West Ham single truck car was tried out on former Ilford tracks, but because of technical difficulties, the experiment was unsuccessful.

345–347, 349. *Croydon Corporation Tramways* Class W/1. 1–3, 5 (1911). Open top, unvestibuled. Car **349** was transferred to work service 98 in Erith. Scrapped in 1935–6.

355. *Croydon Corporation Tramways* Class W/1. 11(1906). Open top, unvestibuled. Scrapped in 1934.

Aside from car **349**, these vehicles usually worked local services 4 and 5.

1427–1440, 1442, 1443, 1445, 1447–1476, 1677–1726. *LCC* Class M (1910). Enclosed top deck, unvestibuled. Cars **1715**, **1723** and **1726** had enclosed top decks and platform screens. Scrapped in 1934–38.

Solidly built and arguably the best of the single truck trams inherited by the LPTB, these vehicles worked in east London, on north Kent services 96 and 98 and very occasionally on services 36/38/44 and 46 from Abbey Wood Depot.

2004–2024, 2031–2041. *Walthamstow Corporation Tramways* 1–32 (1905). Top covered, open balcony, unvestibuled. Scrapped in 1936–37.

2025–2030. *Walthamstow Corporation Tramways* 33–38 (1910). Top covered, open balcony, unvestibuled. Scrapped in 1937.

Walthamstow single truck cars worked East End joint routes and local services 23 and 85.

The following vehicles were transferred to LPTB ownership, but were never renumbered, although some were repainted in London Transport livery. Suffix letters were applied to original fleet numbers:

C = Bexley,
D = Erith,
E = Croydon,
S = South Metropolitan (SMET).

1C–16C. *Bexley Council Tramways* Class A (1903–4). Open top, unvestibuled. Scrapped in 1933–34.

17C–33C. *Bexley Council Tramways* Class B (1903). Enclosed top decks, unvestibuled, acquired from the LCC in 1914–18. Scrapped in 1933–34.

1D–6D, 9D. *Erith Council Tramways* (1906). Open top, unvestibuled. Scrapped in 1933–34.

7D, 8D, 10D–14D. *Erith Council Tramways* (1906). Top covered, open balcony, unvestibuled. All seven cars received ex-Croydon Brill 21E trucks. They were repainted in LPTB livery, but not renumbered in the main London Transport series. Scrapped in 1935–36.

6E–20E. *Croydon Corporation Tramways* (1906–07). Open top, unvestibuled. Scrapped in 1933–34.

1S–15S. *SMET* Type J/1 (1906). All cars repainted in LPTB livery. Open top, unvestibuled. Scrapped in 1935–36.

17S–25S. *SMET* Type K/2 (1902). Open top, unvestibuled, Scrapped in 1934.

36S–46S, 48S–51S. *SMET* Type M (1906). Open top, unvestibuled. Scrapped in 1936.

17S, 21S, 47S, 52S. *SMET* Type P (1901–07). Open top, unvestibuled. Scrapped in 1934.

8-Wheel, Bogie Tramcars

1. *LCC* Luxury car (1931). All enclosed, intended as the forerunner of a new fleet, but the establishment of the LPTB intervened. Car christened 'Bluebird' on account of its blue and white livery. Repainted red and cream in 1938. Sold to Leeds in 1951. Saved for preservation, now at Crich, awaiting full restoration.

2. *London Transport* (1935). All enclosed, domed roof, complete rebuild of accident victim car 1370. Scrapped in 1952.

81–100. *East Ham Corporation* 51–70 (1927–28). Enclosed top deck, unvestibuled (later received platform screens). Worked first on East End trunk routes, then transferred to Abbey Wood Depot. Worked services 36/38, 44 and 46. Scrapped in 1952.

101–159. *LCC* Class HR/2. All enclosed. Conduit only, no trolley poles. Worked mainly on routes 11, 35 and Dog Kennel Hill services 56, 58, 60, 62 and 84. Cars **112**, **123–125**, **129–131**, **148** were destroyed by enemy action. Car **127** reconditioned after bomb damage in 1940. Rest scrapped in 1951–52.

160. *LCC* Class E/3. All enclosed. Conduit only, original equal wheel trucks removed for use under car 1. Often worked service 31. Scrapped in 1952.

161–210. *Leyton Council Tramways* [operated by the LCC] (1931) Class E/3. All enclosed. Worked service 29 and East End trunk routes, particularly service 61. Later transferred to south London. Car **192** was painted medium blue and cream in 1934. Experimental livery was not pursued and the car was repainted in standard colours. Scrapped in 1952–53. Car **179** was the last London tramcar to be sacrificed on 29th January 1953.

Car 2 has been claimed as London Transport's only 'new' tramcar. In fact it was a complete rebuild of badly damaged car 1370. Although sporting a fairly traditional body layout, a concession to modernity was the domed roof. *Roy Hubble/LCCT Trust*

unvestibuled. Cars **326**, **327** and **330** were later fitted with windscreens. They served as staff cars at the CRD in Charlton. **325** scrapped in 1947, **328** and **329** in 1949. Rest scrapped in 1951.

331–343. *West Ham Corporation Tramways* 125–137 (1925). Enclosed top deck, unvestibuled (later received platform screens). Like their sister cars all worked in the East End until transfer to south London. **331** scrapped in 1951. Rest scrapped in 1952.

344. *West Ham Corporation Tramways* 138 (1928). Enclosed top deck, unvestibuled (later received platform screens). Scrapped in 1952.

365–374. *Croydon Corporation Tramways* Class B/2. 21–30 (1902). Top covered, open staircases, unvestibuled. Worked Croydon local service 42. Scrapped in 1936.

375–399. *Croydon Corporation Tramways* Class E/1. 31–55 (1927–28). Enclosed top cover, unvestibuled (later received platform screens). Cars **376**, **379**, **380** and **398** reconditioned in November/December 1936. **396** damaged by enemy action in 1940. **376** destroyed by fire in 1945. Rest scrapped in 1951–52.

402–551. *LCC* Class E (1906). Enclosed top deck, unvestibuled. Cars **420** and **454** were rebuilt after accident damage. 420 was renumbered **1597** and reclassified E/1. It was scrapped in 1951. Rest scrapped in 1936–38.

above Part of the Leyton E/3 class, car 186 later found itself deployed in Southeast London. This tram retained its original windscreens, unlike many other members of its class, which were equipped with the less attractive Charlton Works wooden ones. It is pictured at Eltham Green. Note the 1930s tram shelter in the background.
Don Thompson/LCCT Trust

right West Ham car 68 was renumbered 295 by London Transport. This transformation was recorded on film outside the depot in Greengate Street. The Corporation Tramways livery was described as Munich lake/rich maroon and deep cream, with a red coloured diamond shape surrounding the headlamps.

295. *West Ham Corporation Tramways* 68 (1931). All enclosed. Worked in the East End and subsequently from Abbey Wood Depot on services 36, 38, 44 and 46. Scrapped in 1952.

296–312. *West Ham Corporation Tramways* 69–85 (1929–30). All enclosed. Worked in the East End until transferred to south London. **303** destroyed by enemy action. Scrapped in 1952.

313–324. *West Ham Corporation Tramways* 107–118 (1911). Top covered, open balcony, unvestibuled. Scrapped in 1938.

325–330. *West Ham Corporation Tramways* 119–124 (1925). Enclosed top deck,

552–601. *LCC* Class E/1 (1930). Enclosed top deck, unvestibuled (later received platform screens). New bodies with trucks and electrical gear from scrapped F and G class cars – The original LCC car 600 was retained as a works vehicle (qv). **583** and **597** were destroyed by enemy action. Rest scrapped in 1950–52.

602–751. *LCC* Class E (1906). Enclosed top deck, unvestibuled. Scrapped in 1936–38.

752–1426. *LCC* Class E/1 (1907–10). Enclosed top deck, unvestibuled (later some cars received platform screens). **826, 962, 972, 1023, 1028, 1241, 1351, 1371, 1373, 1394, 1403, 1421** were destroyed by enemy action. Car **1025** preserved by London Transport. Rest scrapped in 1939–52.

1441, 1444. *LCC* Class ME/3 (1932). All enclosed. Rebuilt from single truck Class M cars. LCC car 1446 was similarly rebuilt and renumbered **1370**. Car **1441** was destroyed by enemy action in 1944. Car **1444** scrapped in 1951 and car **1370** in 1952.

1477–1676. *LCC* Class E/1 (1911–12). Enclosed top deck, unvestibuled (later some cars received platform screens). **1490, 1515, 1523, 1524, 1526, 1536, 1543, 1575, 1578, 1580, 1586, 1591, 1600, 1649** were destroyed by enemy action. Car **1622** restored by LCC Tramways Trust volunteers and National Tramway Museum staff at Crich. Rest scrapped in 1939–52.

1727–1851. *LCC* Class E/1 (1922). Enclosed top deck, unvestibuled (later received platform screens). These cars were particularly associated with services operated by Clapham Depot. Cars **1736, 1799, 1807, 1808, 1821, 1825, 1842** were destroyed by enemy action. Rest scrapped in 1945–52.

1852. *LCC* Class HR/1 (1929). Enclosed top deck, unvestibuled (later received platform screens). Car destroyed in September 1940 raid on Camberwell Depot.

1853. *LCC* Class HR/2 (1929). Enclosed top deck, unvestibuled (later received platform screens). Car destroyed in September 1940 raid on Camberwell Depot.

1854–1903. *LCC* Class HR/2 (1930). Enclosed top deck, unvestibuled (later received platform screens). **1865, 1889, 1898–1903** lost in the Camberwell Depot raid of 1940. Car **1893** repaired with new top deck after bomb damage. Car **1858** preserved by P. J. Davis and it now resides at Carlton Colville. Rest scrapped in 1952.

Car 1852 was a one off. It formed the entirety of class HR/1. It is seen on route 60 at the top of the four track layout on Dog Kennel Hill. Unfortunately this vehicle had a relatively short career and it perished in an enemy air raid. Note the truck mounted plough carrier.

1904–2003. *LCC* Class E/3 (1930). Enclosed top deck, unvestibuled (later received platform screens). **1967, 1972, 1973, 1976, 1978, 1982, 1983, 1985** destroyed by enemy action. This class mainly worked Kingsway Subway routes 31, 33 and 35. Scrapped in 1952.

2042–2053. *Walthamstow Corporation Tramways* 51–62 (1926). Enclosed top deck, unvestibuled (later received platform screens). These fast cars were well travelled. They worked East End trunk routes, north London services and were later transferred to south London. **2044** and **2051** were wartime casualties. Rest scrapped in 1952.

2054–2061. *Walthamstow Corporation Tramways* 39–46 (1932). All enclosed. Had a similar career to the previous batch. Scrapped in 1952.

2066–2119. *Metropolitan Electric Tramways* Type UCC Feltham 319, 321–329, 332–375 (1930–31). All enclosed, driver's cabs, separate entrances and exits, air operated doors. These vehicles worked the north London trunk routes until transfer to Streatham Depot. At a length of 40ft 6ins (12.3 metres) over the fenders they were the longest trams in the fleet. **2109** and **2113** were destroyed by enemy action. **2067** and **2091** were scrapped in 1947–9. Rest sold to Leeds in 1950–51. Car **2099** was later preserved by London Transport. Car **2085** crossed the Atlantic to reside at the Seashore Electric Railway Museum in Maine; however, it was neglected and is now in an appalling condition. Rest of the MET Felthams scrapped in 1959.

2120–2165. *London United Tramways* Type UCC Feltham 351–396 (1930–31). Specifications as the MET batch. The LUT Felthams were supplied without conduit gear. They worked Hanwell Depot routes 7 and 55. Later transferred to south London. Car **2165** rode on trucks from car **2317** 'Poppy' and was chronically underpowered. **2122, 2130, 2163, 2165** scrapped in 1947–49. Cars **2144** and **2162** scrapped in 1951. Rest sold to Leeds in 1950–51. Scrapped in 1959.

2166. *Metropolitan Electric Tramways* Type UCC Experimental Feltham 320 (1929). All enclosed, driver's cabs, air operated doors. Worked the Finchley to Cricklewood service, until replaced by trolleybuses. As a non-standard vehicle it was considered surplus to requirements. Scrapped in September 1937.

2167. *Metropolitan Electric Tramways* Type UCC Experimental Feltham 330 (1929). All enclosed, driver's cabs, air operated doors. Transferred to south London in 1938. Scrapped in 1949.

2168. *Metropolitan Electric Tramways* Type UCC Experimental Feltham 331 (1930). All enclosed, driver's cabs, air operated centre doors. Sold to Sunderland in 1937. Preserved as MET 331 at Crich.

2169–2254. *Metropolitan Electric Tramways* Type H 2, 12, 22, 31, 46, 82, 237–316 (1910–12). Enclosed top deck, unvestibuled (later some 37 cars received platform screens). Some vehicles were reconstructed from earlier open top types. Car **2243** was the subject of a preservation attempt by the LRTL. Unfortunately, no

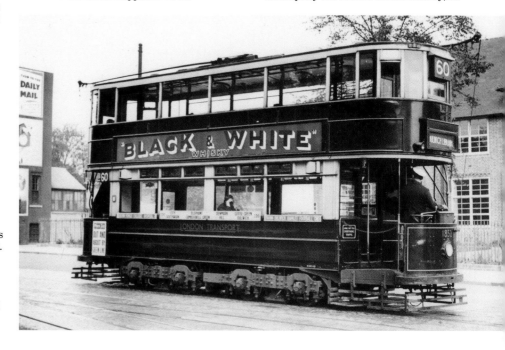

below The lower saloon of type G car 2265 looks inviting, if you can ignore the used tickets on the floor. Many LRTL members and north Londoners believed that the scrapping of the reconditioned ex-MET vehicles was a mistake, bearing in mind it was claimed they could have supplied more years of faithful service south of the River Thames.

top and above The type UCC, Feltham trams set a new standard in passenger comfort. Quite simply there were luxury vehicles on rails. There were heaters to take the chill off the ride home in winter. In the lower saloon a double row of comfortable seats leads to a platform with the stairs and entrance and exit doors. Beyond is the driver's cabin. The upper saloon, where the smokers congregated, is furnished with leather seats. Passengers sitting at the ends of the car had a fine view of the landscape, as the tram made progress in all weathers.
London Transport Museum

suitable accommodation could be found and the car was later scrapped. These trams worked in north London until 1939. Scrapped 1938–39.

2255. *Metropolitan Electric Tramways* 'Bluebell' 318 (1927). All enclosed, driver's cabs, platform doors. Rebuilt after accidental damage in 1928. Car was originally painted a medium blue colour. Worked former MET services 40 and 45. Claimed as London's first modern tram, but was non-standard. Scrapped in 1937.

2256–2260. *Metropolitan Electric Tramways* Type F 212–216 (1908). Enclosed top deck, unvestibuled (later received platform screens). Scrapped in 1938.

2261–2281. *Metropolitan Electric Tramways* Type G 217–236, 317 (1909). All enclosed. Scrapped in 1938–39.

2282–2301. *Metropolitan Electric Tramways* Type C/1 192–211 (1907–08). Enclosed top deck, unvestibuled (later received platform screens). Scrapped 1936–38.

2317. *London United Tramways* 'Poppy' 350 (1929). Enclosed top deck, unvestibuled driver's cabs. Constructed at Chiswick by the London General Omnibus Company, this vehicle resembled two NS type bus bodies stuck together. Worked former LUT service 57. Non-standard and scrapped in 1935. Trucks retained for use under **2165** (qv).

2318–2357. *London United Tramways* Type T 301–340 (1906). Top covered, open balcony, some cars unvestibuled. Once the pride of the LUT and nicknamed 'Palace Cars', because of their superior furnishings. Worked mainly on former LUT service 7. Scrapped in 1936.

2358–2402. *London United Tramways* Type U 151, 154, 158, 204, 205, 210, 212, 224, 235–6, 250–1, 255, 262, 265–74, 276–9, 281–7, 290–7, 299, 300 (1902). Top covered, open staircases, unvestibuled. Nicknamed 'influenza cars' because their poorly fitted top covers let in the wind and rain, they worked on former SMET route 7 and were then transferred to work the 'western' routes of the former MET. Scrapped in 1936.

top Quite frankly, there were some tramcars in the LPTB fleet that just looked plain unattractive. Although, of course, most folk in North Finchley would probably not have given a second glance to car 2407. Officially classed as a member of type WT, this former London United vehicle has been considerably reconstructed since its arrival in 1906. It was scrapped in August 1936.

above Official records state that car 2522 met its end in Hampstead Depot in November 1935. This photo proves that the health and safety rules in those days were pretty rudimentary! A few metal parts were salvaged, but the bulk of the wooden body was later burnt. With the exception of a few preserved vehicles the whole of the London tram fleet eventually ended up in this sorry state.
London Transport Museum

2403–2405. *London United Tramways* Type U/2 155, 199, 288 (1902). Top covered, open staircases, unvestibuled. Scrapped in 1936.

2406–2410. *London United Tramways* Type WT 157, 161, 211, 243, 261 (1902). Top covered, open balcony, unvestibuled. Scrapped in 1936.

2411. *London United Tramways* Type XU 247 (1902). Top covered, open staircases, unvestibuled. Scrapped in 1936.

2412. *Metropolitan Electric Tramways* Type A 77 (1904). Enclosed top deck, domed roof, unvestibuled. Nicknamed the 'Silver Queen' after being rebuilt in 1929 at Hendon Works. Scrapped in 1936.

2413–2466. *Metropolitan Electric Tramways* Type A 71–76, 78–81, 83–103, 105, 107–117, 119–122, 124–130 (1904). Top covered, open staircases, unvestibuled. Scrapped in 1935–36.

2467–2482. *Metropolitan Electric Tramways* Type B/2 3–5, 7, 9–11, 13, 15, 16, 19, 24, 26, 27, 30, 34 (1904–05). Top covered, open balcony, unvestibuled. Scrapped in 1935–36.

2483–2497. *Metropolitan Electric Tramways* Type C/2 151–165 (1907–08). Top covered, open balcony, unvestibuled. Scrapped in 1936.

2498–2521. *Metropolitan Electric Tramways* Type B 6, 14, 20, 38, 55, 62–64, 68, 70 (1904–05). Top covered, open balcony, unvestibuled. The full series of LPTB fleet numbers was never applied, as some vehicles retained their MET numbers until scrapping. Rest scrapped in 1935–36.

2522–2529. *London United Tramways* Type W 165, 173, 182, 185, 200, 240, 254, 259 (1902). Open top, unvestibuled. The most 'antique' looking vehicles to receive London Transport livery. Scrapped in 1935.

Bogie trams transferred to the LPTB, but never renumbered.

15D–18D. *Erith Council Tramways* (1902). Open top, unvestibuled. Acquired second hand from the LUT. Scrapped in 1933–34.

19D. *Erith Council Tramways* (1903). Top covered, open staircases, unvestibuled. Acquired second hand from Hull. Nicknamed 'The Tank' at Erith. Scrapped in 1933.

30S, **32S–34S**. *South Metropolitan Electric Tramways* Type O (1902). Open top, unvestibuled. Acquired second hand from Gravesend & Northfleet. Scrapped in 1934.

Walthamstow single deck, unvestibuled cars 47–50 were allocated **2062–2065** LPTB numbers, but never carried them.

Part of Fulwell Depot was used as the former LUT 'bone yard'. Instructions from on high in the Combine to clean up the place, in view of the impending arrival of important visitors to inspect the new trolleybuses, fell on deaf ears. A number of semi-derelict tramcars remained stubbornly in residence in the period 1931–34. These relics were disposed of very early in the LPTB regime. However, one of the LUT vehicles to survive is car 159, which has been restored to pristine condition at Crich.

Works Car Fleet

The average Londoner was probably unaware of the existence of the works car fleet. In the early years of electric traction the larger metropolitan tramway operators ensured that they possessed suitable auxiliary rolling stock to transfer stores and equipment between depots. Works trams fitted with water tanks helped still the dust and wash away the detritus on Edwardian streets. Water cars could also be fitted with carborundum blocks, which were lowered on to the track in order to smooth out corrugations and imperfections in the rail surface. These vehicles were known as rail grinders. Specialist functions performed by other cars included the transport of sand, wheels, axles and running gear between yards and repair facilities.

The Combine company tramways supplied a motley collection of rolling stock, including breakdown cars and engineering vehicles equipped with small cranes and chain hoists. Non-passenger trams with the highest public profile were the snowbrooms, which appeared in the depths of winter. The ex-LCC snowbrooms and ploughs were formerly passenger cars of classes B and C. The LPTB deemed snowbrooms more effective than the ploughs.

Many of the tasks allotted to works cars were later taken over by motor vehicles. Scrapping took place throughout the period 1933–38. Generally the ex-LCC fleet lasted

above Car 011 was designed as a wheel carrier in the former LCC fleet of works cars. As can be seen, this vehicle lacked trolley gear and could only work over conduit equipped lines. Its task was to carry wheel sets, miscellaneous running gear and electrical parts from depot to depot. There was precious little protection against the elements for the motorman. Car 011 is pictured in Woolwich Road, Charlton. D. A. Thompson/ LCCT Trust

below Snowbroom 048 was a former member of the LCC fleet. Here it is stationed at Stonebridge Park Depot. This car and others like it performed sterling service in keeping the tracks clear of snow and ice.

longer and many cars survived until the end of the system in 1952. All vehicles were four wheel, single truck, unless stated otherwise.

Former LCC Vehicles
016–037, 040–043, 048. LCC Snowbroom. **O22** preserved and restored as Class B car 106 at Crich.
038, 039, 044, 046, 047, 049–054. LCC Snow Plough. **037** and **048** converted in 1935 to snowbrooms.
01–04, 013, 014. LCC Rail Grinder.
05, 06. LCC Small Stores Van.
07–010. LCC Large Stores Van.

LCC Class G car 600 was the sole survivor of the former Kingsway Subway single deck trams. It was retained at Holloway Depot as a 'tool van'. Still painted in LCC livery, it was never renumbered as a LPTB vehicle. Richard Elliott, one time employee at Charlton Works, in conversation with the author, related that car 600 had been equipped temporarily with a trolley pole, in order that it could travel beyond the confines of the conduit system. No photographic or textual evidence has come to light to support this statement. However, it is certain that car 600 was used as a works vehicle in the first few months of the LPTB and as such may well have traversed overhead wire equipped lines.

Former Municipal Vehicles
055. *West Ham* Water Car.
1A. *West Ham* Water Car/Broom.
056. *Croydon* Welding Car.
363/19E. *Croydon* Snowbroom.
057. *Ilford* Water Car.
20D. *Erith* Water Car.
63K. *Walthamstow* Rail Grinder.

Former Combine Vehicles

02. *MET* Crane Car/Wheel Carrier. Bogie car.
04. *MET* Rail Grinder.
05. *MET* Sand Carrier.
07. *MET* Breakdown Van.
08. *MET* Stores Carrier. Bogie car.
09. *MET* Salt Car.
010–014. *MET* Breakdown Van.
001, 003. *LUT* Rail Grinder.
005. *LUT* Crane Car/Wheel Carrier. Bogie car.
006. *LUT* Rail Grinder.
148. *LUT* Vacuum Cleaner. Converted from a Type X passenger car. Bogie car.
19S. *SMET* Breakdown Car.

The open top works car **148** was an ingenious specimen. It was employed at Hanwell Depot as a mobile valeting gantry. Parked alongside a Feltham, cleaning staff on the top deck of car **148** would then feed vacuum hoses through the upper saloon windows of the Feltham, so that the interior floor and furnishings could be thoroughly cleaned.

List of Reconditioned Tramcars

Experimental Rehabs:
 2, 467, 936, 962, 982, 1001, 1038, 1103, 1144, 1260, 1370, 1373, 1397, 1441, 1444.

E/1 Class Rehabs – Main Batch:
 826, 827, 836, 839, 940, 947, 948, 953, 960, 972, 978, 981, 984, 985, 993–996.

1003, 1009, 1017, 1022, 1024, 1033, 1042, 1078, 1087–1090, 1177, 1190, 1191, 1195, 1212, 1215, 1216, 1223, 1226, 1227, 1246–1248, 1275.

1310, 1351–1353, 1357, 1359, 1364–1366, 1368, 1369, 1375, 1377, 1380–1382, 1384–1388, 1391–1393, 1396, 1398–1402, 1408, 1421, 1422, 1481, 1491, 1492.

1500, 1502, 1506–1508, 1514, 1517, 1520, 1521, 1534, 1538, 1541, 1545, 1547, 1553, 1563, 1564, 1566, 1569, 1572, 1574, 1576, 1577, 1579, 1587, 1590, 1599.

1606, 1608, 1610, 1614, 1619, 1636, 1642, 1643, 1645, 1647, 1648, 1650, 1652, 1654–1656, 1661, 1668, 1676.

1727, 1730, 1743, 1744, 1758, 1761–1763, 1766, 1768–1772, 1775.

HR/2 Class Rehabs:
 127, 1884, 1885, 1887, 1890, 1893.

Former Croydon E/1 Class:
 376, 379, 380, 398.

The date is 29th June 1935. In the yard of Hanwell Depot former LUT crane car leads car 148, once of type X. Car 005 perished at Walthamstow in December 1936. Car 148 should have been preserved, as it was one of the vehicles to inaugurate electric tramways in the capital, but it met the same fate as car 005.
D. W. K. Jones/National Tramway Museum

The following roster has been included as an example of the mix of vehicles employed on one particular London trunk service. It was compiled from eye witness information received from D. H. Johnson, and was checked by John Barrie. It represents a fairly typical weekday on route 29 from Enfield to Tottenham Court Road. Each car had a running number and the roster is published in numerical order – car **2076** was No. 1 and car **2093** No. 31.

The running number (not to be confused with the route or service number) appeared on a small metal disc, mounted on the side of the car. In type UCC (Feltham) vehicles the number was displayed in the cab window at both ends.

Trams on the 29 worked from either Holloway Depot or from the former MET establishment at Wood Green. In 1936 the roster list included Felthams, ex-Leyton E/3 and ex-Walthamstow cars.

1. **2076**. UCC. Wood Green.
2. **166**. E/3. Holloway.
3. **2059**. Walthamstow. Holloway.
4. **169**. E/3. Holloway.
5. **165**. E/3. Holloway.
6. **2083**. UCC. Wood Green.
7. **2091**. UCC. Wood Green.
8. **2042**. Walthamstow. Holloway.
9. **162**. E/3. Holloway.
10. **2100**. UCC. Wood Green.

11. **2049**. Walthamstow. Holloway.
12. **170**. E/3. Holloway.
13. **2084**. UCC. Wood Green.
14. **2073**. UCC. Wood Green.
15. **2044**. Walthamstow. Holloway.
16. **2099**. UCC. Wood Green.
17. **168**. E/3. Holloway.
18. **2077**. UCC. Wood Green.
19. **2061**. Walthamstow. Holloway.
20. **167**. E/3. Holloway.

21. **2094**. UCC. Wood Green.
22. **2060**. Walthamstow. Holloway.
23. **163**. E/3. Wood Green.
24. **2053**. Walthamstow. Holloway.
25. **2082**. UCC. Wood Green.
26. **2097**. UCC. Wood Green.
27. **2055**. Walthamstow. Holloway.
28. **2080**. UCC. Wood Green.
29. **164**. E/3. Wood Green.
30. **2057**. Walthamstow. Holloway.
31. **2093**. UCC. Wood Green.

According to official LPTB fleet allocation lists cars **163** and **164** were housed at Wood Green in 1936. The Sunday service on route 29 involved 28 or 29 vehicles. The ex-Leyton E/3s were replaced by cars from the main LCC batch **1927–1949**. On Bank Holidays there was a real assortment of trams, which could include ex-MET types H, G and C/1.

A small blue running number of 14 is displayed on the side of car 2049, which is pictured on route 29 at Enfield terminus. On another weekday roster it sometimes ran as number 11. The running number was an indication to staff of a particular car's position relative to other vehicles working the same service. G. N. Southerden

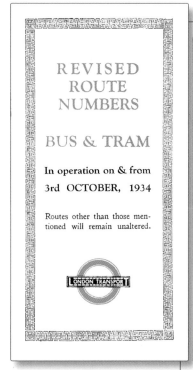

REVISED ROUTE NUMBERS

BUS & TRAM

In operation on & from 3rd OCTOBER, 1934

Routes other than those mentioned will remain unaltered.

LONDON TRANSPORT

NOTICE

ON and from Wednesday, 3rd October, 1934, the following revision to bus and tram route numbers will come into force.

The revision has been found necessary owing to the duplication of numbers now used. Further, the numbering of the routes is simplified to assist the travelling public in identifying the route they require.

Some of the tram routes will be numbered for the first time.

NEW NUMBERS ARE SHOWN IN RED.

In certain cases, not shown in this leaflet, where a suffix letter is used at present the number will remain the same but without the suffix.

BUS ROUTES (Central).

Old No.	New No.	From	To
20	21A	WOOD GREEN	WELLING
26	25A	VICTORIA STATION	LAMBOURNE END
41A	232	HIGHGATE STATION	CROUCH END B'WAY
41B	41	CROUCH END B'WAY	WALTHAMSTOW (NR. BLACKHORSE LANE)
50	5	MITCHAM COMMON	STREATHAM COM.
58	59	CAMDEN TOWN	CHIPSTEAD VALLEY ROAD
61	217	KINGSTON BUS STN.	STAINES
62	218	KINGSTON BUS STN.	STAINES
64	6A	HACKNEY WICK	WATERLOO STATION
79	219	KINGSTON BUS STN.	WOKING
87	234	STREATHAM COM.	PURLEY
92	9	BARNES	ROMFORD (NEW MILL INN)
100	10A	ELEPHANT & CASTLE	EPPING TOWN
103	200	WIMBLEDON STN.	RAYNES PARK (RAYNES PK. HOTEL)
104	240	GOLDERS GREEN STATION	EDGWARE STATION
105	201	LAMPTON	KINGSTON BUS STN.
108B	108	BROMLEY-BY-BOW	CRYSTAL PALACE
108D	208	CLAPTON POND	BROMLEY-BY-BOW
109	227	PENGE (CROOKED BILLET)	WELLING
110	210	FINSBURY PK. STN.	GOLDERS GN. STN.
111	212	FINSBURY PK. STN.	MUSWELL HILL BROADWAY
112	12	HARLESDEN	EAST DULWICH
113	213	KINGSTON BUS STN.	BELMONT
115	215	KINGSTON BUS STN.	GUILDFORD
118	18A	ACTON STATION (G.W.R.)	LONDON BRIDGE STATION

2

TRAM ROUTES.

Old No.	New No.	From	To
2	1A	UPTON PARK (BOLEYN)	STRATFORD BROADWAY
2	42	CROYDON (GREYHOUND)	THORNTON HEATH
3	23	WOODFORD (NAPIER ARMS)	WALTHAMSTOW (FERRY LANE)
5	95	WANSTEAD FLATS	CANNING TOWN
5	85	HIGHAM HILL	LEYTON (MARKHOUSE RD.)
6	69	STRATFORD BROADWAY	CANNING TOWN
7	97	CHINGFORD MOUNT	VICTORIA & ALBERT DOCKS
8	87	LEYTON (BAKERS ARMS)	VICTORIA & ALBERT DOCKS
9	99	STRATFORD BROADWAY	VICTORIA & ALBERT DOCKS
18	39A	BRUCE GROVE	ENFIELD
26	49A	ENFIELD	PONDERS END
32	37	WOOD GREEN	ALEXANDRA PALACE
34	39	BRUCE GROVE "WELLINGTON"	MUSWELL HILL ALEXANDRA PALACE
40	45	WHETSTONE	CRICKLEWOOD
—	73	WANSTEAD PARK	ROYAL ALBERT DOCKS
—	91	BARKING BROADWAY	BARKINGSIDE
—	93	BARKING BROADWAY	CHADWELL HEATH
—	96	WOOLWICH (BERESFORD SQUARE)	HORNS CROSS
—	98	ABBEY WOOD	BEXLEY HEATH

9

10

Tram Routes/Night Services

March 1935

ROUTE/SERVICE numbers were displayed on vehicles. Destinations and important intermediate stopping places appeared on indicator blinds and on side route boards, affixed usually outside the car under the windows of the lower saloon. Unlike some other British cities, in LPTB days there was no colour coding of routes, nor were special symbols adopted. Early in the LCC electric era a system of three different coloured lights was instituted on vehicles. It was assumed in the 1930s the higher standard of literacy among the travelling public rendered such methods unnecessary.

In 1912 the LCC allotted even numbers to services in the Southern Division and odd numbers to those north of the Thames. Kingsway Subway routes **31**, **33** and **35** crossed the divide. It was more practical for the LPTB to retain LCC service numbers, as well as the system of route pairing (**2/4**, **16/18** etc) with trams using the Victoria Embankment as a loop terminus to return to south London. As has been mentioned in the text, there were still anomalies in the timetable, especially when it came to duplicates (**7** to Uxbridge, **7** to Holborn etc).

The letters EX, displayed on a tram, denoted an extra vehicle to augment the normal service. Obviously, bearing in mind the diverse nature of the rolling stock inherited by the LPTB, destination displays varied according to the vehicle. Indeed, some metropolitan tramway operators, like Bexley, Erith and Ilford, managed with no route numbers at all. Most ex-LCC trams working on the Hampstead routes had larger, three line indicator boxes at each end of the car. A fare chart, including route details, was positioned in one of the lower saloon bulkheads. This would also give information on concessionary fares and special journeys, usually in connection with peak hour extensions or depot workings.

After the route number and places served, the interval between cars is given in minutes, followed by the total journey time. The through fare is quoted in old currency – 12 pence (3d, 7½d etc) in a shilling (1/-, one shilling and a penny was commonly written 1/1), and 20 shillings (20/-) in a pound (£1). In 1971 the former British monetary system was replaced by decimal coinage (£1=100p).

In March 1935, traffic congestion on main roads into London was beginning to affect journey times and service intervals. Lines of trams sometimes built up at traffic 'hot spots' such as Aldgate terminus, New Cross Gate by the depot and on the approaches to the Elephant and Castle junction. At times of traffic congestion or in bad weather conditions, trams running late could be turned short of their respective termini. However, it was a golden rule that the last scheduled tram of the day always completed its journey.

This timetable shows only the basic services. On weekends and in rush hours some routes were extended. An example of this practice is the **31**, which was prolonged on Sundays as far as Leyton (Bakers Arms). The busiest trunk routes operated at headways of two minutes between cars; the longest wait for any passenger was on the rural Dartford to Horns Cross section of route **96**, where an interval of 24 minutes separated the trams.

The service offered by trams in London, while not quite in the modern sense of 24/7, was almost round the clock with the exception of a gap of a few hours early on Sunday mornings. Normal service cars overlapped with the All-Nighters. An example was the 3:35am departure on route **46** of the first car of the day from New Cross to Eltham. The last **46** of the day left Beresford Square for New Cross Depot at 1:32am!

1. East Ham – West Ham – Stratford Broadway. 4-10mins. 21mins. 3d.

1A. Upton Park – West Ham – Stratford Broadway. 4-10mins. 14mins. 2½d.

2/4. Wimbledon – Kennington – Embankment.
2 via Westminster Bridge.
4 via Blackfriars Bridge.
4mins. 54mins. 5d.

2A/4A. Streatham Library – Tooting – Embankment.
2A via Westminster Bridge.
4A via Blackfriars Bridge.
Weekday Rush Hours Only. 4mins. 50mins. 5d.

3. Hampstead – Camden Town – Holborn. 5-7mins. 25mins. 4d.

5. Crystal Palace (High Level) – West Croydon. 5-7mins. 28mins. 4d.

5. Hampstead – Camden Town – Moorgate. 4-5mins. 32mins. 4d.

6. Tooting Junction – Southwark (City). 5-8mins. 44mins. 5d.

7. Parliament Hill Fields – Holborn. 5-8mins. 24mins. 3d.

7. Sutton – Wallington – West Croydon. 4-10mins. 31mins. 6d.

7. Shepherds Bush – Ealing – Uxbridge. 2-12mins. 67mins. 1/-.

8/20. Tooting Broadway – Victoria Station.
8 via Streatham.
20 via Clapham.
5-6mins. 34mins via Clapham, 44mins via Streatham. 5d.

9. North Finchley – Highgate – Moorgate. 6-8mins. 50mins. 7d.

10. Stratford – Upton Park – Stratford (Circle). 10-11mins. 33mins. 2½d.
Stratford – Upton Park.

10. Tooting Broadway – Southwark (City). 4-12mins. 48mins. 5d.

11. Highgate Village – Moorgate. 3-4mins. 31mins. 4d.

12. Tooting Junction – London Bridge (Borough). 5-8mins. 57mins. 5d.

13. Highgate – Highbury – Aldersgate. 6mins. 25mins. 4d.

14. Wandsworth – Embankment – London Bridge (Borough). 12mins. 46mins. 5d.

15. Parliament Hill Fields – Moorgate. 6-8mins. 33mins. 4d.

16/18. Purley – Kennington – Embankment.
16 via Westminster Bridge.
18 via Blackfriars Bridge.
3-4mins. 71mins. 1/-.

17. Highgate – Kings Cross – Farringdon Street. 2-8mins. 26mins. 3d.

19. Barnet – Highgate – Tottenham Court Road. 6-8mins. 54mins. 8d.

21. North Finchley – Wood Green – Holborn. 4-5mins. 60mins. 8d.

22/24. Tooting Broadway – Streatham-Embankment.
22 via Westminster Bridge.
24 via Blackfriars Bridge.
4mins. 47mins. 5d.

23. Woodford (Napier Arms) – Walthamstow (Ferry Lane). 3-5mins. 19mins. 3d.

25. Parliament Hill Fields – Tottenham Court Road. 8mins. 18mins. 2d.

26. Kew Bridge – Putney – London Bridge (Borough). 3-8mins. 83mins. 7d.

27. Edmonton – Finsbury Park – Tottenham Court Road. 3-8mins. 47mins. 7d.

28. Victoria – Putney – Craven Park. 5-8mins. 87mins. 9d.

29. Enfield – Finsbury Park – Tottenham Court Road. 4-6mins. 58mins. 8d.

30. Harrow Road (Scrubs Lane) – West Croydon. 5-6mins. 81mins. 1/-.

31. Wandsworth – Embankment – Hackney. 5-8mins. 70mins. 8d.

32. Clapham (Plough) – Chelsea Bridge. 5-6mins. 12mins. 2d.

33. West Norwood – Embankment – Manor House. 5-10mins. 68mins. 8d.

34. Chelsea (Kings Road) – Blackfriars. 4-8mins. 58mins. 5d.

35. Forest Hill – Embankment – Highgate. 6-10mins. 85mins. 9d.

36/38. Abbey Wood – New Cross – Embankment.
36 via Blackfriars Bridge.
38 via Westminster Bridge.
2-4mins. 70mins. 5d.

37. Wood Green – Alexandra Palace. 5-8mins. 9mins. 1d.

39. Bruce Grove – Muswell Hill. 6-12mins. 22mins. 4d.

39. Wood Green (Wellington) – Alexandra Palace. 7-9mins (Afternoons Only). 13mins. 2d.

39A. Bruce Grove – Wood Green – Enfield. 8mins. 34mins. 6d.

40. Abbey Wood – New Cross – Kennington – Embankment. 4-10mins. 75mins. 5d.

41. Manor House – Moorgate. 2-8mins. 23mins. 3d.

42. Croydon (Greyhound) – Thornton Heath. 3-5mins. 16mins. 2d.

43. Stamford Hill – Dalston – Holborn. 4-10mins. 33mins. 4d.

44. Woolwich – Shooters Hill – Eltham. 8-10mins. 18mins. 3d.

45. Whetstone (Totteridge Lane) – Cricklewood. 2-8mins. 30mins. 4d.

46. Woolwich (Beresford Square) – Southwark (City). 4-10mins. 64mins. 5d.

47. Stamford Hill – London Docks. 2-4mins. 30mins. 4d.

48. West Norwood – Southwark (City). 5-10mins. 37mins. 4d.

49. Edmonton – Dalston – Liverpool Street Station. 3-6mins. 44mins. 6d.

49A. Enfield – Ponders End. 6-8mins. 6mins. 1d.

51. Muswell Hill – Angel – Aldersgate. 8-12mins. 42mins. 6d.

52. Grove Park – Southwark (City). 4-5mins. 53mins. 5d.

53. Tottenham Court Road – Aldgate. 6mins. 64mins. 6d.

54. Grove Park – New Cross – Victoria. 2-4mins. 60mins. 5d.

55. Brentford – Hanwell. 7-10mins. 13mins. 2d.

55. Leyton – Hackney – Bloomsbury. 4-8mins. 48mins. 5d.

56/84. Peckham Rye – Embankment.
56 via Westminster Bridge.
84 via Blackfriars Bridge.
3-6mins. 35mins. 4d.

57. Chingford Mount – Liverpool Street Station. 4-8mins. 55mins. 6½d.

57. Hounslow – Shepherds Bush. 4-10mins. 40mins. 6d.

58. Blackwall Tunnel – Victoria. 4-10mins. 72mins. 5d.

59. Waltham Cross – Kings Cross – Holborn. 6-8mins. 75mins. 1/-.

60. Dulwich Library – Southwark (City). 5-6mins. 33mins. 4d.

60. North Finchley – Paddington (Edgware Road). 6-8mins. 64mins. 11d.

61. Leyton – Stratford – Aldgate. 3-4mins. 47mins. 6d.

62. Sudbury – Paddington (Edgware Road). 6-10mins. 40mins. 7d.

62. Blackwall Tunnel – Embankment (Savoy Street). 8-10mins. 79mins. 5d.

63. Ilford – Stratford – Aldgate. 2-4mins. 42mins. 6d.

63. Kew Bridge – Shepherds Bush. 4-6mins. 19mins. 3d.

64. Edgware – Paddington (Edgware Road). 8mins. 62mins. 10d.

65. Poplar (Blackwall Tunnel) – Bloomsbury. 2-3mins. 32mins. 3d.

66. Forest Hill – Embankment (Savoy Street). 12mins. 53mins. 5d.

66. Canons Park – Hendon – Acton. 4-8mins. 62mins. 9d.

67. Hampton Court – Hammersmith. 6-10mins. 62mins. 10d.

67. Barking – Poplar – Aldgate. 2-4mins. 45mins. 5½d.

68. Greenwich Church – Waterloo Station. 5-6mins. 34mins. 5d.

68. Acton – Harlesden – Craven Park. 2-8mins. 17mins. 3d.

69. Stratford – Plaistow – Canning Town. 4-6mins. 18mins. 2d.

70. Greenwich Church – London Bridge Station. 2-6mins. 25mins. 4d.

71. Aldersgate – Wood Green – Aldgate. 6mins. 95mins. 1/1.
72. Woolwich (Beresford Square) – New Cross – Embankment. 8-10mins. 70mins. 5d.
73. Wanstead Park – Royal Albert Docks. 2-6mins. 24mins. 3½d.
74. Downham – New Cross – Embankment. 6-10mins. 55mins. 5d.
75. Stamford Hill – Holborn. 6-8mins. 32mins. 4d.
77. West India Docks – Aldersgate. 4-8mins. 46mins. 5d.
78. West Norwood – Brixton – Victoria. 5-8mins. 30mins. 4d.
79. Waltham Cross – Finsbury Park – Smithfield. 6-8mins. 73mins. 1/1.
81. Woodford – Leyton – Bloomsbury. 5-8mins. 57mins. 6d.
83. Stamford Hill – Moorgate. 4-8mins. 28mins. 4d.
85. Higham Hill – Blackhorse Road – Leyton. 3-5mins. 16mins. 2d.
87. Leyton (Bakers Arms) – Victoria & Albert Docks. 6-8mins. 46mins. 6d.
89. Acton – Hammersmith. 3-8mins. 19mins. 3d.
91. Barkingside – Barking Broadway. 3-10mins. 32mins. 4d.
93. Barking – Chadwell Heath. 3-8mins. 30mins. 4d.
95. Wanstead Flats – Canning Town. 6-7mins. 23mins. 3d.
96. Woolwich (Beresford Square) – Dartford – Horns Cross. 6-24mins. 76mins. 8d.
97. Chingford Mount – Victoria & Albert Docks. 4-6mins. 59mins. 7½d.
98. Abbey Wood – Bexleyheath. 6-10mins. 34mins. 4d.
99. Stratford – Victoria & Albert Docks. 2-11mins. 21mins. 3½d.

All Night Tram Services
(Saturday Nights Excepted):

Tooting Broadway – Embankment (Circle). 5d.

Tooting Broadway – Embankment (Blackfriars). 5d.

Southcroft Road – Embankment (Circle). 5d.

Poplar – Bloomsbury. 4d.

Stamford Hill – Holborn. 4d.

Hampstead – Holborn. 4d.

Highgate – Bloomsbury. 4d.

Downham – Embankment (Savoy Street). 5d.

New Cross Gate – Embankment (Savoy Street). 4d.

All-Night Services ran at headways between vehicles of one hour or 30 minutes, usually the latter. Only after the war were route numbers allotted to night services. In March 1935, cars would have carried an **EX** designation.

All-Night Services after 18th/19th June 1946:

1. Tooting Broadway – Victoria Embankment.
3. Battersea – Embankment (Blackfriars).
5. Downham – Embankment (Savoy Street).
7. New Cross Gate – Embankment (Savoy Street).
26. Clapham Junction – London Bridge (Borough).
35. Highgate – Bloomsbury. (5:42am journey from Highgate, Archway Station to Westminster Station).

Routes partly or wholly abandoned by the LPTB prior to March 1935:

4. Penge (Entrance to Crystal Palace) – West Croydon. 9mins. 26mins. 4d.
6. Mitcham (Cricket Green) – Southwark (City). 5mins. 52mins. 7d.
14. Wimbledon Station – London Bridge (Borough). 12mins. 73mins. 5d.

Unnumbered. Wilmington – Dartford. 15mins. 7mins. 1d.

Tramway Abandonment Dates

THE DATES given here represent the end of tramway service, often leading to the abandonment of track. Tracks shared with other services were maintained until complete abandonment of the tramway in that locality. Some rail connections were preserved for depot/scrap yard movements or were needed for electrical supply purposes.

In nearly all cases the final journeys began late in the evening and the last tram arrived back at the depot in the early hours of the following morning. As has been mentioned in the main text, some local farewells degenerated into rowdy scenes and the forces of law and order had to be summoned. Other last cars went entirely unmourned. Replacement bus and trolleybus routes (shown in brackets) were sometimes extended past former tram termini to what were judged as 'more suitable traffic objectives'. It will also be noted that, due to shifting patterns of passenger usage, certain tram routes (e.g. routes **13** and **51**) were abandoned altogether and not replaced on a like for like basis.

1933
7th December:
6 Mitcham Fair Green – Mitcham Cricket Green;
4 Anerley, Robin Hood – Penge (bus 12 & 75).

1934
19th April:
Unnumbered Dartford – Wilmington (bus 401).
16th May:
14 Wimbledon Station – Wandsworth (bus 67 & 130).

1935
4th April:
2 Chingford – Leyton;
10 West Ham Circular: Stratford Broadway – Stratford Broadway.

A trial trolleybus stops opposite one of the doomed trams at Barnet Church terminus. LPTB planners were fortunate at this location, because the highway was wide enough to instal a trolleybus turning circle. Car 2253 was scrapped in October 1938.

27th October:
  57 Hounslow – Shepherds Bush &
  63 Kew Bridge – Shepherds Bush
  (trolleybus 657);
  67 Hampton Court – Hammersmith
  (trolleybus 667).
10th November:
  98 Abbey Wood – Bexleyheath Clock
  Tower (trolleybus 698).
24th November:
  96 Woolwich – Dartford, Horns Cross
  (trolleybus 696, bus 480)
8th December:
  7 West Croydon – Sutton (trolleybus 654).

1936
8th February:
  5 West Croydon – Crystal Palace
  (trolleybus 654).
5th April:
  89 Acton – Hammersmith (trolleybus
  660).
5th July:
  66 Canons Park – Acton &
  68 Acton – Craven Park (trolleybus 666).
2nd August:
  45 Whetstone – Cricklewood &
  60 North Finchley – Paddington
  (trolleybus 645 & 660).
23rd August:
  62 Sudbury – Paddington (trolleybus 662);
  64 Edgware – Paddington (trolleybus
  664).
7th October:
  73 Wanstead Park – Royal Albert Docks
  (bus 101).
18th October:
  23 Woodford – Walthamstow (trolleybus
  623).
15th November:
  7 Shepherds Bush – Uxbridge (trolleybus
  607).
13th December:
  55 Brentford – Hanwell (trolleybus 655).

1937
17th January:
  85 Higham Hill – Leyton (trolleybus 685).
6th June:
  57 Chingford Mount – Leyton (trolleybus
  687);
  69 Stratford – Canning Town (trolleybus
  669);
  87 Leyton – Victoria & Albert Docks
  (trolleybus 687);
  97 Chingford Mount – Victoria & Albert
  Docks (trolleybus 697);
  99 Stratford – Victoria & Albert Docks
  (trolleybus 699).
8th September:
  32 Clapham – Chelsea Bridge (bus 137).
12th September:
  1/1A East Ham – Stratford Broadway
  (trolleybus 689);

95 Wanstead Flats – Canning Town
(trolleybus 685);
12 Wandsworth – Tooting Junction
(trolleybus 612).
30 Harrow Road – West Croydon
(trolleybus 630);
26 Hammersmith – Clapham Junction
(trolleybus 626);
28 Harlesden – Clapham Junction
(trolleybus 628);
6 Tooting, Amen Corner – Mitcham Fair
Green (trolleybus 612 & 630).

1938
6th February:
  91 Barkingside – Barking Broadway
  (trolleybus 691);
  93 Barking – Chadwell Heath (trolleybus
  693).
23rd February:
  37 Wood Green – Alexandra Palace (bus
  241/233);
  39 Wood Green – Alexandra Palace &
  51 Muswell Hill – Turnpike Lane Station
  (bus 144, 144A, 144B, 233).
6th March:
  9 North Finchley – Moorgate (trolleybus
  609).
  13 Highgate – Aldersgate.
  17 Highgate – Farringdon Street
  (trolleybus 517/617);
  19 Barnet – Tottenham Court Road
  (trolleybus 609 & 651, bus 134);
  21 North Finchley – Holborn (trolleybus
  521/621);
  39A Bruce Grove – Enfield;
  51 Turnpike Lane Station – Aldersgate.
8th May:
  29 Enfield – Tottenham Court Road
  (trolleybus 629);
  41 Winchmore Hill – Moorgate (trolleybus
  641).
10th July:
  3 Hampstead – Holborn (trolleybus
  513/613);
  5 Hampstead – Moorgate (trolleybus 639);
  7 Parliament Hill Fields – Holborn
  (trolleybus 513/613);
  15 Parliament Hill Fields – Moorgate
  (trolleybus 615);
  Unnumbered: All-Night Hampstead
  – Holborn (trolleybus).
3rd August:
  99A West Ham Stadium – Plaistow (bus
  106).
16th October:
  49 Stamford Hill – Enfield (trolleybus 649,
  bus 107);
  49A Enfield – Ponders End (bus 107);
  59 Waltham Cross – Holborn (trolleybus
  659);
  79 Waltham Cross – Smithfield (trolleybus
  679).
6th November:
  27 Edmonton – Tottenham Court Road
  (trolleybus 627).

1939
5th February
  43 Stamford Hill – Holborn (trolleybus
  543/643);
  47 Stamford Hill – London Docks
  (trolleybus 647);
  49 Stamford Hill – Liverpool Street
  Station (trolleybus 649);
  71 Aldersgate – Aldgate (trolleybus 643,
  bus 42);
  75 Stamford Hill – Holborn.
  83 Stamford Hill – Moorgate (trolleybus
  683);
  Unnumbered All-Night Stamford Hill
  – Holborn (trolleybus).
5th March:
  53 Tottenham Court Road – Aldgate
  (trolleybus 653).
11th June:
  55 Leyton – Bloomsbury (trolleybus 555).
  57 Leyton – Liverpool Street Station
  (trolleybus 557);
  81 Woodford – Bloomsbury (trolleybus
  581).
2nd August:
  14 Wandsworth – London Bridge
  (Borough).
10th September:
  77 West India Docks – Aldersgate
  (trolleybus 677).
5th November 1939.
  61 Leyton – Aldgate (trolleybus 661);
  63 Ilford – Aldgate (trolleybus 663).
10th December:
  11 Highgate Village – Moorgate
  (trolleybus 611);
  31 Rosebery Avenue – Hackney (trolleybus
  555 & 581).

1940
9th June:
  65 Poplar – Bloomsbury &
  67 Barking – Aldgate (trolleybus 565, 567,
  665).

Thus ended the trolleybus conversion years 1931–1940. After the Second World War motor buses replaced the remaining trams in stages from 1st October 1950 to 5th July 1952. The trolleybuses, which had replaced trams, were themselves ousted by diesel buses in stages from 3rd March 1959 to 8th May 1962.

15th December 1933.

THIS INTERNAL document was sent to Lord Ashfield, Frank Pick and other members of the Board. One assumes they all needed to be 'au fait' with current policy in regards to parts of the tramway system. The report can be viewed as the first stage of the new regime's annihilation of trams in London. Many of the points raised were disputed by advocates of tramway modernisation. They argued that the trolleybus was just as route bound as the tramcar and that promises to extend trolleybuses into 'developing areas' would never be fulfilled in any meaningful way. It was also quite clear that the search for suitable trolleybus turning points would be a contentious issue in some quarters. Although the tone of this memorandum is measured in setting out the pros and cons of the trolleybus conversion scheme – it hints at, but does not state a case for total tramway abandonment – there can be no doubt as to the importance of this document in formulating future policy.

The principal advantages which the trolley bus has over the tramcar so far as the public are concerned are :

1. The trolley bus can draw alongside the pavement for the purpose of picking up and setting down passengers.

2. The greater comfort which it is possible to provide on a vehicle which only travels in one direction.

3. The elimination of delays due to other vehicles breaking down on tramway tracks.

4. It conforms with the other traffic of the street and thus conduces to greater flexibility.

The proposals of the Board for the conversion of tramways to trolley buses fall into three parts:

(i) The complete change over of an entire system.

(ii) The conversion of sections of tramways which cannot be operated satisfactorily for physical or other reasons.

(iii) The partial conversion of an 'in town' route for the purpose of providing a through service to and from the suburbs.

(i) The complete change over of an entire system.

Coming within the first category is the proposal regarding Erith, Bexley and Dartford.

These systems were formerly operated in two parts, by Erith and by a joint committee of Bexley and Dartford. There was in the case

of Erith a wide interval through service to Bexley Market Place via Northumberland Heath, and between Bexley and the London County Council system via Wickham Lane and Plumstead to Woolwich. These systems both as regards their rolling stock and permanent way are approaching the end of their life and it is urgently necessary, both on safety and economic grounds, to take steps either to renew the tramways or adopt another means of transport.

In the case of Bexley and Dartford, the system consists very largely of long lengths of single track with passing places; for that reason and the condition of the cars and track the average speed is only 8 mph. The nature of the traffic in this area is not of such a character as would justify the laying of a new permanent way throughout, and in view of the availability of electricity supply and the existence of overhead equipment, it is considered that a trolley bus system is the most suitable.

The route mileage which it is proposed to convert is 14½ miles, but it is desired to provide for trolley bus operation over the existing tramway between Abbey Wood and Woolwich in order that through services may be operated to the latter point.

At the present time there is a through tramway service to Woolwich from Bexley, but there is no connection between Erith and the London system at Abbey Wood.

It is desired to retain the tramway between Woolwich and Abbey Wood in order that the through services of tramcars from London may be maintained.

(ii) The conversion of sections of tramways which cannot be operated satisfactorily for physical or other reasons.

Most of the remainder of the proposals come within this category. The tramways in Croydon between West Croydon Station and Selby Road consist mainly of single track with its disadvantages in operation and the swinging out of cars at the points, creating risk of danger to overtaking vehicles.

The nature of traffic between West Croydon and Crystal Palace and Sutton and Croydon is such that it can be dealt with more efficiently by trolley bus than by tramway.

It will be noticed that an extension is proposed from the present tramway terminus at Sutton along the High Street to the corner of Bushey Road. The main object of this proposal is to provide a suitable turning point for trolley buses, but it is also of traffic value.

The tramway routes between Brentford and Hounslow and to Hampton Court via Hampton Hill are of similar character to those which have already been converted, such as Teddington, Kingston and Surbiton.

The conversion of the remainder of the

routes in this area will provide means for improving the facilities which are now limited by the fact that tramway and trolley bus systems are at present in operation.

A similar case for conversion exists along the Uxbridge Road, where between Southall and Uxbridge there are long lengths of single line which are difficult to operate and unnecessarily reduce speed.

The complete conversion of what was the London United system to Shepherds Bush and Hammersmith is desirable in order to provide through services.

Power is being sought for an extension from the existing Hounslow tramway terminus along the Staines Road and Martindale Road returning via the Bath Road; this would provide travelling facilities for the developing area between the Staines and Bath Roads, and at the same time is a convenient means for turning the vehicles.

The same need for conversion arises as between Sudbury and Willesden and Canons Park and Cricklewood, the completion of this part of the system to Paddington and Acton is necessary in order to avoid a change of vehicle.

It is proposed to extend from the present terminus at Sudbury along the Watford Road for about half a mile into a developing area where a turning point is available. At Paddington the existing tramway terminus is not conveniently situated and in order to avoid turning round at the junction of Harrow Road and Edgware Road it is proposed to proceed via Paddington Green, Church Street and Edgware Road into Harrow Road.

As between Wood Green and North Finchley on the one hand and Enfield on the other, the question arises as to whether the tramway shall be renewed over a considerable area or another system of transport adopted and the answer appears to be that the character of traffic in these districts is not such as to justify a retention of the tramway system.

As between Wood Green and Finsbury Park, the traffic is of a heavier character, but it would be impracticable to compel a change of vehicles at Wood Green which would be necessary if the conversion were to cease at that point.

(iii) The partial conversion of an 'in town' route for the purpose of providing a through service to and from the suburbs.

In the third category is the tramway between Euston Road and Finsbury Park. This is constructed on the conduit system and in order to provide a London connection from Wood Green, Finchley and Enfield, it is necessary to erect overhead wires to permit of through trolley bus services being operated. It will, however, be necessary to retain the tramways over part of this section of the route, in order to permit through serv-

ices from London terminals to operate via Finsbury Park and Manor House to Tottenham and Edmonton.

It will be obvious that if the tracks are not retained between the Nags Head, Holloway and Manor House, the tramway services which now operate through the Caledonian Road and Holloway Road via the Seven Sisters Road would have to be turned back at the Nags Head and Manor House respectively.

For the same reason it will be necessary to retain the tramway as between Mornington Crescent and Park Street in order to permit of through tramway services being operated via Crowndale Road and High Street, Camden Town to Hampstead.

It is also desired in this area to provide for access to the tramway depot in Holloway Road by trolley buses, and in order to do this, it will be necessary to erect overhead wires between the Nags Head and Pemberton Gardens.

It is obvious from examination of the map that the Euston Road tramway terminus is a very poor one from a traffic point of view as it stops short of the point to which most passengers would desire to travel

It would also be difficult to provide for the turning of a trolley bus at the present terminus. For these reasons the extension via Tottenham Court Road is proposed. To provide adequately for traffic requirements the extension should go as far as New Oxford Street, but it was appreciated that it would not be reasonable to suggest turning round at the junction of Tottenham Court Road and New Oxford Street; alternatives were, therefore, considered with a view to providing for public requirements with a minimum of inconvenience to other traffic. With that end in view, it is proposed to turn from Tottenham Court Road into Bayley Street, thence along the West Side of Bedford Square, Caroline Street and Bedford Avenue, back into Tottenham Court Road.

Other means of turning were considered, such as turning out of Tottenham Court Road into Bedford Avenue and back via Gt. Russell Street, there might be difficulty in emerging from Gt. Russell Street into Tottenham Court Road.

General.

It will be recognised that the process of converting large blocks of the Board's tramway system for trolley bus operation will involve some temporary alteration in existing facilities pending the completion of the conversion of the whole of an area. It is, however, felt by the Board that a substantial start should be made in providing the newest form of transport wherever practicable in areas which make such a course desirable from the point of view of the greater convenience of the travelling public

and the economic operation of the Board's services.

The experience already gained in the London area is such as to encourage the Board to be confident as to the results to be obtained from a further conversion of tramways to trolley bus operation.

Conversion of tramways from conduit to overhead.

A large section of London's tramways lie under the severe handicap of conduit operation. In addition to the economic and operating difficulties of this system, there is the grave disadvantage of a change over at the many points of connection with overhead tramways. In order to obviate this, at one point at least, it is proposed to erect overhead work from Aldgate to the junction of Mile End Road with Grove Rd. – a distance of 1.9 miles. This would enable the through services between Aldgate and Leyton and Ilford to be operated on one system of traction, thus eliminating the change point at Grove Road. Congestion is caused by the delay to tramcars at the latter point.

1934 INTERNAL LPTB BRIEFING NOTE TO FRANK PICK

THE DEPUTY Chairman liked to be well briefed. He had a deserved reputation of having the facts at his finger tips when being questioned on the Board's policies by the press or by Parliamentary committees. This document, prepared in advance of the 1934 legislation, contains the claim that trams were actually cheaper to run than motor buses. In fact, the official line states categorically that the complete annihilation of tramways in London is not on the negotiating table. However, it was important for Lord Ashfield that the trolleybus bandwagon was given a Parliamentary push to enable it to roll. Hence the tone of the second section of the document.

On the one hand the inference is 'if it ain't broke, don't fix it' – thus securing a role for the tramcar in the future plans of the LPTB. On the other, in a section possibly written by a different advisor, sufficient doubt is implanted in the minds of the reader and listener as to the economic viability of continued tramway operation.

As the average distance travelled by tram exceeds that by bus, the cheapness is more marked. On this basis the cost per mile for the tram is 0.5d. and for the bus 0.85d.

There is a general objection to tramways often expressed in these days which the Board could not fail to note. In part it is founded on prejudice.

Admittedly, in narrow streets they are a cause of congestion by reason of their presence in the centre of the roadway. Admittedly, they are a contributing cause to accidents by reason of their tracks, and in the case of conduit tramways, of the slot for current supply, as well as by reason of the fact that passengers must cross to and from the centre of the roadway to board or alight from the cars.

Still in wide roads where there is space for two free moving lines of traffic in each direction, apart from the tramways, and where central loading platforms can be installed, tramways can perform an effective and economic public service especially where there are heavy volumes of traffic to be carried in peak periods.

The Board would not wish it to be supposed that the proposals for trolley buses included in the Bill are a condemnation of tramways in all circumstances, quite apart from the particular financial and operating problems which the existence of the tramways raises at the present moment. The Board has considerable investment in tramways which it must conserve as far as it is able.

From an examination of the loadings of the tramways of the Board it was apparent that upon many miles of route the loadings were light and the services relatively infrequent. The presence, therefore, of the tramways was not entirely justified.

In the Bexley – Dartford area, for example, the density of service was 74,000 car miles per annum per mile of route, and the average load per car was 15 passengers. The average seating capacity of the cars themselves was only 56 passengers.

In the Croydon – Sutton area, for another example, the density of service was 117,000 car miles per annum per mile of route, and the average load per car was 17 passengers. The average seating capacity of the cars themselves was only 55 passengers.

Finally, on the ex-London United Tramways System not already converted to trolley bus operation, the density of service was 178,000 car miles per annum per mile of route, and the average load per car was 18 passengers. The average seating capacity of the cars themselves was only 68 passengers.

All these services and the traffics which they carried were capable of being effectively dealt with by a trolley bus.

For comparison, the density of service upon the London County Council tramway system was 414,000 car miles per annum per mile of route, and the average load per car was 20 passengers, which is still sufficiently low to show that even this includes a good many route miles of tramway of relatively light traffic.

THE FOLLOWING information is based partly on official reports from the era. It has been supplemented considerably by notes made by eye witnesses. Some details from this period of British history are still rather sketchy. It has to be remembered that government censorship was enforced in an attempt to preserve civilian morale and to deny the enemy knowledge of damage to important thoroughfares, strategic factories, warehouses and docks.

The gathering of information at this time of national emergency sometimes had its darkly comic side. An observer in his late teens, who was writing down tramcar numbers on Wednesday, 11th September 1940, at Vauxhall Cross, was challenged by an official and then escorted to the nearest police station. Our youthful enthusiast, on protesting his innocence that he was not a German spy, was informed by a burly desk sergeant that, if Nazi parachutists disguised as nuns had caught the Belgians napping (a widespread belief at the time), then even the apparently innocuous hobby of tram spotting could hide a multitude of sins! Luckily for tramway scholarship, the enthusiast's mum then arrived to bail him out.

Incidents not featuring on the list include short breaks in service, occasioned by rubble being strew across streets that was cleared quickly by civil defence personnel. Bomb craters caused by a direct hit often left highways impassable with gaping holes, broken, twisted tram rails and smashed water mains and sewers. Where bombs struck neighbouring buildings, conduit tracks were normally less susceptible to blast damage than overhead wires. The presence of the latter could also hinder the progress of fire fighters and their ladders. Even though all citizens were asked to carry masks, at no stage was poisoned gas used by the enemy in the Blitz.

The list of service disruptions was originally collated after the war by south London tram enthusiasts, particularly D. W. Smithson of Lewisham. The usual caveat applies to the information contained therein. There may be omissions and mistakes. Where possible, the exact text of the original hand written notes, often jotted down in haste at the scene of an incident, has been retained.

UXB denotes unexploded bomb. Street names are quoted as they were in 1940–1.

1940

6th September
Rubble from bombed buildings blocks Borough High Street. Tram routes 6, 10 and 48 diverted via Southwark Bridge Road. Track restored on 16th September.

7th September
Widespread bomb damage at Camberwell and Clapham depots.

8th September
Bomb crater in Balls Pond Road curtails service 33 short of Manor House terminus. Brixton Road impassable. Routes 10, 16, 18, 22, 24 and 33 diverted via Stockwell. Track reopened on 7th October. UXB outside New Cross Gate Station causes trams to reverse at Marquis of Granby and New Cross Gate crossovers. Further incendiary damage to Camberwell Depot. Trams in store at Hampstead sent through the Subway to assist south London services.

9th September
Southwark Bridge closed to traffic. Trams diverted to Borough terminus. Bomb damage closes Westminster Bridge until evening rush hour. UXB at Well Hall Roundabout, Eltham interrupts services 44, 46 and 72 for three days. Rubble blocks Camberwell New Road. Trams diverted via Walworth Road.

10th September
Car 1385 destroyed at Kennington, The Horns. Tracks also damaged. Trams diverted via Kennington Park Road. Bomb craters on the Embankment force all services to turn short, until tracks reopen on 18th September. Harleyford Road, the Oval blocked. Services 54, 58 and 66 diverted via Elephant and Castle.

11th September
A tram hold up at Vauxhall Cross. Long lines of cars wait to cross the junction. All caused by so many emergency service diversions. Only a 30 minutes delay to all routes at this location in the evening rush hour! Earlier in the day widespread failure in electrical supply after damage to feeder cables at Greenwich Power Station.

12th September
Continuing problems with power supply. Service 34 still operating from Brixton to Camberwell; Services 16/18 operating from Brixton to Purley. Emergency bus service from Streatham to London termini.

13th September
Trams isolated at Norwood Depot due to damaged tracks in Milkwood Road and Effra Road. Clapham Road closed north of Stockwell. Bomb damage at Clapham Common blocks local tram routes. Services to Peckham Rye disrupted. Cars on routes 56 and 84 terminate at Nunhead Lane. Lower Road, Rotherhithe blocked, affecting routes 68 and 70. Centre of Greenwich impassable. Trams on services 36, 38, 40 and 58 reverse either side of the craters. Track damaged at Bellingham, cutting off Downham and Grove Park from the network.

14th September
Bomb crater on Albert Embankment. Cars turn short at Vauxhall. Further air raid on Clapham Depot damages trams.

15th September
High explosive bombs cut tracks at Well Hall Road, Eltham Common. Emergency bus service from Woolwich to Eltham. Much damage in Lewisham and Greenwich causing many services to be curtailed or diverted. UXB in Bromley Road, Catford. Emergency bus services from Grove Park to Lewisham and on towards Blackwall Tunnel. A motley collection of buses using side streets to get round obstructions.

17th September
Destruction in the Clapham Junction area including the closure of Lavender Hill and Wandsworth Road. Services 26, 28 and 34 diverted via Battersea Park Road. UXB between Streatham and Tooting causes suspension of tram services. Cars on routes 16/18 unable to proceed past Norbury, because of bomb damage at Streatham. Vauxhall becomes terminus of all routes normally bound for Victoria. Tracks damaged in Vauxhall Bridge Road.

18th September
Temporary rail bridges span craters on the Victoria Embankment. Trams obliged to coast across the gaps in the conduit. Bomb damage in the Herne Hill area affecting services 33 and 48. UXB closes Denmark Hill. Trams forced to reverse either side at Camberwell Green and Champion Park. Trafalgar Road, Greenwich and Woolwich Road impassable for trams.

19th September
Tracks cleared at New Cross Gate, Kennington Road and Brixton Hill, but Brixton Road still closed. Emergency bus service Blackfriars to Streatham.

20th September
Damage to overhead wires at Well Hall Roundabout. UXB in Eltham Hill causes three day delay to service 46 cars. Bomb then explodes, creating craters in the roadway. West Norwood to Herne Hill lines reopened, but Effra Road and Dulwich Road still closed to trams. Cars on route 33 diverted via Loughborough Junction.

21st September
Evelyn Street and Creek Road closed to trams. Cars on routes 68 and 70 terminate at Rotherhithe.

23rd September
Stanstead Road again passable for cars heading for Catford.

26th September
Widespread destruction in the Kennington area, cars on routes 40, 54,

58, 66 and 72 diverted via Walworth Road. Clapham Road impassable north of Stockwell.

27th September
Southwark Bridge Road closed. Route 12 diverted via Borough Road, Borough High Street and Marshalsea Road. No trams operating between Tooting Broadway and Clapham South tube station. Emergency bus service from Tooting to Victoria. Feltham car 2142 damaged by explosion in South Lambeth Road. Bomb landed in nearby garden and shattered car windows. Injured passengers treated on the spot or taken to hospital. Tram covered with earth. Large bush removed from its roof.

28th September
Former Poplar Depot cars, stored at Hampstead, appear on route 33 between Bloomsbury and Balls Pond Road and on service 35 from Bloomsbury to Highgate. Most of these are unvestibuled and still have fare charts relating to routes 65 and 67, replaced by trolleybuses in the summer of 1940. Cars observed include 1000, 1005, 1049, 1050, 1073, 1107, 1124, 1166, 1217, 1252, 1259, 1262, 1302 and 1304. UXB at Holborn Hall affects routes 33 and 35.

30th September
Kingsway Subway routes back to normal working. Track repairs at Kennington Gate completed.

1st October
Cars on route 26 stop at Blackfriars. Southwark Street impassable for trams. Vauxhall Bridge Road closed. Trams to Victoria as far as Grosvenor Road. Passengers then change to replacement bus service to Victoria.

2nd October
Emergency track repairs at Kennington cause diversions. Route 10 temporarily replaced by bus service.

3rd October
Track damaged in London Road, Thornton Heath. Road impassable for trams at Thornton Heath Pond. Emergency bus service Thornton Heath to Purley.

4th October
Woolwich Road and New Cross Gate hit by bombs. Eastern side of triangle in New Cross Road unusable for trams. Old Kent Road services use western side and then reverse in Queens Road.

5th October
Track repairs in Brixton Road. Cars 1484, 1741, 1765 and 1776, formerly stored at Purley Depot, are seen on emergency shuttle service, covering routes 16, 18 and 42, from Purley to London Road, Thornton Heath.

7th October
Track damaged in Shardeloes Road,

Brockley. Route 35 diverted via Lewisham and Catford. Cars on route 74 curtailed to work Brockley to Catford. Brixton Road reopened to trams.

8th October
Nazi fighter planes in daylight low level raid machine gun two trams at the Elephant and Castle in the morning rush hour. Loss of life among passengers.

9th October
Service 34 returns to normal Chelsea to Blackfriars route.

10th October
Lines cut by bomb damage in Bromley Road. Services 52, 54 and 74 to Grove Park disrupted.

11th October
Track repairs at Tooting Broadway force services 8 and 20 to be worked in two sections.

12th October
Services restored through Thornton Heath after track and overhead repairs completed. Single line working at first past bomb craters.

14th October
Vauxhall Bridge Road again passable for trams to reach Victoria.
Bomb craters block Eltham Hill and tracks at Well Hall Roundabout. Cars on routes 44 and 46 terminate at Eltham Church after Well Hall Circus is cleared. Bus route 21 runs extra journeys to replace service 46 west of Eltham Church. Lewisham Road and Greenwich South Street impassable for trams. Routes 58 and 62 curtailed at Catford and Lewisham.
Bromley Road damaged again. Emergency bus service between Grove Park and Blackwall Tunnel. South Lambeth Road closed. Services diverted via Kennington and Stockwell.

15th October
Vauxhall Cross gyratory system hit by bombs. Wandsworth Road impassable for trams. Routes 12, 26 and 28 diverted via Cedars Road, Clapham and Stockwell. Craters in Balham High Road force curtailment of tram services. A route 88 bus falls into one of the craters.
UXB at the Angel, Islington. Route 33 cars terminate at Bloomsbury. Holloway Depot and New Cross Depot damaged in air raids.

17th October
Much damage across south London. Railway bridge at New Cross Gate destroyed. Trams reverse at the Marquis of Granby and at New Cross Gate either side of the gap. Car 1499, badly damaged and left abandoned on the up line some yards east of New Cross Gate Station. Emergency circular tram service

instituted: Marquis – Lewisham – Catford – Stanstead Road – Brockley – Marquis. Emergency bus service between Greenwich and Church Lane, Charlton. Old Kent Road blocked at Dunton Road. Dulwich Road, Herne Hill blocked. Routes 33 and 78 diverted via Loughborough Junction. Holloway Depot again hit by bombs.

18th October
Overhead wires down at Thornton Heath. Repaired by evening rush hour. Single line working between the Pond and Mayday Road crossover. Mitcham Lane impassable for trams. Emergency bus service Streatham to Tooting. Routes 33 and 35 affected by a UXB in Theobalds Road and another at the Angel, Islington.

20th October
Through tram services restored to London Road, Thornton Heath. Temporary track laid across craters. Motor traffic unable to pass until highway fully repaired at Christmas.

21st October
Southwark Bridge Road, Blackfriars Road and Old Kent all impassable for trams. Bomb damage at Vauxhall Cross. Routes 4, 18 and 34 terminate at the Elephant and Castle. Route 12 curtailed at St George's Circus and routes 8, 20, 28 and 78 at Vauxhall. Obstructions soon cleared. Route 46 worked in three sections: Southwark Bridge to Dunton Road crossover, single line working along part of Old Kent Road to New Cross Gate, then Marquis of Granby to Eltham.

25th October
One of the worst incidents of the war. In the morning five trams in a queue at Blackfriars Road receive a direct hit. Large loss of life. Wreckage and casualties cleared by evening rush hour.

26th October
Walworth Road partly blocked. Single line working. Services 34 and 48 diverted via Kennington. Feltham car 2113 destroyed in Stockwell Road.

28th October
Stockwell Road impassable for trams. Route 34 operated in two sections: Chelsea – Stockwell, Brixton Road – Blackfriars.

29th October
Lordship Lane impassable for trams. Services 58 and 62 from London terminate at Dulwich Library. Shuttle service of Felthams between Victoria and Camberwell New Road. Tracks at Vauxhall Cross repaired.

31st October
Route 33 restored from Bloomsbury to Balls Pond Road. Tracks damaged at Kennington Gate.

4th November
UXB at Brixton Hill delays tram services.

6th November
Widespread damage to tracks. Streatham High Road, Balham Hill, Balham High Road and Thornton Heath High Street blocked. UXB in Wandsworth Road and Southwark Bridge Road.

7th November
Single line working instituted in Lordship Lane between Horniman Museum and the Grove Hotel. Pointsmen stationed at each end. Cars passed through with single line token. Service 58 restored to Greenwich. Abbey Wood Depot damaged in air raid.

8th November
Bomb crater damage to tracks in Mitcham Road, Tooting. Trams curtailed at Amen Corner. Walworth Road, Lewisham High Street and Woolwich Church Street impassable for trams.

11th November
Emulating the 88 bus, a tram at Streatham Common is stranded in a bomb crater. Tracks blocked, trams curtailed at Hermitage Bridge, Norbury.

13th November
Streatham Hill impassable for trams. Emergency bus service Telford Avenue to Streatham Common.

15th November
Waterloo Road impassable for trams. Route 68 cars reverse in Blackfriars Road.

17th November
Large crater in High Street, Colliers Wood. Shuttle service to Wimbledon maintained by cars 1659, 1801 and 1844. Shuttle service Tooting Broadway to Streatham via Southcroft Road operated by Felthams 2078, 2121, 2130 and 2161.

18th November
UXB in Queens Road, Peckham. Lewisham High Street impassable for trams. Service 54 diverted via Brockley.

20th November
Southern portal of Kingsway Subway hit, causing broken gas main and explosion. Eight trams caught in the blast.

21st November
Single line working from Aldwych Tram Station to the Embankment.

23rd November
Single track restored over New Cross Gate railway bridge only for depot workings and workmen's cars. Abbey Wood Depot hit in air raid.

25th November
Streatham Hill reopened for single track working.

27th November
Large crater at Streatham Common bridged by temporary track. Single line working for restored services 16 and 18.

3rd December
Services 10, 16 and 18 operating normally in Streatham Hill.

8th December
Tracks damaged at Kennington Gate. Routes 40 and 72 diverted via Vauxhall.

13th December
Temporary crossovers installed at the Horns, Kennington.

17th December
Tracks at Elephant and Castle and in Walworth Road and New Kent Road damaged by enemy action.

18th December
Double track working restored to Kingsway Subway.

22nd December
Demolition of unstable buildings in Thornton Heath High Street curtails route 42.

27th December
Land mines dropped on New Cross Depot – late Christmas present from the Hun? Front of depot completely demolished. Most trams out on the road during the air raid.

30th December
Great fire raid on the City. Blackfriars Bridge and Victoria Embankment closed. Southwark Street and Theobalds Road blocked. Destroyed tram on the Embankment near Westminster.

31st December
Great Dover Street blocked. Routes 46 and 52 diverted via Elephant and Castle.

1941

1st January
Restricted service north of Kennington due to unsafe buildings.

5th January
Theobalds Road reopened. Car 1937 on route 35 first tram through at 11:50am.

6th January
Routes 2 and 4 restored from London to Wimbledon.

13th January
St. George's Road impassable for trams. Streatham Hill blocked again.

14th January
Blackfriars Bridge closed. Southwark Street blocked. Cars on route 26 diverted via Borough Road and Southwark Bridge Road.

15th January
Blackfriars Bridge and Great Dover Street reopened. Normal service on the 46 and 52.

16th January
UXB outside Swan and Sugar Loaf pub in South Croydon.
Delayed action bomb explodes in Old Kent Road. Tramlines laid across the crater. Near normal service restored.

20th January
Double track over New Cross Gate railway bridge restored. New Kent Road blocked due to unsafe buildings. Old Kent Road closed to motor traffic, only trams allowed.

24th January
Southwark Street reopened to route 26 cars.

28th January
Grand Depot Road, Woolwich blocked. Single line working for routes 44, 46 and 72 via Woolwich New Road. UXB in Holloway Road cuts access to Holloway Depot. Shuttle service of two trams on route 35 tracks between Highgate and Holloway.

1st February
Crater at West Norwood on non-conduit section. Temporary tracks laid round the obstruction. Road closed to motor traffic.

9th February
Replacement trackwork in Streatham Hill. New crossover installed at Christchurch Road.

14th February
St. George's Road reopened to trams. First through cars on route 33 from West Norwood to Manor House. Strict speed limits imposed over temporary trackwork.

17th February
Double track restored in Stockwell Road. Near normal service resumed.

9th March
Essex Road impassable for trams on route 33 and for trolleybuses. Cars 1928, 1995 and 1996 stranded between Balls Pond Road and Manor House. Rest of route 33 cars diverted to Highgate.
Tracks destroyed by bomb crater at the corner of Christchurch Road and Streatham Hill. Emergency buses between Telford Avenue and Brixton Hill Depot diverted via side streets.

12th March
Single line working restored on Streatham Hill.

24th March
Single line working restored on Essex Road. Stranded trams now able to reach rest of the network.

7th April
Full double line working restored in Essex Road. Service 33 back to normal.

16th April
Night raid causes widespread destruction. South west area hit badly. Tram services curtailed at Kennington. Large crater on Victoria Embankment. Several land mines damage Charing Cross Station. Many

service diversions south of the River. London Road, Southwark closed due to fire hoses blocking the way. Walworth Road, Newington Causeway and Rosebery Avenue impassable for trams. Two trams stranded on Borough High Street. Clapham Depot damaged, sub-station destroyed. Wandsworth Road blocked by fire hoses. Brixton Road impassable for trams due to large bomb crater. Feltham 2090 stranded at Brixton Station. Car 2089 stuck just north of Stockwell Road. Coldharbour Lane and Effra Road impassable for trams. Car 389 abandoned at Kennington. Restricted tram service West Norwood to Herne Hill only.

18th April

The grand clear up continues. Clapham Road now open as far as the depot. Abandoned trams observed being shunted back to their home depots – often the long way round due to blocked streets. Power supplies restored to Clapham area. Electricity provided courtesy of the Northern Line tube supply.

19th April

Enemy raiders back on Saturday night. Goose Green to Peckham Rye tracks damaged. No service on routes 56 and 84. No trams south of Catford. Downham and Grove Park again cut off from the network. Blackwall Lane blocked. Routes 58 and 62 curtailed to Trafalgar Road, Greenwich. Routes 36 and 38 and trolleybuses 696 and 698 curtailed at Plumstead because of craters in Basildon Road and Wickham Lane. Peckham High Street impassable for trams.
Islington sub-station hit. No power north of Bloomsbury. Theobalds Road blocked by rubble. Route 35 curtailed at Holborn Tram Station.
Large crater at the Horns, Kennington.

21st April

Another grand clear up! Single line working between Rye Lane and Harders Road, Peckham. Double track restored on Streatham Hill.

23rd April

Kennington to Victoria reopened. Cars on routes 40 and 72 diverted via Vauxhall. Routes 10, 16 and 18 now working between Angell Road, Brixton and London termini.

24th April

Service 35 restored north of Bloomsbury. Service 34 working Chelsea to Loughborough Junction.

25th April

Service 34 restored to full length. Temporary tracks laid across crater at the Horns, Kennington.

28th April

Cars on route 46 unable to reach Eltham. Curtailed at Lee Green. Route 48 back to normal service. Late evening test tram sent through on 16/18 from Purley to Brixton Station. Normal service in the morning.

2nd May

UXB in Eltham Road. Cars on 46 and 72 curtailed at Sidcup Road crossover. Cars on the 44 work as far as the Yorkshire Grey Roundabout. Emergency buses Eltham Church to Sidcup Road corner via Middle Park Estate.

4th May

Double track restored at the Horns. Nice touch – cars on the 33 working between Angell Road, Brixton and the Angel, Islington!

8th May

Herne Hill to Brixton reopened for trams only. Motor traffic uses side streets. Temporary track laid round crater in Effra Road.

11th May

Great fire raid – widespread destruction. Luftwaffe attempts to burn down London. Land mines and incendiaries cause many roads to be blocked. UXBs in London Road, Southwark, in the Old Kent Road, at the Elephant and at Balham Grove. Vauxhall Cross badly hit. UXB in Parry Street. Embankment, Blackfriars Road, Westminster Bridge Road, Waterloo Road, Walworth Road, Peckham Road, Peckham Rye, New Kent Road, Great Dover Street, Tower Bridge Road, Tooley Street, Creek Road, Greenwich Road and Trafalgar Road all impassable for trams. Emergency bus service London Bridge to Greenwich Church. Southern portal of Kingsway Subway hit again. Overhead wires down in Plumstead High Street and in Norwood Road. Norwood Depot roof damaged. Car 396 destroyed outside Croydon Bus Garage. Tram conductor and bus staff killed in the raid.

12th May

Clear up continues. Huge fire at the Elephant now under control. Roads blocked by rubble or closed because of unsafe buildings. UXBs have been removed. Trams diverted via Stockwell and Vauxhall to County Hall. Vauxhall Bridge tracks closed. Shuttle tram service either side. Route 35 operates in two halves, Forest Hill to Blackfriars and Highgate to Aldwych Tram Station. Track repaired in Essex Road.

15th May

Routes 36/38 worked in three sections: Embankment to Old Kent Road, Canal Bridge, Old Kent Road to King William Street, Greenwich, Blackwall Lane to Abbey Wood. Route 68 Bricklayers Arms to Greenwich Church. Route 46 Woolwich to Canal Bridge, Old Kent Road. Still no service south of Catford. Routes 4 and 18 curtailed at Blackfriars. Routes 16 and 33 working only to Christ Church, Lambeth.

16th May

Westminster Bridge Road reopened.

18th May

Kingsway Subway reopened with large hole in the roof.

20th May

Service 12 restored through to Southwark. Large crater at northern end of Southwark Bridge cuts off tracks. City terminus for trams moved on to the bridge short of the crater. Old Kent Road reopened for trams.

22nd May

Double track restored in Walworth Road.

27th May

Single line working in Trafalgar Road, Greenwich. Test tram finally reaches tramless outpost of Grove Park. Normal service south of Catford replaces emergency buses.

The detailed notes from our gallant scribes then cease. The Blitz was over and throughout the month of June 1941 all tram services returned to normal or near normal operation. Bomb craters were filled in and temporary trackwork was gradually replaced by standard rails and, if necessary, regular conduit components. Overhead wire crews occasionally used standard trolleybus fittings, where no suitable tramway ones were available.

THE CONDUIT SYSTEM OF CURRENT COLLECTION

THE CONDUIT system of electric current supply, compared with the more conventional overhead wire method of current collection, was expensive to build and costly to maintain. In the opening years of the twentieth century, supporters claimed its aesthetic qualities outweighed any financial considerations. A open skyline, they suggested, was easier on the eye than a web of overhead wires. Many inner London councils agreed, even where the architectural merits of some of the streets and surrounding buildings were highly questionable. Some voices in the LCC, alarmed at escalating costs, maintained that the offer of installing electric lighting on traction standards could have swayed some boroughs into accepting the cheaper overhead wire alternative. As it was, the opportunity was lost and many metropolitan thoroughfares remained poorly illuminated at night by flickering gas lamps.

Technical aspects of the conduit can best be explained by reference to the accompanying diagrams and pictures. Trams using the conduit system collected electric current through a device known as a 'plough', which conveniently was housed in a 'plough carrier' attached to the underside of each tramcar. The plough could move transversely across the width of the tram. Track construction demanded that a deep trough was dug to accommodate the pair of conductor T rails, their insulators and the U shaped yokes supporting the rails and feeding the drains. Hidden from public view was the complex mechanism needed to operate double tongue points, which also had to ensure that the plough attached to each tramcar took the required direction.

Drainage of surface water was essential. Snow and bad weather presented other challenges to the efficiency of the conduit. Periodic cleaning was required to remove mud and debris which fell through the open slot. Man made hazards included any metal object, such as a bolt of a chain, being jammed in the slot. Failure to remove an obstruction could break the fragile plough or cause a short circuit between the positive and negative T rails. Dr Gerald Druce suspects 'a plane of weakness' was deliberately built into the plough to minimise damage in the event of an accident.

Broken plough carriers were a significant cause of hold ups. After the breakdown squad arrived on the scene, the fractured iron channel of the carrier had to be extracted, thus blocking the nearside carriageway; then the plough had to be removed. If possible, the stricken vehicle could then be manoeuvred to the nearest access point in the conduit. The hatches in the tramcar's lower deck floor were often opened to aid the extraction of the plough. Dr Druce observed a similar incident outside Telford Avenue Depot. The whole process took about 20 minutes, until the resumption of normal service, and was conducted in the knowledge that the power supply was live at all times!

Another weakness of the conduit occurred at points, where tram routes diverged. There had to be a break in electrical supply, because the +ve and -ve T rails had to cross. The motorman would put the controller to OFF and then coast. However, if traffic conditions caused him to halt during this critical time, the tram he was driving was effectively stranded without power. On such occasions, the driver had to wait for a following vehicle to 'bump start' him in order to resume his journey. In tramway parlance this form of minor embarrassment was known as being 'stuck on a dead'!

The first LCC conduit line opened in May 1903 and it was followed by further construction of routes on both sides of the Thames. Londoners accepted trams working 'on the third rail' as part of the street landscape. When the LCC lines met those of other metropolitan operators at the county boundary,

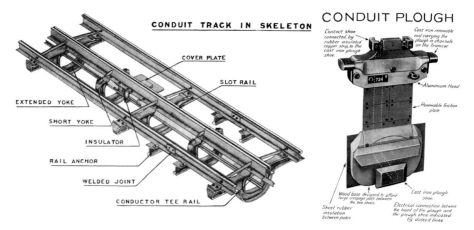

CONDUIT TRACK IN SKELETON

COVER PLATE
SLOT RAIL
EXTENDED YOKE
SHORT YOKE
INSULATOR
RAIL ANCHOR
WELDED JOINT
CONDUCTOR TEE RAIL

CONDUIT PLOUGH

Contact shoe connected by rubber insulated copper strip to the cast iron plough shoe.
Cast iron renewable end carrying the plough in channels on the Tramcar.
Aluminium Head
Renewable friction plate
Cast iron plough shoe.
Wood base designed to afford large creepage path between the two shoes.
Sheet rubber insulation between poles
Electrical connection between the head of the plough and the plough shoe indicated by dotted lines

the need soon became apparent to devise an efficient changeover method between the two systems of current collection.

Conduit tramways existed in major cities of the globe including, Washington DC, New York, Paris and Brussels, but the design of the LCC change pit or ploughshift was unique in the tramway world. The LCC's initial overhead wire equipped line from Woolwich to Plumstead was inaugurated on 17th April 1908, and the first change pits at Gresham Road and Coldharbour Lane opened for traffic in November 1908. Members of the council's tramways committee soon cottoned on to the fact that the overhead trolley method of current collection was more suitable for suburban extensions.

Thus, the network inherited by the LPTB in 1933 included both conduit and overhead wire equipped tramways. The Board also took possession of a fleet of passenger and works vehicles, many of which had both trolley and conduit equipment.

Just before they reached transfer points (change pits), trams leaving the conduit would halt to give the conductor time to raise the trolley pole and place it on the overhead. Sometimes this took some skill, especially in fog or bad light. The motorman would then operate a changeover switch to complete the electrical circuit for trolley operation. The tram would proceed towards the change pit, where the plough then moved sideways across the carrier and, guided by the conduit slot which intersected the running rail nearest the centre of the road, it parted company from the carrier. Once free of the tram, ejected ploughs ended up in a Y shaped junction. These were subsequently reused for trams going in the opposite direction.

In the opposite direction the conduit slot again crossed the running rail to resume its position in the centre of the track. Ploughs were guided by the attendant's fork and inserted into the carriers of city bound vehicles. When ready, the attendant banged on the side of the tram with the hooked rod he employed to pull the ploughs into position. The car crept forward so that the plough slid neatly into the carrier. The tram then halted again to allow the conductor to pull down the trolley arm into the retaining hook on the roof. After he had completed this task, the conductor would check the trolley rope was neatly fastened to a cleat in the dash of the tram. During this time the driver would lock the controller at OFF, to release a key so that he could operated the changeover switch located under the stairs. After a brief check to see all was well, the tram would then move off, while drawing power from the conduit.

This process at change pits went on hundreds of times a day, usually without any trouble at all. It was normal policy to have a stop sign at each change pit, however, sometimes no official halt was made and the plough could be expelled from the car at a velocity somewhat quicker than walking pace.

Outside the Fire Station at Lee Green was a good place to observe the practice of cars on routes 46 and 72 'shooting the plough' and it was enjoyed by boys of all ages. Although, of course, change pit attendants had to step lively to make sure their feet were nowhere near the plough, as it emerged at speed from the passing tramcar.

The following list of change pits indicates the principal connections between the central LCC conduit network and the other constituent systems of the LPTB:

North of the Thames

Highgate Archway Tavern, Archway Road. LCC -> MET.

Manor House, Seven Sisters Road. LCC -> MET.

Manor House, Green Lanes. LCC -> MET.

(A further ploughshift existed at Finsbury Park. The section from here to Manor House was equipped for both conduit and overhead trolley.)

Stamford Hill, Amhurst Park. LCC -> LCC.

Stamford Hill opposite Egerton Road. LCC -> MET.

Lea Bridge Road at junction with Clapton Road. LCC -> Leyton.

Well Street, Hackney. LCC -> LCC.

Grove Road at junction with Mile End Road. LCC -> LCC.

Mile End Road by Mile End tube station. LCC -> LCC/West Ham.

Burdett Road at junction with East India Dock Road. LCC -> LCC.

Iron Bridge Canning Town. LCC -> West Ham.

South of the Thames

Woolwich, Market Hill. LCC -> LCC.

Lee Green, Eltham Road. LCC -> LCC.

Downham Way at junction with Bromley Road. LCC -> LCC.

Coldharbour Lane at junction with Denmark Hill. LCC -> LCC.

Gresham Road at junction with Brixton Road. LCC -> LCC.

Effra Road at junction with Brixton Hill. LCC -> LCC.

Streatham High Road by Gleneagle Road. LCC -> LCC/Croydon.

Mitcham Road, Tooting Junction. LCC -> SMET.

Tooting High Street by Longley Road. LCC -> LCC (LUT).

Summerstown, Plough Lane. LCC -> LCC (LUT).

Putney Bridge Road at junction with Wandsworth High Street. LCC -> LCC.

At change pits there was an inevitable overlap between conduit and overhead wires. At Lee Green, for example, trolley wires were erected in Lee High Road in advance

above A close up of the conduit plough being guided into the plough carrier by the attendant's fork. Once lodged in the carrier, the plough could move laterally to follow the position of the conduit rails. B. T. Cooke

right The conduit or 'third rail' as most Londoners called it, exercised a certain fascination. Although it was expensive to maintain, it did leave streets pleasantly uncluttered and free from overhead wires. Track layouts such as this trailing crossover had a quality of artistic symmetry about them.

of the Tigers Head road junction, so that tram conductors could raise the trolley pole some distance before the actual change pit in Eltham Road, opposite Meadowcourt Road. This procedure of stopping ahead of traffic lights was calculated to cause less traffic congestion.

In the East End, southbound trams on route 77 changed from conduit to trolley at Well Street, Hackney and were then on the overhead as far as the terminus at West India Dock. However, just before the crossing with Mile End Road a change pit was installed to enable trams to use a connecting conduit track to the Mile End Road (routes 61, 63). The same arrangement occurred at Limehouse, where a double track conduit connection led to the East India Dock Road (routes 65, 67). The LCC electrified route 77 after the First World War, when economic considerations ruled out another purely conduit equipped line.

The longest dual equipped section was from Finsbury Park to Manor House (routes 21, 27, 29, 53, 59, 71 and 79). This stretch of track was originally owned by the MET and built with overhead wires. It was later purchased by the LCC and the conduit was then extended the length of Seven Sisters Road from the Nags Head to Manor House.

This very practical arrangement permitted conduit only vehicles to terminate at Manor House and, more importantly, the existence of overhead wires allowed MET trams without conduit equipment to reach their prime traffic objective of Finsbury Park, which was a vital interchange point for passengers transferring to the Piccadilly tube line.

Ploughshifts at Longley Road, Tooting (routes 2, 4) and at Summerstown (route 14) originally joined LCC tracks with those owned by the LUT. However, through services at these locations were operated until 1933 exclusively by the LCC.

Routes such as the 30, 34 and 53 passed two change pits on their journeys. Change pits also existed away from main highways. One was installed at the entrance to Brixton Hill Depot and another was positioned at Charlton. Entry into the CRD required vehicles to eject their ploughs. Trams were then shunted around the works by a converted Fordson tractor.

The last on-street ploughshifts to be constructed were at Summerstown in April 1931 and at Iron Bridge, Canning Town (routes 65, 67) in January 1933. The remodelled highway at Canning Town, which linked East India Dock Road with Barking Road, bypassed the original tramway alignment. This was closed on 14th January 1933. The change pit then lay derelict. It

outlived the replacing trolleybuses and was the subject of an archaeological dig, which resulted in the whole structure being removed for preservation.

Dr. Gerald Druce comments:

From personal experience of the run-down London tramways between 1945 and 1952, when much of my travelling was on ex-Croydon Corporation track with overhead wires, I am firmly of the opinion that the decision to adopt the conduit system of current collection was a disaster. It was a cause of additional operating expense, the hollow conduit weakened the foundations of the track, it was the source of many breakdowns and hence delays; in the Kingsway Subway the hollow trough amplified the noise. The conduit slot was also the worst danger for cyclists. These faults combined to give much ammunition to the anti-tram lobby. Probably not considered when the tramway was constructed, the cost of removing unwanted conduit track from the highway far exceeded that of conventional track consisting of rails and tiebars.

For the record the last conduit line in Paris survived until 1936. In London the system was in use up to abandonment on the night of 5th/6th July 1952. The final application of this ingenious, but expensive method of current collection was in Washington DC. It ceased on 28th January 1962.

Time Test
– Grove Road/Bow Road Change Pit . . .
Monday, 18th June 1934.

This internal document was circulated in the T & T section in preparation for the overhead electrification of Mile End Road, proposed in the 1934 Act. It is probably the only time and motion study of a change pit. Ironically, no action was later taken to abandon the Grove Road/Bow Road change pit, until trolleybuses arrived on the scene. An interesting exercise was thus rendered wholly academic.

Method of Test.
Up track. Cars timed when brought to a standstill at or approaching change-pit, until starting away to cross Grove Road. The time taken thus includes the time occupied in the various operations of changing from overhead to conduit operation, and also the traffic delay resulting from Cross traffic.

Down track. Cars timed when brought to a standstill at or approaching stopping place until starting away to cross Grove Road. The time taken thus includes the time occupied in operating the changeover switch and raising trolley, and also the traffic delay resulting from cross traffic.

RESULTS.
Up track.
Total cars (7am – 7.30pm) = 535.
Total delay = 969 mins. 25 secs.
Average delay per car = 1 min. 49 secs.

Down track.
Total cars (7am – 7.30pm) = 526.
Total delay = 451 mins. 39 secs.
Average delay per car = 52 secs.

In order to separate the delay due to change-over operations from the delay due to traffic crossing, a separate test was made on Tuesday and Wednesday, June 19th and 20th.

The actual delay occasioned by traffic was taken, cars being timed after all change-over operations were completed, until starting to cross Grove Road.

RESULTS.
Up track.
Cars = 534. Delay = 269 mins. 24 secs.
Average delay per car = 30 secs.

Down Track.
Cars = 526. Delay = 243 mins. 51 secs.
Average delay per car = 28 secs.

Total delay attributable to change-over up and down tracks 907 mins.
49 secs. = 15 car hours.

The Mile End twins were minor celebrities in tramway circles. The job of change pit attendant obviously ran in the family. At the nearby Mile End Station, construction work is taking place in connection with the Central Line eastern extension. Out on the highway the driver of oncoming car 190 eases his charge over track works in advance of the change pit. This was the change pit mentioned in the 1934 time and motion study.
Henry Priestley/National Tramway Museum

APPENDIX
DEPOTS AND YARDS

MENTION HAS already been made in the main text of the range of depots and yards inherited by the LPTB in 1933. In the former LCC Northern Division exclusively conduit depots were situated at Hampstead, Holloway, Stamford Hill, Hackney and Poplar. Bow Depot was all trolley. South of the Thames car sheds at Wandsworth, Clapham, Streatham, Camberwell and New Cross were all conduit. Brixton Hill was equipped for overhead wire operation, even though the access was by conduit tracks. Abbey Wood and Norwood depots were all trolley, as were Hammersmith (situated to serve the western lines of the LCC) and Chiswick (acquired from the LUT). The Combine tramways contributed 12 depots to the new organisation, the municipal systems nine. In the second year of LPTB ownership the number of staff employed at depots was 2,456 people. The total for all depots, repair works and yards was 4,020.

Depots and yards are grouped according to their former owners. Also listed are their street addresses, their respective London postal districts and, where applicable, their pre-1965 counties. Opening dates are given in brackets, followed by vehicle capacity. This last calculation was often based on the maximum number of tramcars that could fill a particular building. In practice this figure was almost always an overestimate. Obviously car length played a part in the calculations and a rough estimate was six E/1s = five Felthams. The year of final tramway usage is given, plus the fate of said depot. Standard London Transport garage letter codes were never carried by the trams, however, those appearing on buses and trolleybuses are printed in square brackets.

In London trams and trolleybuses were housed in depots, but motor buses resided in garages.

LCC

Abbey Wood
Abbey Wood Road, SE2. (1910–14). 86 trams. Converted to bus garage [AW] in 1952. Closed in October 1981. Demolished.

Bow
Fairfield Road, E3. (1908–10). 79 trams. Converted to trolleybus depot in 1939; to bus garage [BW] in 1959.

Brixton Hill
219 Brixton Hill, SW2. (1924). 46 trams. Used as an annexe to Streatham Depot. Closed in 1951. Now used as a bus garage.

Camberwell
Camberwell Green. Camberwell New Road, SE5. (1903–5, 1913). 131 trams. Converted to bus garage [WL] in 1951. Renamed Walworth Garage.

Chiswick
Chiswick High Road, W4. (1883, 1901). 75 trams. Purchased in 1922 from the LUT. Used mainly as a store. Disconnected from the network in 1935. Renamed Stamford Brook [V] Garage. Partly demolished.

Clapham
Clapham High Street, SW4. (1903). 164 trams. Converted to bus garage [CA] in 1951. Closed in 1987. Demolished.

Cars 1221 and 1482 rest behind closed gates at Abbey Wood Depot in this pre-war view. One suspects the metal gates were later prime candidates for the wartime scrap drive to melt down railings. Car 1221 was scrapped at Hampstead in June 1939; car 1482 was stored during the conflict and was disposed of at Purley Depot in November 1945. Former members of the East and West Ham fleets took the place of these trams at Abbey Wood. C. Carter

A number of cleaners' gantries add interest to this view of the interior of Clapham Depot. Note the maintenance pits with the shielding for the conduit T rails. This was a necessary precaution to prevent accidents to maintenance and repair staff working on running and electrical gear. W. J. Haynes

Hampstead Depot is the last resting place of former MET car 2231. It was scrapped in November 1938. A happier fate awaits car 589. It was fitted with driver's windscreens in August 1938 and it survived until 1951.

Hackney
Bohemia Place, E8. (1882, 1909). 120 trams. Converted to trolleybus depot in 1940; to bus garage [CT] in 1959. Renamed Clapton Garage.

Hammersmith
Great Church Lane, W6. (1906–1911). 59 trams. Converted to trolleybus depot in 1937; to bus garage [HB] in 1960. Closed in 1966. Demolished.

Hampstead
Cressy Road, NW3. (1913–14). 150 trams. Closed to service cars in 1939. Retained as a store/scrap yard until the end of the war. Demolished.

Holloway
Holloway Road. Pemberton Gardens, N19. (1907–9). 307 trams. Dual tram/trolleybus operation 1938–52. Trolleybus depot to 1961, then bus garage [HT]. Renamed Highgate and subsequently reverted to Holloway Garage.

Leyton
Lea Bridge Road, E10. (1889, 1906). 50 trams. Operated by the LCC from 1921. Converted to trolleybus depot in 1939. Renamed Lea Bridge [LB]. Closed in 1959. Demolished.

New Cross
New Cross Road, SE14. (1906). 314 trams. Converted to bus garage [NX] in 1952.

Norwood
Norwood Road, SE27. (1909). 64 trams. Partly demolished.

Poplar
Leven Road, E14. (1906). 96 trams. Also used as a PW store. Converted to trolleybus depot in 1940; to bus garage [PR] in 1959.

Stamford Hill
Rookwood Road, N16. (1907). 140 trams. Converted to trolleybus depot in 1939; to bus garage [SF] in 1961.

Streatham Telford Avenue
Streatham Hill, SW2. (1892, 1904–13). 108 trams. Converted to bus garage [BN] in 1951. Renamed Brixton Garage.

centre E/1 rehab car 1507 awaits its turn to enter the imposing portals of Norwood Depot. The LCC architectural style could be described as functional and workmanlike, however, it was not unpleasant on the eye. John H.Meredith

right Former Leyton E/3 class car 206 stands outside the entrance to Telford Avenue Depot, Streatham. Built on the site of a former cable tram depot, the reconstructed LCC establishment opened on 3rd February 1906. It was enlarged in 1937 to receive Felthams. After the demise of the trams it was razed to the ground and rebuilt as Brixton Bus Garage. A. V. Mace

Wandsworth
Jews Row, SW18. (1883, 1906). 95 trams. Dual tram/trolleybus operation 1937–50, then bus garage [WD].

Central Repair Depot, Charlton
Woolwich Road, SE7. (1911). Closed to trams in 1952 and to trolleybuses in 1959. Demolished. Access road renamed Felltram Way after A. L. C. Fell, former LCC Tramways General Manager.

Deptford PW Yard
Greenwich High Road, SE10. (1871, 1907). Demolished.

Battersea PW Yard
Battersea Bridge Road, S. W. 11. (1909). Demolished.

Peckham
Rye Lane. Bellenden Road, SE15. (1885, 1909). Former depot used by PW department. Converted to bus garage [RL] 1952. Demolished.

right Rail carrier 139A, registered AGJ 912, poses for the photographer at Deptford PW Wharf by Deptford Creek. This green painted Albion lorry was attached to the LT yard at Bowles Road, just off the Old Kent Road. Note the stack of conduit 'yokes' on the left of the picture. This permanent way yard had a track connection with routes 36, 38 and 40 in Greenwich High Road. LCC Tramways Trust

below A variety of ex MET tramcars are being sheltered under the depot roof at Finchley. The figures painted on the roof valance are clearly visible and they indicate stabling roads, of which there were fifteen in number. These tracks led to a traverser situated at the back of the depot. Note the open doors of the tower wagon annexe. The pile of sand and aggregate on the right of the picture indicates that work is in progress to convert this establishment into a trolleybus depot.

Combine

– MET, LUT, SMET.

Acton (LUT)
Acton High Street, W5. (1895, 1901). 35 trams. Closed to trams in 1937; temporary trolleybus depot. Converted to bus garage [AT]. Demolished.

Edmonton (MET)
Tramway Avenue, N9. (1880, 1905). 66 trams. Converted to trolleybus depot 1938; to bus garage [EM] 1961. Demolished.

Finchley (MET)
Rosemont Avenue, N12. (1905). 60 trams. Converted to trolleybus depot 1936; to bus garage [FY] 1962. Demolished.

Fulwell (LUT)
Wellington Road, Hampton, Middlesex. (1903). 191 trams. Also used as works/repair depot/store/scrap yard. Converted to trolleybus depot 1931–5; to bus garage [FW] 1962. Now divided into two bus garages.

Hanwell (LUT)
Hanwell Broadway, W7. (1901). Converted to trolleybus depot 1936; to bus garage [HL] 1960. Demolished.

Hendon (MET)
Edgware Road, NW9. (1904). 32 trams. Also used as works/repair depot. Converted to trolleybus depot 1936. Renamed Colindale Depot [CE]. Closed in 1962. Demolished.

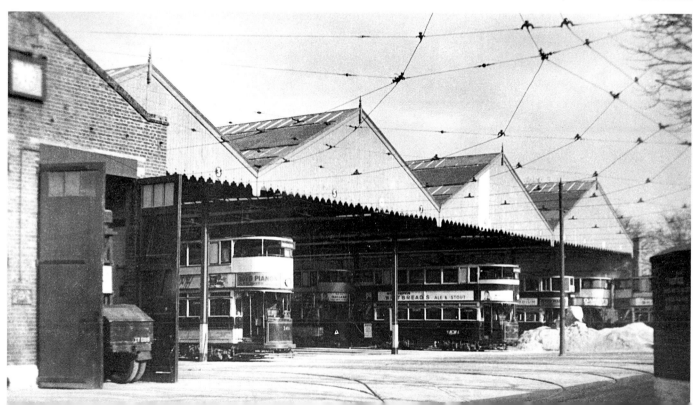

The London United under the stewardship of Sir James Clifton Robinson certainly had great style and this is reflected in the ornate gates to Chiswick Depot and Power House. This photo was taken in the 1950s, when the place had been demoted to the status of a storage facility. The glory days were well and truly over! Some of the original pointwork can be glimpsed in the yard.
N.Rayfield

Bexleyheath. Broadway, Bexleyheath, Kent. (1903). 34 trams. Closed in 1935. Demolished.

East Ham. Nelson Street, E6. (1901). 48 trams. Closed in 1933.

Erith. Walnut Tree Rd, Erith, Kent. (1905). 19 trams. Closed in 1933. Demolished.

Ilford. Ley Street, Ilford, Essex. (1903). 40 trams. Converted to trolleybus depot 1938. [ID]. Closed in 1959.

Purley. Brighton Road, South Croydon, Surrey. (1901). 20 trams. Used at various times as a store/repair depot/scrap yard. Closed in 1951. Demolished.

Hounslow (LUT)
London Road, Isleworth, Middlesex. (1901). 40 trams. Converted to trolleybus depot 1935. Renamed Isleworth Depot [ID]. Closed in 1962.

Mitcham (SMET)
Aurelia Road, Croydon, Surrey. (1906). 20 trams. Latterly used as a store/scrap yard. Closed in 1937. Demolished.

Penge (SMET)
Oakgrove Road, SE20. (1906). 25 trams. Latterly used as a scrap yard. Closed in 1936. Demolished. Former site now called Tramway Close.

Stonebridge Park (MET)
Harrow Road, NW10. (1906). 48 trams. Converted to trolleybus depot 1936; to bus garage [SE] 1962. Demolished.

Sutton (SMET)
Westmead Road, Sutton, Surrey. (1906). 60 trams. Converted to trolleybus depot 1935; to bus garage [CN] 1959. Renamed Carshalton Garage. Closed in 1964.

Wood Green (MET)
High Road, N22. (1895, 1904). 87 trams. Converted to trolleybus depot 1938; to bus garage [WN] 1961.

Brentford PW Yard
High Street, Brentford, Middlesex. (1898, 1904). Closed in 1936. Demolished.

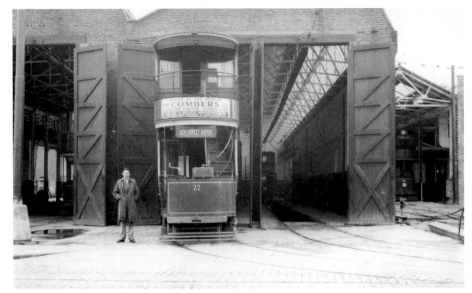

above right Ley Street Depot was once home to the Ilford fleet. Car 22, working route 91, awaits its crew. Of interest is car 261 stationed to the far right of the picture. This ex-West Ham vehicle failed to impress when tested on local tracks, with considerable wheel spin which was attributed to Ilford's non-standard wheel profiles.
W. A. Camwell/National Tramway Museum

right Walthamstow Depot yard is the setting for a varied collection of tramcars. In the centre is a former Walthamstow single truck veteran, repainted by London Transport, but not expected to survive the forthcoming trolleybus onslaught. The two other trams are from the LCC 552–601 series, which was subsequently transferred to south London. Works car 014 with the two water tanks was employed on rail grinding duties. It had a useful life with its new owners and wandered far and wide over the system, even getting as far as Dartford.

Thornton Heath. London Road, Thornton Heath, Surrey. (1879, 1901). 37 trams. Converted to bus garage [TH] in 1950.

Walthamstow. Chingford Road, E17. (1905). 62 trams. Partly used as a scrap yard. Converted to trolleybus depot 1937; to bus garage [WW] 1960. Demolished, except for the former Walthamstow Corporation Tramway Offices.

West Ham. Greengate Street, E13. (1906). 150 trams. Also used as works/repair depot. Converted to trolleybus depot 1937–40; to bus garage [WH] 1960. Demolished.

Municipal depots also had facilities for repair work. As can be seen from the list, some tram depots underwent rebuilding for trolleybuses and, when electric traction went out of favour, were later reconfigured for diesel buses. An interesting situation arose with the old Bexley tram depot at Bexleyheath Broadway. According to the wording of the 1934 Act, powers were being sought by the LPTB for a new tram and trolleybus depot in the area. It was rumoured among tram crews that temporary tracks would be laid in the modern structure. However, plans were altered and Bexleyheath trolleybus depot opened on Erith Road in 1935, without any tramway connections. The old Bexley tram depot was handed back to the local council and dust carts replaced tramcars under its roof!

After the Second World War extensive reconstruction of former depots, such as happened at New Cross, Streatham, Camberwell and Thornton Heath, completely obliterated any traces of tramway heritage. At the time of writing, decades of urban redevelopment have accounted for most of the establishments on the list. Sometimes the odd retaining wall is spared demolition, but this is poor recompense for the preservation of an intact structure. The latest casualty of gross civic vandalism was Acton Tram Depot. Of the very few remaining buildings of interest to industrial archaeologists, the most noteworthy structures are at Bow, Brixton Hill, Chiswick, East Ham, Fulwell and Walthamstow.

In an area otherwise devoid of great architectural merit, Bow Depot in Fairfield Road, is probably the best preserved of the original LCC car sheds. Brixton Hill was designed by G. Topham Forrest, Chief Architect for the LCC. Tram track is still visible inside the building. Chiswick Depot and associated Power House were designed by William Curtis Green. The Power House is a Grade II listed building, currently home to a music industry and entertainment complex. The old car sheds of East Ham Corporation have been refurbished and restored externally with a plaque depicting two tramcars on the former depot wall.

The erstwhile LUT main depot at Fulwell stands out because of its size. Sadly, the interesting tram track layouts in the two large depot yards, which survived the trolleybuses, have been another casualty of progress. The Tramway Offices at the depot site in Walthamstow have been preserved and are Grade II listed buildings. Unfortunately, they now suffer the indignity of having a street address of 23, Omnibus Way!

Those lovers of the grimly utilitarian may fancy a visit to Ley Street, Ilford, to Westmead Road, Sutton, to Leven Road, Poplar or to London Road, Isleworth, where some former tramway buildings still stand. How long this will remain the case is anyone's guess. Stamford Hill is another ex-LCC depot worth seeing. The establishment still in the public transport domain with the oldest provenance is probably Wood Green. Whatever the location, potential tramway industrial archaeologists are politely reminded that security, health and safety concerns dictate that official permission must be obtained before any exploration of former depot buildings, especially if they are now used for the current London bus fleet.

The melancholy fate of three ex Ilford trams is depicted here on the scrap siding behind Walthamstow Depot. Such wanton destruction of historic vehicles now seems barbaric to us, but in the late 1930s it was a price worth paying to get to the future. At that time scenes like this were repeated all over the country, as town after town dispensed with its trams.

A CONDUCTOR'S LIFE – Fares and Tickets

WORKMEN'S FARES were a feature of every-day travel. They were available on London's tramways (and later on replacing trolleybuses), but were not offered on buses. This institution of discounting the normal stage fare tariff for bone fide workpeople and artisans had its roots in the horse tramway era. The London Street Tramways Act of 1870 obliged operators to run cars for workmen on six days of the week except on Sundays. Exclusions also applied to Christmas Day and Good Friday. Cars were to run not later than 7am and the return workmen's journeys were not to commence before 6pm. Fares at affordable rates, usually up to one penny a mile, were fixed by the Board of Trade. This statutory framework for workmen's fares lasted for trams in the London Transport area until 1st October 1950.

The whole scheme was regarded by legislators and employers as vital for the economic wellbeing of the metropolitan region. Clerks, labourers, shop assistants, dockers and many other workers could now live further than walking distance from their places of employment. It was hoped that the workmen's fare strategy would act as a stimulus for people to forsake crowded inner city areas in favour of healthier homes and lodgings in the suburbs.

Electric trams had fixed stops and therefore it was a straightforward matter to divide routes into recognised fare stages. Charts were posted in every vehicle, so the travelling public could check how much their journeys would cost. The conductor was on hand to give out tickets and collect fare money from passengers. The main accoutrements of this occupation were a stout leather money bag or satchel (a collection of old pennies and other low value pre-decimal coins could weigh quite a bit!), a long and a short ticket rack and a bell punch with canceller harness. A key to operate indicator blinds, a small knife shaped device to clean the ticket slot of the bell punch, a wooden waybill board with a bulldog clip and a whistle attached to a chain were also included in the standard conductor's equipment. Since trams were legally classed as light railways, the conductor needed a whistle, as a guard would on a train. A shrill whistle blast also acted as a convenient sign to the motorman, when the conductor was on the top deck or a starting bell was out of reach.

Before taking charge of his tramcar, the conductor needed training to cope with an array of different coloured tickets at his disposal. Destinations and the names of intermediate locations on any particular route were usually printed in full on each ticket. In order to conserve card, a change was made from July 1940, when the so called deaf and dumb style was adopted. Names of fare stages gave way to a numbered sequence. However, named destinations and transfer points remained on many types of tickets, in combination with numerical fare stages. Tram tickets, unlike those used on the buses, had a white stripe down the centre.

During the LPTB regime, in addition to fares for single journeys, passengers could buy a return ticket, or could avail themselves of a bargain with cheap midday fares. Children under 14 years of age were usually charged half the adult fare. Topping it all was the Shilling All Day, which gave unlimited travel over most of the system. Transfer journeys from one tram route to another were also permitted. Luggage carried on trams was paid for by means of a 2d. ticket. Production of tickets, waybills, some maps and other printed material was kept in house at the former LCC Tramways establishment at 51–53 Effra Road, Brixton. Rolls of thin white card, each around 4,000 feet (1,207 metres) long, supplied the raw material for 450,000 tickets.

Lord Ashfield and his Board were reluctant to draw criticism by imposing regular fare increases, but the inevitable happened on 11th July 1939, when the cost of travel went up. Another increase occurred on 3rd July 1940. Running public services in wartime was an expensive business and each passenger was expected to pay his or her fair share. However, at a time of great stress for the population common sense dictated that for the rest of the war years there was only a very moderate adjustment in some local fares, although this did involve the scrapping of the Shilling All Day, the 6d Evening Tourist and the 6d Child Day tickets in October 1942.

After the return of peace, fares remained stable until 9th February 1947. In spite of rises in costs the whole essence of tram travel lay in the availability of affordable transport for business and for pleasure. When the sparkling modern looking buses appeared to drive the trams off the road, there was a consensus that the brave new world foisted on Londoners would have to be paid for out of passengers' pockets. Many then quit public transport altogether and bought a car. The rest is history.

APPENDIX
BIBLIOGRAPHY

The sequel to the current work is:

London Tramway Twilight 1949–1952, published by Capital Transport in 2000. ISBN 185414 234 8.

Other books by the author include:

LCC Electric Tramways, Capital Transport, 2002. ISBN 1 85414 256 9

Croydon Tramways, Capital Transport, 2004. ISBN 185414 278 X

North London Trams, Capital Transport, 2008. ISBN 978 1 58414 314 3

London United Electric Tramways, Capital Transport, 2010. ISBN 978 1 85414 338 9

London Transport Trams – A black and white album, Capital Transport, 2012. ISBN 978 1 85414 365 5

The following reference works on London mention tramways:

London. A Social History, *Roy Porter*, Penguin, 1994. ISBN 0 14 024238 4

The Times History of London, *Hugh Clout*, 1997, ISBN 0 7230 1030 7

The Face of London, *Harold P. Clunn*, Simpkin Marshall, 1932.

London: The Unique City, *Steen Eiler Rasmussen*, Macmillan, 1937.

The County Books.
London is covered in six volumes:
The Northern Reaches,
The Western Reaches,
South London, East London,
West of the Bars, The City, 1949.
General Editor, *Brian Vesey-Fitzgerald.*

A reliable street map always comes in handy. The metropolis has changed much since the demise of the trams. For a good guide to the era the following are recommended:

Bartholomew's Handy Reference Atlas of London, Sixth Edition, 1930. (Tramways are clearly marked).

Geographers' Atlas of Greater London, First Edition, Geographers' Map Company, 1947–8. (Clear mapping, easy on the eye).

London A-Z Street Atlas – Historical Edition of 1938, Geographers' Map Company. ISBN 978 1 84348 639 8 (Pocket edition reprint – bus routes and tramways are clearly marked.)

The LPTB issued a range of maps covering all their transport operations.

The Tram & Trolleybus Map & List of Services went through a number of editions in the period 1933–1950. Copies of these maps are usually only available on the second hand market or through dealers of transport memorabilia.

The moving image is very evocative of times past. The best DVD on the subject is **London Trams: Part One** produced from amateur and professional, colour and black and white film sources by *Martin Jenkins and Wilf Watters* of Online Video, in cooperation with the Huntley Archive.

London's trams in the lptb era (1933–1947) have been the subject of many publications directed mainly towards the enthusiast and local history market. The standard and content of these works varies from detailed technical offerings to wide ranging picture albums. Books on this list can be enjoyed by the serious student and the general reader.

A History of London Transport, Volume II, *T. C. Barker and Michael Robbins*, George Allen & Unwin, 1974. ISBN 0 04 385067 7

The Man Who Built London Transport: A Biography of Frank Pick, *Christian Barman*, David & Charles, 1979. ISBN 0 7153 7753 1

Herbert Morrison – Portrait of a Politician, *Bernard Donoughue & G. W. Jones*, Phoenix Press, 2001. ISBN 1 84212 441 2

Labour Relations in London Transport, *H. A. Clegg*, Blackwell Oxford, 1950.

London's Passenger Transport Problem, *Gilbert J. Ponsonby*, King & Son London, 1932.

Socialisation and Transport, *Herbert Morrison*, Constable & Co London, 1933.

Street Traffic Flow, *Henry Watson*, Chapman & Hall, 1933.

The London Tramcar 1861–1952, *R. W. Kidner*, Oakwood Press LP7, 1992. ISBN 0 85361 433 4

The Felthams, *Ken Blacker*, Dryhurst Publications, 1962.

Tramway London – Background to the abandonment of London's trams 1931–1952, *Martin Higginson*, LRTA, 1993. ISBN 0 948106 16 6

London Transport Tramways Handbook, *D. W. Willoughby & E. R. Oakley*, 1972. ISBN 0 903479 00 1

London Transport Tramways 1933–1952, *E. R. Oakley & C. E. Holland*, London Tramways History Group, 1998. ISBN 0 9513001 2 1

The Wheels Used To Talk To Us, *Stan Collins. Edited by Terence Cooper*, Tallis Publishing, 1977. ISBN 0 9505458 0 5

North London's Tramways 1938–1952, *John Barrie*, LRTL, 1969.

The Tramways of Croydon, *G. E. Baddeley*, LRTA, 1983. ISBN 0 900433 90 6

The Tramways of East London, *Rodinglea*, TLRS/LRTL. 1967.

Tramways in Metropolitan Essex, Volume 2, *Vernon Burrows*, 1976.

The Metropolitan Electric Tramways, 2 volumes, *Cyril Smeeton*, TLRS/LRTA, 1984/1987. ISBN 0 900433 94 9/0 948106 00 X

The London United Tramways, 2 volumes, *Cyril Smeeton*, TLRS/LRTA, 1994/2000. ISBN 0 948106 13 1/0 948106 24 7

The Tramways of Woolwich and South East London, *Southeastern*, TLRS/LRTL, 1963.

London United Tramways, *Geoffrey Wilson*, George Allen & Unwin, 1971. ISBN 0 04 388001 0

London Trams: A View From The Past, *Paul Collins*. Ian Allan, 2001. ISBN 0 7110 2741 2

Tramway Classics.
A series of picture albums covering all London's tramways on a geographical basis. Middleton Press.

The development of British tramcar design, including London examples, can be studied in the following four copiously illustrated volumes:

Modern Tramcar Types, *Gerald Druce*, Light Railway Transport League, 1951.

Classic Tramcars, *R. J. S. Wiseman*, Ian Allan, 1986. ISBN 0 7110 1560 0

The Classic Trams, *Peter Waller*, Ian Allan, 1993. ISBN 0 7110 2160 0

English Electric Tramcar Album, *Geoff Lumb*, Ian Allan, 1998. ISBN 0 7110 2613 0

Last but not least, a book first published in 1961, which is an absolute must for all those wishing to further their knowledge of British tramways. It also includes much material on London.

The Golden Age of Tramways, *Charles Klapper*, Routledge & Keegan Paul. Revised edition, 1974, David & Charles. ISBN 978 0715364581

The abandonment of London's tramways in favour of trolleybuses features in the following books:

The London Trolleybus, Volume 1, 1931–1945/ Volume 2, 1946–1962, *Ken Blacker*, Capital Transport, 2002/2004. ISBN 185414 260 7/185414 285 2

London Trolleybus Routes, *Hugh Taylor*, Capital Transport, 1994. ISBN 185414 155 4

London Trolleybus Chronology 1931–1962, *Mick Webber,* Ian Allan, 1997. ISBN 0 7110 2528 2

Works by Ken Glazier are detailed histories of London's buses, but they do contain much relevant information about trams and trolleybuses.

London Buses Before The War, Capital Transport, 1995. ISBN 185414 182 1

London Buses and the Second World War, Capital Transport, 1991. ISBN 185414 136 8

Routes to Recovery, Capital Transport, 2000. ISBN 185414 236 4

INDEX OF PEOPLE

An evocative scene at Wood Green Depot, as the pride of the former Metropolitan Electric Tramways fleet line up after a hard day's work. Note the contrasting body styles between the Felthams and the more traditional rolling stock. A. V. Mace

GENERAL INDEX

'Bluebird' car 1 revisits Purley on an 'Extra Special' organised by tram enthusiasts in post war days. Ahead is a Feltham on route 16. A. V. Mace

Faretable as displayed inside every tram in service. The production and printing details appearing along the base are as follows: 1147/2432 Ex/180cards. 40paper. 24496R. Knapp, Drewett & Sons Ltd., London and Kingston-on-Thames Route 68, November 1947